T0214097

Lecture Notes in Computer Science 12637

More information about this subseries at http://www.springer.com/series/7410

Gabriela Nicolescu · Assia Tria ·
José M. Fernandez · Jean-Yves Marion ·
Joaquin Garcia-Alfaro (Eds.)

Foundations and Practice of Security

13th International Symposium, FPS 2020
Montreal, QC, Canada, December 1–3, 2020
Revised Selected Papers

 Springer

Editors
Gabriela Nicolescu
Polytechnique Montréal
Montréal, QC, Canada

José M. Fernandez 🆔
Polytechnique Montréal
Montréal, QC, Canada

Joaquin Garcia-Alfaro 🆔
Télécom SudParis
Evry, France

Assia Tria
CEA-Leti Technology Research Institute
Grenoble, France

Jean-Yves Marion
University of Lorraine
Vandœuvre lès Nancy, France

ISSN 0302-9743   ISSN 1611-3349   (electronic)
Lecture Notes in Computer Science
ISBN 978-3-030-70880-1   ISBN 978-3-030-70881-8   (eBook)
https://doi.org/10.1007/978-3-030-70881-8

LNCS Sublibrary: SL4 – Security and Cryptology

This Springer imprint is published by the registered company Springer Nature Switzerland AG
The registered company address is: Gewerbestrasse 11, 6330 Cham, Switzerland

Preface

This volume contains the papers presented at the 13th International Symposium on Foundations and Practice of Security (FPS 2020). The symposium was scheduled to be held at Polytechnique Montréal (Canada) on 1, 2, and 3 December 2020. Exceptionally, due to COVID-19, FPS 2020 was held as a virtual event.

The symposium received 23 submissions, from countries all over the world. At least two reviews were made for each paper. The Program Committee selected 11 full papers and 1 short paper. The program covers diverse security research themes including Analysis and Detection, Prevention and Efficiency, Privacy by Design, and Digital Identities. The program was complemented with two keynote presentations by Christine Beauchamp (from the Canadian Centre for Cyber Security, Canada) and Dr. Syrine Tlili, (from the National Digital Certification Agency, Tunisia); and some panel discussions.

We would like to thank all the authors who submitted their research results, allowing us to create the 2020 program of FPS. We greatly thank the local organization committee, Militza Jean, Kacem Khaled, and Henrique Amaral Misson (all three from Polytechnique Montréal); as well as the external reviewers, the steering committee members, and the publications chair, Joaquin Garcia-Alfaro. We also want to express our gratitude to all the attendees. Last, but by no means least, we want to thank all the sponsors for making the event possible.

We hope the articles contained in this proceedings volume will be valuable for your professional activities in the area.

January 2021

José M. Fernandez
Jean-Yves Marion
Gabriela Nicolescu
Assia Tria

Organization

General Chairs

Jose Fernandez   Polytechnique Montréal, Canada
Jean-Yves Marion   Université de Lorraine, LORIA, France

Program Committee Chairs

Gabriela Nicolescu   Polytechnique Montréal, Canada
Assia Tria   CEA, France

Publications Chair

Joaquin Garcia-Alfaro   Télécom SudParis, France

Local Organizing Committee

Militza Jean   Polytechnique Montréal, Canada
Kacem Khaled   Polytechnique Montréal, Canada
Henrique Amaral Misson   HumanITas Solutions, Canada

Program Committee

Abdelmalek Benzekri   Université Toulouse 3 Paul Sabatier, France
Guillaume Bonfante   Université de Lorraine, LORIA, France
Driss Bouzidi   Mohammed V University in Rabat, Morocco
Jordi Castellà-Roca   Universitat Rovira i Virgili, Spain
Ana Rosa Cavalli   Télécom SudParis, France
Frédéric Cuppens   Polytechnique Montréal, Canada
Nora Cuppens-Boulahia   Polytechnique Montréal, Canada
Mila Dalla Preda   University of Verona, Italy
Mourad Debbabi   Concordia University, Canada
Josep Domingo-Ferrer   Universitat Rovira i Virgili, Spain
Nicola Dragoni   DTU Informatics, Technical University of Denmark, Denmark
Sébastien Gambs   Université du Québec à Montréal, France
Guang Gong   University of Waterloo, Canada
Abdelwahab Hamou-Lhadj   Concordia University, Canada
Guy-Vincent Jourdan   University of Ottawa, Canada

Steering Committee

Additional Reviewers

Carles Angles-Tafalla
Pradeep K. Atrey
Stefano Berlato
Anis Bkakria
Andrey Chechulin
Cristofol Dauden-Esmel
Edlira Dushku
Shihui Fu
Fadi Hassan
Vinh Hoa La
Najeeb Jebreel

Abdelkader Lahmadi
Wissam Mallouli
Kalikinkar Mandal
Catherine Meadows
Huu Nghia Nguyen
Octavio Perez-Kempner
Maxime Puys
Veena Ravishankar
Yusuke Sakai
Giada Sciarretta

Contents

Privacy by Design

Analysis and Detection

New Wrapper Feature Selection Algorithm for Anomaly-Based Intrusion Detection Systems

Meriem Kherbache[1(✉)], David Espes[2], and Kamal Amroun[1]

[1] Limed Laboratory, Faculty of Exact Sciences, University Abderrahmane Mira, Bejaia, Algeria
kherbache.meriem1@gmail.com, kamalamroun@gmail.com
[2] University of Western Brittany, Brest, France
david.espes@univ-brest.fr

Abstract. With advanced persistent and zero-days threats, the threat landscape is constantly evolving. Signature-based defense is ineffective against these new attacks. Anomaly-based intrusion detection systems rely on classification models, trained on specific datasets, to detect them. Their efficiency is related to the features used by the classifier. Feature selection is a fundamental phase of anomaly-based intrusion detection systems. It selects the near-optimal subset of features in order to improve the detection accuracy and reduce the classification time. This paper introduces a new wrapper method based on two phases. The first phase adopts a correlation analysis between two variables as a measure of feature quality. This phase aims to select the features that contribute the most to the classification by selecting the ones that highly correlated to either the normal or attack traffic but not both. The second phase is used to search for a proper subset that improves the detection accuracy. Our approach is evaluated using three well-known datasets: NSL-KDD, UNSW-NB15 and CICIDS2017. The evaluation results show that our algorithm significantly increases the detection accuracy and improves the detection time. Moreover, it is particularly efficient on stealthy attacks.

Keywords: Intrusion detection system · Correlation · Support vector machine · Feature selection

1 Introduction

To circumvent the increase in protection mechanisms' quality, attackers use new patterns to reach their target. Intrusion Detection Systems (IDS) play an essential role in achieving the security of networking resources and infrastructures. However, signature-based IDS are not able to detect these new threats. Unlike them, anomaly-based IDS is a system designed to monitor network traffic for any suspicious activity and sends alerts while any such activity is discovered.

Anomaly-based IDS are dealing with data traffic that is increasing day by day. The performance of the IDS is highly dependent on the data features they use in

© Springer Nature Switzerland AG 2021
G. Nicolescu et al. (Eds.): FPS 2020, LNCS 12637, pp. 3–19, 2021.
https://doi.org/10.1007/978-3-030-70881-8_1

their model. Irrelevant features affect the quality of an IDS and cause an increase in false alarms which involve a significant workload for the administrators. For each class of attack, they have to use the most relevant features and remove irrelevant or redundant ones.

Feature Selection (FS) is one of the most important step for anomaly-based detection systems. It is applied either to eliminate redundant and irrelevant features from the network traffic data or to select the optimal features for detection accuracy. FS methods can be divided into two types [1]: wrapper and filter methods.

Wrapper methods exploit machine learning algorithms to test different sets of features and evaluate their accuracy. They select more suitable features than filter methods since they employ the performance of the learning algorithm as an evaluation criterion, but they are highly computational demanding.

Filter method does not use any machine learning algorithm to filter out the irrelevant and redundant features [10]. Rather, they utilize statistical methods, such as distance [17], information gain [2], gain ratio [11], correlation [15] and principal components analysis [6,12] methods, on the underlying features of the training data to evaluate their relevance. These methods are known for their speed. However, the resulting feature set may not be the best one.

Filter and wrapper methods have both strengths and weaknesses. Same if filter methods are faster than wrapper methods, they form a feature set that is independent from the learning algorithm and so have a lower detection accuracy. In enterprise, the computational time for training a model is not as important as the detection accuracy. Most of the time, the model can be trained offline. As wrapper methods can find the best feature set, they are more suitable to detect new threats and improve the overall security of an enterprise (e.g. attacks difficult to detect due to the little traffic used and similarities with normal traffic).

In this paper, a new wrapper feature selection method is proposed. The main objective of our wrapper method is twofold: 1) increase the detection accuracy on stealthy and persistent attacks and 2) distinguish the attack that triggers the alarm. Persistent attacks (They are performed during a long period of time and use few traffic to reach the target. Unlike noisy attacks and stealthy ones (e.g., Denial of Service, user to remote, Shellcode, etc.), they are particularly difficult to detect due to the little traffic used and similarities with normal traffic. Our algorithm is based on a feature-class correlation approach to select the most relevant feature sets for a class of attack. The best set of feature candidates is then chosen by the classifier, based on the best first strategy. The performance of a given feature set is so measured by its ability to predict the class that not only increases the detection accuracy but also improves the distinguishability of the attacks. This last factor is important because it helps the operator to respond to an attack appropriately.

To show the efficiency of our method, we present an extensive experimental comparison on three well-known intrusion detection datasets: the NSL-KDD, the UNSW2015 and the CICIDS2017. The approach is effective not only for stealthy and persistent attacks but also for the most noisy ones.

This paper is organized as follows: Sect. 2 introduces the concept of FS and recent feature selection algorithms, then, Sect. 3 formalizes the feature selection problem introduced by correlation-based methods. Section 4 presents the proposed model. Section 5 describes the experimental details and results. Finally, a summary of the paper is drawn in Sect. 6.

2 Related Works

Recently wrapper methods are the most common FS methods because they generally perform better than filter methods. However, they require more computational power than filter methods due to the use of successive iterations to find the best feature candidates.

Wrapper methods are principally composed of two steps: the search step and the evaluation step. The search step consists of selecting several sets of features using different methods such as bio-inspired, statistical or both. The evaluation step tests the previous feature sets to select the best one i.e., the one with the highest detection accuracy. The most recent methods are presented below and classified regarding their search methods.

Bio-Inspired-Based Search Methods: Genetic algorithms are widely used in feature selection methods. They are a good way to realize a search method, called genetic search, because they use probabilistic selection rules. Moreover, unlike traditional methods, they have the ability to avoid being trapped in a local optimal solution.

In [13], the authors use a genetic algorithm (GA) to form several set of features. The decision tree learning algorithm is then used to find the most relevant features to detect complex attacks i.e., attacks that use a few traffic to be performed. This method is tested on the NSL-KDD dataset and shows significant improvement in the detection rate of U2R and R2L attacks.

The authors in [9] propose a method that is based on a genetic algorithm as a search strategy and logistic regression as a learning algorithm. The proposed approach is based on three stages: a pre-processing phase, a feature selection phase, and a classification stage. Some experiments are conducted on KDD99 and UNSW-NB15 datasets. The method is good to detect noisy attacks. However, stealthy attacks (such as U2r attack for KDD99 or Backdoor, Analysis, Shellcode and DoS attacks for UNSW-NB15) are not well detected.

The authors in [3] propose a neural networks with 2 hidden layers for feature selection architecture and compares two commonly used normalization preprocessing techniques. They find that using ZScore normalization increased the performance of their model.

Statistical-Based Search Methods: Some papers propose to use a statistical method during the search phase. Unlike filter methods, statistical methods are used to form several sets of relevant features.

The authors in [18] propose a new wrapper feature selection algorithm based on feature augmentation. Using the logarithm marginal density ratios transformation, they obtain new transformed features of better quality. During the evaluation step, the support vector machine (SVM) algorithm is applied with these augmented features. Applied to NSL-KDD, the results show that it achieves a better and more robust performance than existing methods in terms of accuracy, detection rate, false alarm rate, and training speed.

Hybrid-Based Search Methods: Some works do not limit their approach to only one search strategy. They combine a bio-inspired method with a statistical one in order to increase the detection rate of the IDS.

In a study conducted in [4], the authors propose a hybrid-based search method combining a statistical algorithm, the linear correlation coefficient algorithm, and a bio-inspired algorithm, the cuttlefish algorithm. The decision tree classifier is used in the evaluation phase to select the best set of features. For performance verification, the proposed method is applied to the KDD99 dataset. The results show a high accuracy (95.03%) and detection rate (95.23%) with a low false-positive rate (1.65%).

The authors in [19] combine a statistical method, correlation information entropy, with a bio-inspired algorithm, binary particle swarm optimization algorithm. Correlation information entropy reduces the feature dimension after sorting the features and removing the irrelevant ones. Then, the particle swarm optimization algorithm forms several feature sets and the classifier selects the best one. The results show an improvement in the classification performance and the testing time of a sample is significantly reduced.

In [7], the authors propose a hybrid-based search method for feature selection. First, the proposed model uses the correlation feature selection (CFS) algorithm to remove irrelevant features. Then three different search techniques (best-first, greedy stepwise and genetic algorithms) are used to form several sets of features. The evaluation step uses a random forest classifier to evaluate each of the features that were first selected by the search methods. Applied on KDD99 and DARPA 1999 datasets, the experimental results show that the selected features produce a satisfactory outcome.

Despite its complexity, wrapper methods remain the best in terms of efficiency. As seen in the literature, they are designed to select features as a whole regardless of whether the attack is low or high traffic. The only known method that focuses on the selection of weak signal features is proposed in [9] and [13]. However, the effectiveness of the detection of stealthy and persistent attacks is still not achieved. Our objective is to propose a method that detects stealthy and persistent attacks without degrading the detection rate of the noisy ones.

3   Problem Statement

Correlation is the most widely used technique in statistics to measure the degree of relationship between random variables. Correlation ranges from -1 to 1. When the absolute value of the correlation tends to 1 it implies that the features are linearly correlated. It means that if attribute A increases (resp. decreases), then attribute B also increases (resp. decreases).

Correlation methods are very useful in many applications such as intrusion detection systems. For feature selection, the correlation method is used for finding the association between the features of a dataset. It consists of finding the subset of features that respects these two conditions [5]: 1) good feature sets contain features that are highly correlated with the class, 2) yet uncorrelated with each other. Therefore, the correlation for feature selection can be computed in two ways:

- Feature-class correlation: it indicates the degree of correlation of a feature with a specific class. If the value is higher than the threshold value (e.g., 0.5), then the feature will be selected. Feature-class correlation can be very beneficial when the size of the traffic of the different classes are equal (normal and attack), otherwise correlation tends towards the dominant traffic and it can falsify the good features.
- Feature-feature correlation: it represents the association between two features. It is mainly used to identify and remove unnecessary, irrelevant and redundant features that do not contribute to or decrease the accuracy of the predictive model [8]. If two features are linearly dependent, then their correlation coefficient is +1 or −1. If the features are uncorrelated, the correlation coefficient is 0. As correlated features share the same properties, redundant features do not increase the diversity of the feature set and have to be removed from it. Fewer features usually means a big improvement in speed, and so removing these features can make the learning algorithm faster. However, this may affect the effectiveness of the method because it is possible to remove features that correlate with the class.

For a dataset composed of n samples, the correlation between two features $X = \{x_1, \cdots, x_n\}$ and $Y = \{y_1, \cdots, y_n\}$ is given by the following equation:

$$\rho = corr(X, Y) = \frac{cov(X, Y)}{\sqrt{\sigma^2(X)\sigma^2(Y)}} = \frac{\sum_{i=1}^{n}(x_i - \bar{x}_i)(y_i - \bar{y}_i)}{\sqrt{\sum_{i=1}^{n}(x_i - \bar{x}_i)^2 \sum_{i=1}^{n}(y_i - \bar{y}_i)^2}} \tag{1}$$

where cov is the covariance and σ is the variance.

Same if the correlation is very useful for feature selection in IDS, it may suffer from three problems: 1) difficulty to find the best trade-off between feature-class and feature-feature correlation methods, 2) difficulty to select correlated features with multiple classes and 3) non-dependency of the classifier.

For the first problem, feature-class and feature-feature correlation methods have complementary purpose. The goal of the feature-class correlation method is to select the most relevant features for a specific class and so to increase the overall efficiency of the detection, while the goal of the feature-feature correlation is to remove redundant features and so to decrease the detection time.

Same if their goal is different, these two methods are interdependent. Feature-class correlation selects all the relevant features for a class. It completely disregards the redundancy between features. Unlike it, feature-feature correlation removes redundant features. Sometimes redundant features are necessary to increase the efficiency of attacks' detection. They highlight a specific property that can be necessary to detect attacks especially for the advanced persistent ones. A trade-off has to be found between the efficiency and the detection time.

The second problem concerns the correlation of some features with multiple classes. If the classes only represent different attacks, these features are useful to increase the detection efficiency but it decreases attacks distinguishability. It may be important for the operator to distinguish between attacks. Most of the time, the response is specific for each attack in order to mitigate it. If the distinguishability is an important factor for the operator, the feature selection algorithm should be tuned to consider it.

The correlation of a feature with an attack class is not enough to increase the detection efficiency. The correlation with other classes must also be considered. If a feature correlates highly with both a normal and an attack classes, the features is not relevant to detect the attack. The classification will tend to follow the distribution of classes in the corpus i.e., the sample will be classified in the majority class that is, most of the time, the normal class. The rate of false-positive results would be greatly increased.

For the last problem, the correlation is not enough to determine the efficiency of a feature selection algorithm. Same if it is a good indicator, the relevancy of a feature can only be known after testing it. A feature is relevant for the classification if its removal degrades the detection accuracy. So, the wrapper algorithm should use the same classifier, as the one used for testing, during the evaluation step in order to return the optimal feature set.

As aforementioned, correlation methods have pros and cons. Correlation-based feature selection algorithms have to be designed in such a way that only its benefits remain. In this paper, we propose a new feature selection algorithm that can significantly decrease the training and testing times while maintaining high detection rates and low false-positive rates.

4   New Wrapper Method for Feature Selection

As for other wrapper methods, our proposed model has two steps: a search phase and an evaluation phase. In the first step, the algorithm uses a statistical-based search method. The correlation is used to remove redundant features and find the most relevant ones to increase the detection accuracy. Several sets of features are formed during this stage. The second step uses a classifier to select the best set of features among all the previously formed candidates.

The novelty of the approach is that the search method is specifically designed to solve the problems of correlation-based methods (see Sect. 3). Correlation-based methods usually uses either feature-class correlation or feature-feature correlation. In feature-class correlation, the correlation between features and the class is estimated globally, so it tends to select features that are highly predictive of the class. However, in some cases, some features that represent well the attack class are neglected since the attack traffic is in a small area of the instance space over which normal traffic is dominant. This is typically the case for Stealthy and persistent attacks and so these methods have a low detection accuracy. On the other hand, feature-feature correlation methods are only used to remove redundant features and do not express the relevancy of features to a class.

The proposed model overcome these shortcomings by applying feature-feature correlation in a new way. A feature is relevant to detect an attack if it is highly correlated to either the normal or attack classes but not both. So, our algorithm selects the feature pairs that highly correlate with either the attack class or the normal class but not both. This approach only keeps the advantages of both feature-class correlation and feature-feature correlation. In the evaluation phase, a classifier selects the best set of these pairs of features.

The overall architecture of our approach is depicted in Fig. 1. It shows the two stages of the proposed model and how it is used in conjunction with a machine learning scheme. The approach is generic enough to support all types of classifier. However, to optimize the results, the classifier has to be same in all the stages of the method.

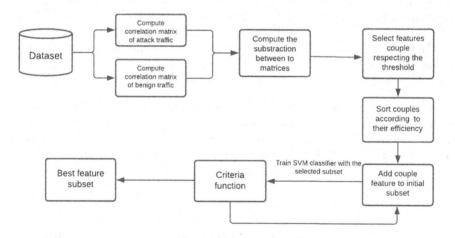

Fig. 1. Architecture of the proposed model

4.1   Search Phase

Each step of our search phase is done to solve the three problems of correlation-based methods. The objective is to only keep the advantages of these methods without retaining their flaws.

1) Difficulty to find the best trade-off between feature-class and feature-feature correlation methods:

The selection of relevant features i.e., the ones that optimize the detection accuracy for all classes at the same time, is very difficult. Informative features for a class may be uninformative for another class. In order to avoid such a bias, the attack classes have to be considered individually.

Let's suppose a training dataset D_{train} composed of n classes of attack and 1 class of benign traffic. The training dataset is splitted in $n + 1$ datasets i.e., $D_{train} = \{A_1, ..., A_n, B\}$ where A_i is the dataset of the ith attack class and B the dataset of the benign class.

For each resulting dataset $D \in D_{train}$, any sample d_i is described by a vector of features $d_i = \langle f_{i1}, \cdots, f_{im} \rangle$ where m is the number of features and f_{ij} is the jth feature value of the d_i vector. The function $F(D, j)$ returns a set composed of the jth feature for each sample $d_i \in D$ i.e.,

$$F(D, j) = f_{ij} \mid \forall i \in \{1, n\}, f_{ij} \in d_i$$

As feature-class correlation tends towards the dominant traffic, this correlation method is not suitable to detect stealthy and persistent attacks. So, our approach uses a feature-feature correlation on each class of the training dataset. The feature-feature correlation is applied in this step, not only to remove redundant features but also to analyze the traffic and find similarities.

First, the Pearson's correlation coefficient ρ is computed for each class of traffic using Eq. 1. This joins both features f_i and f_j in such a way that a possible value between -1 and 1 results from a matrix.

Property 1: To avoid bias in the selection of the most relevant features, the feature-feature correlation has to be calculated distinctly not only between attack classes but also between an attack class and the benign class. A correlation matrix for each attack class A and the benign class B are formed:

$$M_a = Corr(F(A, i), F(A, j))$$

$$M_b = Corr(F(B, i), F(B, j))$$

Once the correlation matrix for each category of attack and benign is obtained, a couple of attack and benign matrices are exploited to select feature pairs that are correlated in the first matrix and uncorrelated in the second one (or inversely).

2) Difficulty to select correlated features with multiple classes:

Features that correlate with multiple classes are not relevant especially when these classes contain both attack and normal classes. These features increase the rate of false-positive alerts. The operational cost for operators would significantly increase because they would have to check false alarms that is time consuming.

The feature-feature correlation, computed previously for each class, is a good indicator to determine whether features are correlated either for both, the attack and benign classes, or not (see Property 2).

Property 2: The subtraction between two matrices is applied in order to select features that are weakly correlated with the attack classes and strongly corre-lated with the benign classes or inversely.

$$M_{resu} = Abs(M_b) - Abs(M_a)$$

where *Abs* is a function that computes the absolute value of each element of the matrix.

The resultant matrix, M_{resu}, will be used to analyze the similarities between attack and benign classes. Each value of the matrix close to 1 would indicate that a couple of features is well correlated with an attack class and less correlated with the benign class or inversely. The calculation of the resultant matrix collects couples of features with a correlation difference close to 1. Doing so will prevent the attack traffic from being drowned in by the benign traffic or inversely, which would increase the number of false positives during detection. For this purpose, all couples of features with a value higher than the threshold, $\alpha > 0.5$, is selected as candidates (see Algorithm 1).

The correlation can exist in a spectrum represented by absolute values from 0 to 1. Slightly strong positive correlation can be like 0.5 or 0.7. A very strong correlation ranges from 0.9 to 1. This threshold value is set to select features with a low correlation between attack and benign classes. For example, if we assume for a couple (f_i, f_j) a correlation value that belongs to the interval [0.9–1] for the M_a matrix and [0–0.4] for the M_b matrix, this couple will be a very good candidate because it satisfies the threshold. So, the value of the resultant matrix belongs to the interval [0.5–1].

3) Non-dependency of the classifier:

Same if the previous step results in a reduced dimensional feature space that is composed of the best feature candidates, the correlation is only an indicator of the relevancy of a feature. The detection accuracy can only be known after classification.

The last step of our search method applies a classifier to rank the features in decreasing order of detection accuracy. The few bias, that could be introduced by the correlation approach, would be removed following this step. The best feature candidates are used as initial set in the evaluation phase of our wrapper approach.

Algorithm 1. Find the couples of features

1: **Inputs:**
   $A = \{a_1, \cdots, a_q\}$, $a_i = \langle f_{i1}, \cdots, f_{im} \rangle$ // The attack traffic.
   $B = \{b_1, \cdots, b_p\}$, $b_i = \langle f_{i1}, \cdots, f_{im} \rangle$ //The benign traffic.
2: **Outputs:** C// the couples of features.
3: **Begin**
4: $i = 1; j = 1$
5: **while** $i \leq m$ **do**
6:    **while** $j \leq m$ **do**
7:       $M_a(i,j) = corr(a_i, a_j);$ // see Equation (1)
8:       $M_b(i,j) = corr(b_i, b_j);$
9:       $M_{resu}(i,j) = Abs(M_a(i,j)) - Abs(M_b(i,j))$
10:    **end while**
11: **end while**
12: $\alpha = 0.5; d = 1, i = 1; j = 1;$
13: **while** $i \leq m$ **do**
14:    **while** $j \leq m$ **do**
15:       **if** $M_{resu}(i,j) \geq \alpha$ **then**
16:          $C(d) = (f_i, f_j);$
17:          $d = d + 1;$
18:       **end if**
19:    **end while**
20: **end while**
21: **End**
22: **Return** C ;

4.2   Evaluation Phase

To find the near-optimal subset of features, many search strategies are proposed in the literature that depend on the number of features m. If it is small, the brute force method is applied to scan all these subsets. But when this number becomes large, random search strategies, such as the best first search or genetic algorithm, are usually chosen due to their computational efficiency.

In this work, we opt for the best first search using the SVM classifier, which returns good results for classification in several areas. The best first search method starts with either no feature or all features. The search progresses forward through the search space adding one feature at a time. The advantage of this method is that it can be traced back to the previous subset and continue the search from there [5]. The problem of this method is the choice of the starting point. Selecting a starting point in the feature set space can affect the direction of the search.

Our approach deals with feature couples because the couples are ordered according to their degree of contribution in the classification. The first couple c_1 of this ordered set C is used as starting point. The search progresses forward iteratively through the search space by adding a couple of feature to the initial subset only if it improves the detection rate of SVM classifier. The search stops when the number of couples is reached or the search shows no improvement over the current best subset.

4.3   Complexity

The proposed method is composed of different phases, each with their own complexity. The first phase computes the feature-feature correlation matrix for each class of traffic.

Property 3: The complexity for the first phase is $O(n(m^2 - m))$.

Proof: The first step of the search method computes feature-feature correlation matrices, where n is the number of samples and m is the initial number of features. While in our work the feature-feature correlation matrix is computed twice (for attack and benign traffic), only half of the correlation pairs are computed. Indeed the correlation values of f_{ij} and f_{ji} are the same.

The second phase introduces a higher computational complexity since it uses the SVM classifier and searches for the best subset of features.

Property 4: The complexity for the second phase is $O(n^2(m^2 - m))$.

Proof: The computational complexity of SVM varies greatly according to its kernel. In this paper, the kernel used by SVM is Radial Basis Function (RBF) which has a complexity of $O(n^2)$. The complexity to train the SVM classifier is multiplied by the number of pairs that belong to the subset of features.

According to Properties 3 and 4, the complexity of the method tends to $O(n^2)$. The number of features m is very low compared to the samples in the dataset n i.e., $m \ll n$. So the value m is negligible and most of the computational complexity is due to SVM.

5   Experiments

5.1   Datasets

In our experiments, we have used three different datasets to verify the efficiency of the proposed algorithm. The NSL-KDD dataset[1] is the most popular dataset in the literature, The UNSW-NB15[2] is a recommended dataset for IDS and CICIDS2017 is the most recent one.

The NSL-KDD dataset consists of 125973 vectors, each of which contains 41 features [14,16]. The dataset is fully labeled and contains four classes of attack (denial of service (DoS), unauthorized access to local supervisor privileges (User

---

[1] http://nsl.cs.unb.ca/KDD/NSL-KDD.html.

[2] https://www.unsw.adfa.edu.au/unsw-canberra-cyber/cybersecurity/ADFA-NB15-Datasets/.

to root or U2r), Remote to Local (R2L) and Probe) and the benign class. This dataset is always interesting because all the approaches proposed in the literature encounter difficulties in effectively detecting R2l and U2r.

The UNSW-NB15 dataset contains 2.5 million samples. 49 features are computed from the 100 GB of raw data, captured in a modern network architecture. It has nine attack classes: Backdoor, DoS, Generic, Reconnaissance, Analysis, Fuzzers, Exploit, Shellcode, and Worms. It is considered as a new benchmark dataset that can be used for IDS and is recommended. To improve the results' reproducibility, it comes along with predefined splits of a training set (175,341 samples) and a testing set (82,332 samples) that are used in our work.

The CICIDS2017 dataset is the most recent dataset proposed in the literature. It consists of more than 5 billion of vectors, each of which contains 80 features. These vectors are labeled as either benign or attack, with 14 types of attack. As for NSL-KDD, CICIDS2017 has a large disparity in the number of vectors for each attack. Some attacks such as DoS, DDoS and PortScan generate a dense traffic while the traffic generated by the other ones (Heartbleed, Brute Force, XSS, SQL Injection, Infiltration, Botnet) is quite scarce.

5.2   Preprocessing

Except for UNSW-NB15 where the proposed training and testing datasets are used, the NSL-KDD and CICIDS2017 datasets are randomly split in two: 60% of all the traffic is included in the training dataset and the testing dataset is made up of the remaining 40%.

The two datasets (NSL-KDD and UNSW-NB15) consists of two types: numerical and nominal features. The one-hot encoding is used for non-numerical features. For CICIDS2017, all the features are numerical but the data needs to be cleaned. All missing values were replaced with zeros and the infinite values have been replaced by the average of their attribute value.

After their transformations, the datasets need to be normalized. Indeed, the features provide different scales of value. Some features with large numerical values may dominate the classifier's model compared to features with relatively low numerical values. Therefore, normalization is a scale transformation that allows features to be mapped over a normalized range. A quick and simple approach called minimum-maximum method normalizes a vector X using the following equation:

$$\bar{X} = x - min/(max - min) \tag{2}$$

where $\bar{X}$ denotes the normalized vector, x refers to the corresponding vector value and min and max are the minima and maximum values of the vector.

5.3   Result Analysis

To evaluate the performance of the approach model, four metrics are considered: the Detection Rate, the False Positive Rate, the Precision and the F1 score. They are defined as in the following equations:

– Detection Rate (DR): it is the correctly detected intrusion number divided by the number of attacks in the data set. This metric is the main indicator to identify the capacity of a feature selection algorithm to select the adequate features to classify correctly an attack. It can also show the effectiveness of an FS algorithm to help in the detection of new attacks.

$$DR = Sensitivity = TP/(TP + FN) \qquad (3)$$

Where TP, FP and FN are the number of True positives, False positives and False negatives respectively.

– False Positive Rate (FPR): it is the number of the normal data which is wrongly detected divided by the number of normal connections in the data set. This indicator is important in the field of IDS because it increases the analysis work of the administrator. Each reported alert must be studied. A high rate of false positives complicates his job.

$$FPR = (1 - Specificity) = FP/(TN + FP) \qquad (4)$$

– Precision: it is the ratio of the correctly predicted positive observations to the total predicted positive observations.

$$Precision = TP/(TP + FP) \qquad (5)$$

– F1 score: it is the weighted average of Precision and Recall.

$$F1Score = 2 * (Recall * Precision)/(Recall + Precision) \qquad (6)$$

For selecting the features for each attack we apply the proposed model for each pair (type of attack, normal). In our case, we are dealing with a binary classification problem, where a connection is to be classified either normal or intrusive. The SVM kernel used for classification is RBF.

Table 1 compares the SVM classifier using all the features to the SVM classifier using the features obtained by our wrapper method. The proposed approach obtains good results. Except for the infiltration attack, the features returned by the algorithm allow to exceed a detection rate of 90% systematically. For Heartbleed, Sql-injection and Botnet attacks, a perfect detection rate of 100% is reached.

For the UNSW-NB15, almost all attacks are improved in terms of detection rates. The attacks Fuzzers (resp. Analysis) provides the best Detection rate of classification which is about 99.66% (resp. 99.35%) compared when all the features are used.

In average, the proposed algorithm increases the detection rate of 18.49% (resp. 26.66%, 65.06%) for the NSL-KDD dataset (resp. the CICIDS2017 dataset and UNSW-NB15). Therefore, the proposed method is quite close to the near-optimal set of features for each class of attack. The most innovative point of our method is to find the best trade-off between the variance of the features and the correlation between the benign and attack traffic to obtain a high detection rate.

Table 1. Comparison between SVM with all the features and SVM with reduced features for the different datasets

Dataset		SVM with reduced features				SVM with all features			
	Attack	DR%	FPR%	Precision%	F1 score%	DR%	FPR%	Precision%	F1 score%
CICIDS2017	FTP	99.93	0.07	99.83	99.88	99.67	0.32	97.38	98.53
	SSH	99.96	0.04	99.54	99.75	99.70	0.3	98.77	99.23
	Heartbleed	100	0	100	100	66.66	33.33	100	80
	Sql-injection	100	0	96.31	98.12	0	100	NAN	0
	XSS	99.29	0.71	99.51	99.40	98.23	1.77	91.03	94.49
	Brute	96.46	3.54	99.94	98.17	99.32	0.68	98.81	99.06
	Infiltration	88.23	11.77	98.51	93.09	23.52	76.48	66.91	34.97
	Botnet	96.78	3.22	96.47	96.63	88.88	22.22	91.67	90.25
	Port-Scan	99.97	0.03	99.96	99.97	99.97	0.03	99.96	99.97
	DosSlowloris	99.86	0.14	93.86	96.77	99.12	0.88	99.25	99.21
	DosHulk	96.40	3.60	98.01	97.20	99.95	0.05	99.98	99.96
	DosGoldenEye	98.14	1.86	98.38	98.32	97.90	2.10	99.24	98.51
	DosHTTP	99.50	1.50	99.94	99.72	99.18	0.82	98.80	98.96
NSL-KDD	DOS	99.79	0.21	99.56	99.68	99.81	0.09	99.95	99.88
	Probe	99.31	0.69	99.34	99.23	98.23	1.77	99.51	99.21
	R2L	97.82	2.18	98.25	98.08	91.06	8.94	99.26	94.99
	U2R	93.10	6.90	99.06	97.99	20.68	79.32	99.87	34.24
UNSW-NB15	Reconnaissance	98.66	1.34	93.05	95.73	96.26	3.74	98.43	97.33
	Fuzzers	99.66	0.34	92.23	95.84	95.97	4.03	94.30	95.16
	Worms	93.47	6.53	99.42	96.35	60.06	39.94	99.85	75
	Backdoor	91.56	8.44	98.03	94.59	86.48	13.52	99.49	92.53
	Exploits	97.76	2.24	97.74	97.39	96.32	3.68	97.76	96.99
	Dos	95.33	4.67	97.35	95.23	94.58	5.42	98.61	96.55
	Shellcode	95.68	4.32	96.87	96.27	87.04	12.96	88.41	92.51
	Generic	99.21	0.79	99.92	99.56	98.77	1.23	99.94	99.31
	Analysis	99.35	0.65	98.42	98.89	90.88	9.12	98.87	94.66

Indeed, the it selects all the features with a high variance and returns the ones that are lowly correlated with both the benign traffic and the attack traffic.

In the same way, the false positive rate is significantly reduced. the proposed approach reduces the number of false alerts that are triggered. In addition, it reduces the burden of the administrator work and eases the analysis of the true positive alerts. It also complicates the task of the attacker who can no more hide its real attack in a lot of fake ones to divert the attention of the administrator.

Selecting the best features improves the DR, FPR, Precision and F1 score. Also this method reduces the training and testing times significantly. On average, the proposed method reduces the test time by 27.23 s for the NSL-KDD dataset (the difference between the test time when all features are used and when the reduced set of features is used), 58.98 s for the UNSW-NB15 and 131.12 s for the CICIDS2017 dataset. The execution time of the classifier is highly correlated with the number of features. Indeed, FS reduces the computational cost of training algorithms by reducing the dimension of the vectors of a dataset.

As shown in Table 2, we compare our method with one of the most recent wrapper using a correlation-based search approach [7]. Our method performs

Table 2. Comparing our approach with related works

Category	Kamarudin et al. [7]		Our proposed model	
	DR%	FPR%	DR%	FPR%
Worms	82.60	7.40	**93.47**	6.53
Shellcode	72.35	7.75	**95.68**	4.32
Reconnaissance	93.05	6.95	**98.66**	1.34
Analysis	71.24	28.76	**99.35**	0.65
Generic	99.52	0.68	99.21	0.79
Backdoor	60.31	39.89	**91.56**	8.44
Dos	94.33	5.67	**95.33**	4.67
Fuzzers	98.40	1.60	**99.66**	0.34
Exploits	99.32	0.68	97.76	2.24
Dos	99.54	0.46	**99.79**	0.21
Probe	99.70	0.3	99.31	0.69
R2l	98.06	1.94	97.82	2.18
U2r	72.56	27.64	**93.10**	6.90

significantly better on DR and FPR. It improves the DR of 20.16% (resp. 99.56%) for the NSL-KDD (resp. UNSW-NB15) dataset compared to [7]. This latter encounters difficulty in detecting stealthy attacks such as U2r, Analysis, Backdoor and Shellcode. These results show that our method is very efficient to detect not only stealthy and persistent attacks but also the noisy ones.

From the results, we can see that our method is very efficient for each class of attack in each dataset. Moreover, the problem of misclassification between attack categories disappears and the classification rate is significantly increased.

6   Conclusion

The goal of the proposed model was to take advantage of the correlation measures and propose a new wrapper feature selection model. Feature selection is a fundamental part of anomaly based detection. Beside reducing the classification in terms of time, it improves the efficiency of an IDS.

Our wrapper feature selection method is a combination of two approaches: correlation and SVM. In the first step, the correlation focuses on the reduction of redundant features and selects the most relevant couples of feature that is highly correlated with the class of attack and uncorrelated with the benign traffic or inversely. Then, it selects candidate couples to be treated by SVM to rank them according to their efficiency. The Best first search method is applied to start with the first couple elected as the initial subset. It iteratively continues the search for the optimal subset to improve the performance of the classification.

The proposed approach has been evaluated using three types of datasets: NSL-KDD, UNSW-NB15 and CICIDS2017. The performances of the IDS are greatly improved in terms of detection time, accuracy and detection rate after reducing the features with our algorithm. Moreover, the results show that our main objective is achieved. Indeed it performs very well to detect all types of attack i.e., either stealthy and sophisticated attacks or more noisy ones.

References

1. Aljawarneh, S., Aldwairi, M., Yassein, M.B.: Anomaly-based intrusion detection system through feature selection analysis and building hybrid efficient model. J. Comput. Sci. **25**, 152–160 (2018)
2. Ambusaidi, M.A., He, X., Nanda, P., Tan, Z.: Building an intrusion detection system using a filter-based feature selection algorithm. IEEE Trans. Comput. **65**(10), 2986–2998 (2016)
3. Davis, A., Gill, S., Wong, R., Tayeb, S.: Feature selection for deep neural networks in cyber security applications. In: 2020 IEEE International IOT, Electronics and Mechatronics Conference (IEMTRONICS), pp. 1–7. IEEE (2020)
4. Eesa, A.S., Orman, Z., Brifcani, A.M.A.: A novel feature-selection approach based on the cuttlefish optimization algorithm for intrusion detection systems. Expert Syst. Appl. **42**(5), 2670–2679 (2015)
5. Hall, M.A.: Correlation-based feature selection for machine learning (1999)
6. De la Hoz, E., De La Hoz, E., Ortiz, A., Ortega, J., Prieto, B.: PCA filtering and probabilistic SOM for network intrusion detection. Neurocomputing **164**, 71–81 (2015)
7. Kamarudin, M.H., Maple, C., Watson, T.: Hybrid feature selection technique for intrusion detection system. Int. J. High Perform. Comput. Netw. **13**(2), 232–240 (2019)
8. Karegowda, A.G., Manjunath, A., Jayaram, M.: Comparative study of attribute selection using gain ratio and correlation based feature selection. Int. J. Inf. Technol. Knowl. Manage. **2**(2), 271–277 (2010)
9. Khammassi, C., Krichen, S.: A GA-LR wrapper approach for feature selection in network intrusion detection. Comput. Secur. **70**, 255–277 (2017). https://doi.org/10.1016/j.cose.2017.06.005. http://www.sciencedirect.com/science/article/pii/S0167404817301244
10. Kumari, B., Swarnkar, T.: Filter versus wrapper feature subset selection in large dimensionality micro array: a review (2011)
11. Muttaqien, I.Z., Ahmad, T.: Increasing performance of IDS by selecting and transforming features. In: 2016 IEEE International Conference on Communication, Networks and Satellite (COMNETSAT), pp. 85–90. IEEE (2016)
12. Nskh, P., Varma, M.N., Naik, R.R.: Principle component analysis based intrusion detection system using support vector machine. In: IEEE International Conference on Recent Trends in Electronics, Information & Communication Technology (RTEICT), pp. 1344–1350. IEEE (2016)
13. Papamartzivanos, D., Mármol, F.G., Kambourakis, G.: Dendron: genetic trees driven rule induction for network intrusion detection systems. Future Gener. Comput. Syst. **79**, 558–574 (2018)
14. Revathi, S., Malathi, A.: A detailed analysis on NSL-KDD dataset using various machine learning techniques for intrusion detection. Int. J. Eng. Res. Technol. **2**(12), 1848–1853 (2013)

15. Shahbaz, M.B., Wang, X., Behnad, A., Samarabandu, J.: On efficiency enhancement of the correlation-based feature selection for intrusion detection systems. In: 2016 IEEE 7th Annual Information Technology, Electronics and Mobile Communication Conference (IEMCON), pp. 1–7. IEEE (2016)
16. Tavallaee, M., Bagheri, E., Lu, W., Ghorbani, A.A.: A detailed analysis of the KDD cup 99 data set. In: IEEE Symposium on Computational Intelligence for Security and Defense Applications, 2009. CISDA 2009, pp. 1–6. IEEE (2009)
17. Thaseen, I.S., Kumar, C.A.: Intrusion detection model using chi square feature selection and modified Naïve bayes classifier. In: Vijayakumar, V., Neelanarayanan, V. (eds.) Proceedings of the 3rd International Symposium on Big Data and Cloud Computing Challenges (ISBCC – 16'). SIST, vol. 49, pp. 81–91. Springer, Cham (2016). https://doi.org/10.1007/978-3-319-30348-2_7
18. Wang, H., Gu, J., Wang, S.: An effective intrusion detection framework based on SVM with feature augmentation. Knowl.-Based Syst. **136**, 130–139 (2017)
19. Wang, Y.F., Liu, P.Y., Ren, M., Chen, X.X.: Intrusion detection algorithms based on correlation information entropy and binary particle swarm optimization. In: 2017 13th International Conference on Natural Computation, Fuzzy Systems and Knowledge Discovery (ICNC-FSKD), pp. 2829–2834. IEEE (2017)

Network Security for Home IoT Devices Must Involve the User: A Position Paper

Lorenzo De Carli$^{(\boxtimes)}$ and Antonio Mignano

Worcester Polytechnic Institute, Worcester, MA 01609, USA
ldecarli@wpi.edu

Abstract. Many home IoT devices suffer from poor security design and confusing interfaces, lowering the bar for successful cyberattacks. A popular approach to identify compromised IoT devices is network-based detection, in which network traffic is analyzed to fingerprint and identify such devices. However, while several network-based techniques for identifying misbehaving devices have been proposed, the role of the user in remediating IoT security incidents has been conspicuously overlooked.

In this paper, we argue that successful IoT security must involve the user, even if the user is not a technical expert, and that the form in which security findings are communicated is as important as the technique used to generate such warnings. Finally, we present the design of a research testbed designed to foster further research in IoT security warnings.

1 Introduction

Increasingly, modern homes are incorporating internet-connected sensors and actuators such as smart cameras, lights and locks. These devices promise to bring a host of benefits, such as simplifying management of the home. Unfortunately, the potential benefits of IoT devices are increasingly outweighed by cybersecurity risks. Many IoT devices suffer from poor security design that render them vulnerable to cyberattacks [8,20]. Furthermore, the complexity of a residential network with even just a handful of devices can quickly outgrow the network security skills of a non-technical owner.

Existing efforts to secure the smart home include IoT intrusion detection systems (IDS) which flag abnormal device behavior that may be symptom of compromise, based on analysis of device network traffic (e.g., [17,19]). Typically, in presence of a network attack the IDS is expected to generate a warning signal, but existing works tend to sidestep the question of *who* should receive these warnings and act upon them. Interesting, the intrusion detection techniques now proposed for the IoT network security space (attack signatures, network anomaly detection) tend to be adaptations of approaches previously originated in the enterprise space. However, enterprise network security is based on a specific set of assumptions, which do not necessarily hold true in home IoT security.

One of such assumptions is particularly problematic: the availability of an expert user (network administrator, security officer, etc.) who can understand

© Springer Nature Switzerland AG 2021
G. Nicolescu et al. (Eds.): FPS 2020, LNCS 12637, pp. 20–28, 2021.
https://doi.org/10.1007/978-3-030-70881-8_2

and review the output of an IDS, and take action if necessary. The fact that such an expert *does not* exist in most home setups raises a number of issues, which must be solved to make intrusion detection practical in the home IoT space.

The first issue is what to do with warnings generated by an IDS. The option of letting the system autonomously dealing with attacks (e.g., by blocking malicious flows) is tempting, but we argue that is not viable, both due to infeasibility (no IDS is correct all the time), and for incompatibility with what we consider an important design tenet, that a user must be able to retain *control* of their devices (Sect. 3). Having argued the necessity to keep the human in the loop, we then focus on a second issue: how to precisely involve the users in management of security incidents. Through example scenarios, we highlight that determining how to bring the user in the security loop is a hard problem which warrants further research (Sect. 4). Furthermore, in order to foster further research in IoT network monitoring systems with human in the loop, we describe a testbed for user-centric research on IoT security notifications and interactions (Sect. 5). Finally, using this testbed we collect preliminary user impressions (Sect. 6).

2 Background

In this section, we introduce the threat model for home IoT networks which is assumed throughout the rest of this paper, and we review related work in the area of network security.

2.1 Assumptions and Threat Model

Our goal is to provide guidance to designers of systems that aim at detecting compromised IoT devices via analysis of their traffic. We assume an attacker that can send arbitrary traffic to the home network, with the goal of acquire partial or full control of one or more devices. We assume the detection system has visibility over the traffic within the home network. The system may detect attempts to compromise devices, compromised devices, or both. It would typically run on the residential gateway, but it may also be offloaded to the cloud [24].

2.2 Related Work

While the problem at hand has not extensively studied, there exist relevant work in the areas of general user security attitudes, usability of security warnings, and traffic analysis for IoT networks.

User Security Attitudes and Models: Dourish et al. [10] found that negative attitudes towards computer security dominate user experience. Gross and Rosson [14] found that users are not well supported by technology in managing sensitive data. Grinter et al. [13] discovered that even technically-savvy users find home network management nontrivial. Wash [25] described how users may discard expert security advice based on their models. Nthala et al. [21] found that users oftentimes leverage skilled acquaintances to keep their network secure. In IoT-specific work, Zeng et al. [26] uncovered a variety of issues in the attitude of users towards smart home security. Zheng et al. [27] found users lack awareness of IoT-related privacy risks. Emami-Naeini et al. [11] found that users are consistently concerned about IoT privacy/security after device purchase. Overall, these works consistently found that the interface between users and computing devices (particularly IoTs) is problematic, which is one of the motivating arguments for our work.

Usable Warnings: Akhawe and Porter-Felt [1] highlighted how the formulation of browser security warnings impacts their effectiveness. Anderson et al. [2] and Bravo-Lillo et al. [6] studied the effect of habituation to users' attention in the context of traditional computing devices. However, the results of this line of research cannot be directly ported to the IoT domain, where significantly different interfaces and modes of interaction may be used.

IoT Traffic Analysis: We summarize here a few recent representative works. Bezawada et al. [4] propose a fingerprinting technique to identify device type from network traffic. Miettinen et al. [18] leverage fingerprinting to place devices in different trust classes. The Princeton IoT Inspector project maintains a IoT fingerprinting and browser- based traffic inspection tool [15]. Mirsky et al. [19] describe ensembles of autoencoders as an effective unsupervised anomaly detection technique for the IoT domain. Martin et al. [17] describe a system to identify suspicious traffic and build signatures. While all these works provide an important algorithmic foundation for IoT traffic analysis, they offer limited considerations of the issues arising when attempting to interface with the user.

3   The Case for Involving the User

Cranor, in proposing a framework for integrating humans into security systems, states that a secure system should either keep humans out of the loop, or—if not possible—maximize the chances that the human performs security function successfully [9]. We therefore begin by posing the following question: *can a network intrusion detection system for home IoT devices work fully autonomously?*

We believe the answer is "no". The first reason is Axelsson's insight [3] that most IDS's generate more false positives than true positives. As attacks generally constitute rare events, this is likely to affect even an exceptionally accurate detector. As a case-study, consider the Kitsune detector [19], a state-of-art anomaly-based IDS. An important parameter for a detector is the Bayesian detection rate, i.e., the probability that an alert corresponds to a true attack. The Kitsune authors characterize their algorithm on nine sample attacks, from which the Bayesian detection rate can be computed. Oversimplifying, assume that each attack happens once a day and lasts ten minutes, and that traffic is analyzed in discrete time windows of 1 min. Under these assumptions, Kitsune's Bayesian

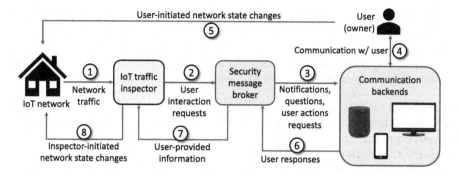

Fig. 1. Overview of proposed architecture

detection rate oscillates between 65% and 0.4%, with a median of 43%. While impressive, these results are not sufficient to allow a system to autonomously decide which flows should be blocked, and which ones should be allowed.

Further, a fully automated system would violate what we believe to be an important tenet in the design of human-centered technology: that the user should retain *control* of their devices, and *understanding* of their action. The relationship between users and the security of consumer devices has long been known to be problematic. Over time, studies on user perception of computer security have found attitudes that express frustration [10], concern [11], difficulty [13], and the necessity to rely on expert friends and relations [21]. In the IoT world, these difficulties are worsened by the deeply invasive nature of security breaches (e.g., access of video/audio from within the home). A device making autonomous, unexplainable, and oftentimes incorrect security decisions carries the risk of further aggravating the situation, by causing unexplained malfunctions (e.g., shutting a Smart TV off the network due to false positives).

Finally, we briefly remark that, even ignoring the two considerations above, securing IoTs occasionally requires manual operations to perform configuration changes, firmware updates [23], reboots, etc.

4 Proposed Architecture and Challenges

Based on the discussion in Sect. 3, we believe that systems that do not involve the user are not viable. In order to productively discuss the challenges of a system that does involve the user, we now propose a general architecture.

4.1 Architecture

We envision an IoT residential network incorporating a monitoring components to identify misbehaving and/or insecure devices, and communicate/interact with users to resolve security-critical situations. The expected system architecture is summarized in Fig. 1. An IoT inspector component analyzes local traffic ①. The analysis may result in various *user interactions*. These include:

1. **Notifications**, in which a security finding is communicated to the IoT user.
2. **Questions**, through which the inspector gathers additional context (e.g., asking the user to describe recent activity to disambiguate findings).
3. **Action requests**, through which the inspector requires manual-only operations (e.g., manual factory reset of a compromised router).

All such interactions are directed towards the user through a message broker ②. This component is necessary as, in a home network, the user can generally be reached using mobile apps, or the IoT devices themselves. It is therefore necessary to determine the best device, among those available, to perform the requested user interaction. The broker performs this function ③. As a result of the communication issued through devices ④, the user may perform actions on the network directly ⑤ (e.g., rebooting a router), or respond to questions ⑥. User responses are received and parsed by the broker, and their content is provided to the inspector ⑦. The inspector may also attempt to automatically resolve issues based on user feedback ⑧.

4.2   Scenarios

In order to highlight the challenges of bringing the user in the loop of a IoT security system, we briefly describe two scenarios. These take place in a hypothetical households which includes a homeowner and a number of smart devices.

Scenario #1: Privacy Violation. The traffic inspector detects unusual bursts of activity from an adjustable home monitoring camera in the living room. Given that the smart speaker and TV are currently off, the message broker issues a notification towards the user smartphone. Upon confirmation that the user is not operating the camera, the inspector informs the user that the camera may have been hacked. The user inspects the camera and realizes that it appears to be re-orienting itself without anyone in the household controlling it. The user suspects this event is related to an abusive former partner and disables the camera.

Scenario #2: Malware Break-In. The traffic inspector generates a notification as the smart fridge is suddenly emitting denial-of-service traffic. It detects that the device is running old firmware with an hardcoded-credential vulnerability. As the smart speaker is currently being used, the broker directs the speaker to enunciate a spoken warning. The warning directs the user to a more extensive smartphone notification which includes instructions on (i) how to reset the appliance's firmware, and (ii) how to perform a step-by-step firmware update.

None of these scenarios is futuristic or far-fetched. All elements, including commandeering of internet-connected cameras [22], vulnerable home appliances [7], the use of IoT devices for domestic abuse [5], hardcoded-credential vulnerabilities [16] and IoT-based DDoS [12] have been observed in the wild. Likewise, research in the IoT space has looked at anomaly detection [19], vulnerability identification [18], and semi-automated firmware updates [23].

4.3   Challenges and Opportunities

The scenarios above highlight a number of open questions which concern the specifics of how warning and interactions are phrased and communicated, including: *(i) Do warnings communicated using different modes (e.g., audio vs text) receive the same attention? (ii) How can we choose the best mode of interaction depending on context? (iii) How can security notifications be formulated to ensure the user understands the situation without receiving undue stress? (iv) How should warnings be managed in a multi-user household? (v) Do warnings and interactions need to be adjusted based on demographics (e.g., age group)?* These questions suggest that, for a network monitoring system, productively cooperating with the user is nontrivial. They also suggest some general directions for future research. First, designers of IoT network monitoring systems should focus on the explainability of their findings (intended as the ability to correlate low-level network behavior, e.g., an increase in short-lived flows, to high-level concepts, e.g., a DDoS). Second, the heterogeneity of IoT devices creates an opportunity to explore user interactions via a variety of modes and interfaces (audio/visual signals, text notifications, haptic, etc.).

5   A Testbed for Evaluating IoT Security Warnings

As an initial exploration in user-interactive IoT monitoring systems, we designed and instantiated a testbed for user studies involving IoT-related security warnings. The design aims at easing common practical issues that affect IoT security and usability research. Not every institution can afford to deploy a dedicated IoT lab. In some case, dedicated space for user studies may not be available, or it may be shared between multiple projects (not all IoT-related). Acquiring the devices may itself be a problem due to the high price of some of them.

Our testbed design implements the components shaded in green in Fig. 1. The software powering the testbed consists of a simple message broker and notification backends for three popular types of IoT devices (we make the software publicly and freely available[1]). We specifically aimed at supporting devices (Android phone; Sonos smart speaker; Raspberry Pi-based Smart TV) which are cheap to acquire and can be deployed and dismantled in a matter of minutes. We hope releasing our testbed software will foster its deployment in research labs, HCI classes, REUs, and other scenarios.

The focus of our testbed is on studying how users receive and understand interaction requests from an IoT monitoring system, and how the phrasing and the mode (audio vs text) of these notifications affect comprehension. The intended mode of use is to have subjects sit through simulated security incidents, where an experimenter generates notifications and questions towards the user. The testbed does not include or propose novel intrusion detection/monitoring algorithms, although such components could easily be interfaced with the broker.

---

[1] https://www.dropbox.com/sh/etkdrmddg2ilkqr/AAC_rctdyOShzMlJu-kCFJoGa.

6 A Preliminary User Study

We conclude this paper by describing a qualitative, IRB-approved user study which we conducted to test-drive the testbed and receive feedback. Recruiting was conducted via on-campus advertising and word-of-mouth. Overall, we recruited 10 participants (all college students from our metro area).

6.1 Experiment Design

Each subject participated in an individual network security exercise. The exercise simulates two different scenarios, both involving an intrusion in the home network to which the testbed devices are connected. The experimenter generates interactions with the participant in order to resolve the issue. Both scenarios are representative of issues where an attacker attempts to masquerade communication to/from an infected device as video streaming from phone or TV.

Prior to the experiment, each subject was informed that during the experiment they would receive notifications about a simulated IT security incident, and they would be requested to pass information to the system. At the end of the experiment, each subject was asked to complete a brief questionnaire.

6.2 Results

Due to the limited sample size and diversity, we do not consider the study sufficient for drawing general conclusions, and we omit a quantitative discussion of the results. However, the study uncovered several interesting user attitudes that highlight some research challenges. We report a few relevant findings.

The most relevant feedback was provided in response to the following question: *How likely would you be to use a system like the one you interacted with in your own home?*. The question required an answer between 1 ("not at all") and 5 ("a lot"), and received the following answers: 3,3,4,2,3,4,4,5,5,3. It further gave each subject the opportunity to provide an unstructured explanation of their answer. Participants who answered in the 4–5 range tended to underscore the importance of keeping the network secure. They also expressed caveats (Subject #6: "How likely I would be to use it is proportional to how accurate it is"). Participants in the range 1–3 expressed, among other concerns, issues with frequent interruptions (Subject #4: "If I was frequently alerted to IT security issues, I would simply stop using the internet."). This is consistent with other user studies that found that convenience tends to trump privacy concerns [27]. Others expressed the concern that the system itself may be prone to security issues (Subject #2: "the notification method itself is prone to security issues").

When asked *What do you think can be improved?*, Subject #10 stated "something that "looks nice" lends it a more professional apperence [sic], and therefore an implicit level of trust on behalf of the user.". Similarly, Subject #6 asked for "An authentication process.". Furthermore, Subject #1 asked "May be [sic] just simple language to define the issues so that even a novice user could understand without having a better network knowledge", and Subject #4 stated "Have the notifications be more educational".

6.3 Discussion

The study found confirmation of the usual hurdle to adoption of a security system: the need to minimize disruption. The issues of security and trust (Subjects 2, 6, 10) are important, as an unprotected notification system may be abused by an attacker. They also suggest that it may be necessary to visually distinguish authenticated notifications. The complaints concerning language (Subjects 1, 4) highlight the difficulty of appropriately phrasing interaction requests. Overall, user feedback suggests that there is interest for technologies, that can help users to identify and understand security issues in their home networks.

7 Conclusion

In this paper, we advocated the need for research on IoT security techniques which are aware of, and involve the user. In particular, we claim that, since most IoT device owners are not security experts, it is necessary to devise novel forms of communication of security findings which are accessible to this population. In order to foster further work in the area, we contributed a general architecture for IoT network monitoring tools, which keeps the user in the loop. Furthermore, we presented the design and implementation of a testbed for research on user-facing network security notifications and feedback requests.

References

1. Akhawe, D., Felt, A.P.: Alice in Warningland: a large-scale field study of browser security warning effectiveness. In: USENIX Security Symposium, p. 17 (2013)
2. Anderson, B.B., Kirwan, C.B., Jenkins, J.L., Eargle, D., Howard, S., Vance, A.: How polymorphic warnings reduce habituation in the brain: insights from an FMRI study. In: CHI (2015)
3. Axelsson, S.: The base-rate fallacy and its implications for the difficulty of intrusion detection. In: Proceedings of the 6th ACM Conference on Computer and communications security - CCS '1999, pp. 1–7. ACM Press (1999)
4. Bezawada, B., Bachani, M., Peterson, J., Shirazi, H., Ray, I., Ray, I.: Behavioral Fingerprinting of IoT Devices. In: ASHES. New York, NY, USA (2018)
5. Bowles, N.: Thermostats, locks and lights: digital tools of domestic abuse (2018). https://www.nytimes.com/2018/06/23/technology/smart-home-devices-domestic-abuse.html
6. Bravo-Lillo, C., Cranor, L., Komanduri, S., Schechter, S., Sleeper, M.: Harder to ignore? In: SOUPS (2014)
7. Chirgwin, R.: Dishwasher has directory traversal bug, March 2017. https://www.theregister.com/2017/03/26/miele_joins_internetofst_hall_of_shame/
8. Cimpanu, C.: Hacker leaks passwords for more than 500,000 servers, routers, and IoT devices, January 2020. https://www.zdnet.com/article/hacker-leaks-passwords-for-more-than-500000-servers-routers-and-iot-devices/
9. Cranor, L.F.: A framework for reasoning about the human in the loop. In: UPSEC (2008)

10. Dourish, P., Grinter, E., Delgado de la Flor, J., Joseph, M.: Security in the wild: user strategies for managing security as an everyday, practical problem. Pers. Ubiquitous Comput. **8**(6), 391–401 (2004)
11. Emami-Naeini, P., Dixon, H., Agarwal, Y., Cranor, L.F.: Exploring how privacy and security factor into IoT device purchase behavior. In: CHI (2019)
12. Goodin, D.: Record-breaking DDOS reportedly delivered by >145k hacked cameras (2016). https://arstechnica.com/information-technology/2016/09/botnet-of-145k-cameras-reportedly-deliver-internets-biggest-ddos-ever
13. Grinter, R.E., et al.: The ins and outs of home networking: the case for useful and usable domestic networking. ACM Trans. Comput.-Hum. Interact. **16**(2), 8:1–8:28 (2009)
14. Gross, J.B., Rosson, M.B.: Looking for trouble: understanding end-user security management. In: CHIMIT (2007)
15. Huang, D.Y., Acar, G., Apthorpe, N., Li, F., Narayanan, A., Feamster, N.: Princeton IoT Inspector, May 2019. https://iot-inspector.princeton.edu
16. Lewellen, T.: CERT/CC Vulnerability Note VU#800094, September 2013. https://www.kb.cert.org
17. Martin, V., Cao, Q., Benson, T.: Fending off IoT-hunting attacks at home networks. In: CAN (2017)
18. Miettinen, M., Marchal, S., Hafeez, I., Asokan, N., Sadeghi, A., Tarkoma, S.: IoT SENTINEL: automated device-type identification for security enforcement in IoT. In: ICDCS (2017)
19. Mirsky, Y., Doitshman, T., Elovici, Y., Shabtai, A.: Kitsune: an ensemble of autoencoders for online network intrusion detection. In: NDSS (2018)
20. Nichols, S.: Don't panic, but your baby monitor can be hacked into a spycam. June 2018. https://www.theregister.co.uk/2018/06/22/baby_monitor_hacked/
21. Nthala, N., Flechais, I.: Informal support networks: an investigation into home data security practices. In: SOUPS (2018)
22. Pascu, L.: Multiple critical security flaws found in nearly 400 IP cameras - Bitdefender BOX Blog, June 2018. https://www.bitdefender.com/box/blog/ip-cameras-vulnerabilities/multiple-critical-security-flaws-found-nearly-400-ip-cameras/
23. Simpson, A.K., Roesner, F., Kohno, T.: Securing vulnerable home IoT devices with an in-hub security manager. In: PerCom Workshop (2017)
24. Taylor, C.R., Shue, C.A., Najd, M.E.: Whole home proxies: bringing enterprise-grade security to residential networks. In: IEEE ICC (2016)
25. Wash, R.: Folk models of home computer security. In: SOUPS (2010)
26. Zeng, E., Mare, S., Roesner, F.: End user security and privacy concerns with smart homes. In: SOUPS (2017)
27. Zheng, S., Apthorpe, N., Chetty, M., Feamster, N.: User perceptions of smart home IoT privacy. Proc. ACM. Hum. Comput. Interact. **2**(CSCW), 200:1–200:20 (2018)

A Quantitative Security Risk Analysis Framework for Modelling and Analyzing Advanced Persistent Threats

Rajesh Kumar[✉], Siddhant Singh, and Rohan Kela

Department of Computer Science and Information Systems,
Birla Institute of Technology and Science, Pilani, India
rajesh.k@pilani.bits-pilani.ac.in

Abstract. Advanced persistent threats (APTs) are different from other computer-based attacks in their target selection, attack technique, and malicious motive. Distinct from script kiddie attacks, these attacks target critical systems to inflict maximum damage, such as to stall critical industrial processes. Standard defenses against APT attack is to deploy security mechanisms that are typically reminiscent of enterprise defense systems such as firewalls, intrusion detection systems, etc. However, given the nature and attack potential of APT attacks, one cannot rely on these security mechanisms alone as they are susceptible to failure, false alarms, and interfere with usability. A yet another problem is to decide on which mechanisms to deploy and at which points to offer maximum coverage against attacks. We believe, given the unique characteristics of APT attacks, one needs a robust and layered defense to protect against APT by timely detection, prevention, mitigation, and emergency plan. One such objective way to determine the countermeasures' efficacy is by modeling and simulating attack behaviour.

In this paper, we propose a two-layer framework to analyze the APT attacks. At the top is the domain model of the Enhanced cyber kill chain. We use it to capture the attack phases, techniques, and processes. The bottom layer is the analytic layer of stochastic timed automata derived from the domain model. Key metrics are obtained using a state-of-the-art statistical model - checking techniques. We argue that such a timed analysis can be used to improve the security posture by putting countermeasures at appropriate positions.

Keywords: Attack trees · Security analysis · Parallel and sequential execution

1 Introduction

Advanced persistent threats (APTs) are relatively newer but sophisticated cyber-attacks. Different from the petty cyber-thefts, these attacks are targeted, typically funded by nation-states, to disrupt critical infrastructure or cyber-espionage [23]. The modus operandi of an APT attack is also different from

© Springer Nature Switzerland AG 2021
G. Nicolescu et al. (Eds.): FPS 2020, LNCS 12637, pp. 29–46, 2021.
https://doi.org/10.1007/978-3-030-70881-8_3

other cyber-attacks in terms of sophistication and craftsmanship [4]. An essential characteristic of these attacks is that they are multi-stage attacks that use diverse propagation paths, combining technical vulnerabilities such as OS, host application, etc., with social engineering. For example, the alleged attack on Iranian facilities by the Stuxnet virus used four zero-day vulnerabilities combining it with social-engineering [21].

In literature, there exists a wide variety of pen-and-pencil security risk assessment methods such as ISO 27001 [29], NIST SP800 [28] These guidelines are in the form of checklists that provide advice on how to manage risk. However, these frameworks are qualitative, i.e., do not offer customized suggestions on reducing risk to a defined acceptance criterion. In a complex system such as the industrial systems, a key challenge for an enterprise manager is to identify the most critical system bottlenecks. These bottlenecks could be a piece of hardware or software that forms the part of an industrial process and whose compromise gives an attacker multiple avenues to attack. Another useful parameter for a security practitioner is to know the timed behavior of an attacker. This information is useful to plan countermeasures to negate the possible attacks. For example, by knowing: "Is it possible for an attacker to be successful in 1 day?" or "Should a crucial vulnerability be patched now?", etc., an enterprise manager can effectively implement hardening controls before an attacker exploits a vulnerability.

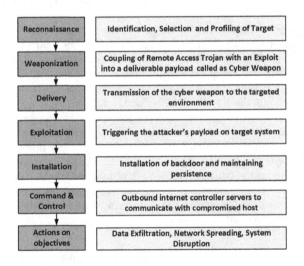

Fig. 1. Cyber-kill chain model.

In this paper, we provide a framework to model and analyze complex multi-stage APT attacks. Similar to the few literature papers on quantitative security risk analysis, for example, the CORAS approach [25], Adversary View Security Evaluation [22], CySeMoL [14], attack tree based methods [7] etc., we aim to equip the security practitioners with a framework that can help assess their security risk posture by doing a scenario analysis. However, different from these papers, our model is customized to model and analyze APT attacks. Our paper leverages the industry-wide popular model of the cyber-kill chain (CKC, [15]), see Fig. 1, to represent the APT attack stages. A CKC model, popular as a military kill chain in defense operations, is a well-defined sequence to represent multi-stage attacks. Here, the disruption at a stage hinders the movement of the malicious actor to the next successive stage. To accommodate the different attack techniques used by the APT actor to execute the attack stages, in this paper, we extend the cyber-kill chain by refining each stage with different techniques. Furthermore, we represent each attack technique as a sequence of atomic events. We call the CKC with these additions as *Enhanced cyber-kill chain* (ECKC).

For quantitative analysis, we consider the atomic events as either *timed events*, i.e., an APT attacker is successful after a duration given by exponential distribution or *probabilistic events* i.e., an APT attacker is successful given by Bernoulli distribution. Technically, to analyze the ECKC model, which cannot be handled otherwise by state-of-the-art analysis techniques, we use the automata-theoretic models. In particular, we provide the stochastic timed automaton (STA, [11]) templates for each element of the ECKC model. Here, rather than building one large STA model, we build the STA models from several smaller STA models. Thus, our models are compositional and easy to extend. We use the Uppaal SMC model checker [10] for probabilistic verification of metrics of interest that are first encoded in temporal logic.

For deriving the analysis results, we use stochastic model checking techniques. Model-checking is a state-of-the-art method for verifying whether the system satisfies the properties of interest. Though powerful and automated, the drawback of the model-checking approach is the state-space explosion. In this paper, we use the statistical model-checking (SMC) approaches that do not require state-space generation [3,20]. Moreover, SMC techniques based on simulations are useful when no closed-form solution is available, as in our case.

Related Work. Different from many other literature papers on APT that provide an informal description of a few APT attacks or enumerate a few historic APT attacks [4,30], in this paper we provide a generic modeling framework rooted in mathematics and formal reasoning. Close to our work there exists few powerful frameworks based on attack tree [7,18,31], attack-fault tree [19], Boolean driven Markov process [26], attack pyramid [13], however, these works are not directed exclusively to APT attacks, hence their terminology is too generic. We believe that a model combining cyber-kill chains and STAs permits systematic brainstorming of attacks belonging to each APT stage and subsequently APT attack technique. Moreover, traditional attack tree analysis methods such as the bottom-up approach do not consider temporal and causal interdependence. Other popular APT analysis techniques are based on machine learning, system-theoretic, etc. [4]. These techniques are interesting to understand the APT behavior. However, they are limited to one or two stages; for example, the authors in paper [33], use DNS and traffic analysis to detect APT attacks when communicating stealthily using back-door channels to a remote server. From our paper's perspective, these techniques form the corpus of defensive measures, whose efficacy can be evaluated based on the metric outlined in the paper.

Cyber-kill chain model has been popularized by Lockheed Martin in [15], In literature, there exist several variants of CKCs, with few modifications, for example, the attack chain model [9], the Unified chain [27], etc. For this paper, we use the initially proposed model of the cyber-kill chain proposed in [15], as it is widely popular in the industry. Statistical model-checking techniques have been popularly used in many domains such as biology, security, reliability [3,17], etc. Petri-net models are an equally powerful and expressive formalism exhibiting concurrency. It has been used in [34], to model APT attacks. The previous paper, however, does not perform quantitative analysis. Other Markov chain based models are popular in reliability and safety domains, for example, in [6].

2   Description of the Framework

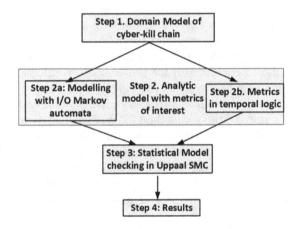

Fig. 2. Framework of the proposed approach for APT analysis.

In Fig. 2, we briefly outline the steps of our framework.

– Step 1 is to construct the domain model. To do this, one collects contextual information on vulnerabilities and actors using red teaming exercises and penetration testing. The information gathered is arranged in the form of an Enhanced Cyber Kill Chain (ECKC) domain model. ECKC is an extended cyber kill chain whose stages are enumerated with the different attack techniques and attack process. We provide the details on the ECKC model in Sect. 2.1.
– Step 2 is the construction of the analytic model from the ECKC model. Alongside this, we also encode the metrics of interest into temporal logic. Both these steps are pre-processing steps to perform model-checking. In this paper, we evaluate two metrics:

- *As-is scenario* aims to find the probability of APT success within a mission time of one year.
- *What-if scenario* aims to find the probability of APT success within a mission time of one year when detection measures are implemented.

We provide the details on STA model in Sect. 2.2.

- Step 3 is to perform statistical model checking (SMC). SMC is a promising technique that allows to verify automata for probabilistic performance properties, reachability analysis, and expected values. It is a compromise between the traditional testing techniques and the complete model checking. The key idea behind SMC consists largely of two steps:
  - monitor some individual paths of the system,
  - use statistical evaluation such as hypothesis testing to infer whether the property is satisfied with a certain degree of confidence over those paths.

  Note that SMC techniques are based on simulations and only provide statistical confidence intervals and not the exact result, and if one needs tighter confidence bound, one needs a large sample size.
- Step 4 is to run the tool and plot the results. Here, we use the popular statistical model-checker of Uppaal SMC to obtain the results.

Below, we discuss each step of our framework in details.

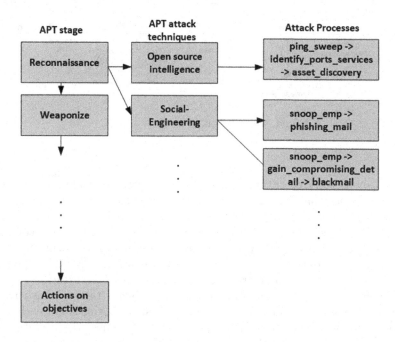

Fig. 3. The ECKC model.

2.1   Step 1. Modelling with Cyber-Kill Chains

Step 1 is to construct the ECKC model, see Fig. 3, by narrowing the problem-of-interest. This can be a post-incident APT attack scenario that one needs to analyze or a system description with known assets for which one needs to perform the security risk assessment proactively. In both cases, along with the stakeholder, we collect the information to obtain contextual details on assets, attack environment, and APT actor (For example, network elements, security policies, etc.). Based on the gathered information, and using the popular attack catalogs such as CAPEC [1] and ATT&CK [2], we build the ECKC model by arranging the attack techniques used at each APT stage. To succeed in their goal, an attacker needs to successfully execute all attack stages in a sequence, where a failure in one stage hinders the attacker's progress to the successive stage.

Below, we showcase the ECKC model using the Stuxnet APT attack. In Sect. 3, we use the example to demonstrate our results.

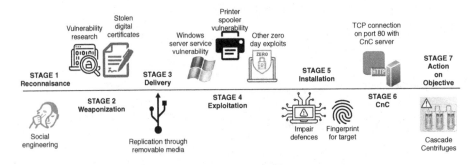

Fig. 4. Stuxnet computer virus attack.

Stuxnet Computer Virus. Stuxnet is a computer worm that allegedly targeted the Iranian nuclear facilities [21]. Due to its multi-stage nature, use of multiple zero-day exploits, and multiple propagation paths, it remains one of the most researched attack scenarios. The information on the Stuxnet attack computer worm is scattered in different peer and non-peer-reviewed literature including industrial forensic reports, blogs and research papers. In Fig. 4, we give the attack stages. Below, we summarize the characteristics of the attack.

In Table 1, we tabulate the information on Stuxnet attack to construct the ECKC model The ECKC model for Stuxnet consists of 7 stages. For each stage, we referred to the literature to find appropriate techniques (the literature references are given in the fourth column of the table). For example, the stage of "Reconnaissance" consists of two attack techniques – "Open source intelligence" and "Social engineering", the success of any techniques mentioned above leads to successful reconnaissance. Each attack technique is distilled into one or more

Table 1. Cyber kill chain stages, attack techniques and attack processes for the case study of Stuxnet computer virus.

Cyber kill chain stage	APT attack technique	Attack processes	Remarks/References
Reconnaissance	Open source intelligence	`ping_sweep -> identify_ports_services -> asset_discovery`	The attack vectors for reconnaissance stage for Stuxnet are speculative [12]. Below, we provided an example attack technique from [24].
	Social Engineering	`snoop_emp -> phishing_mail`	Two forms of social-engineering techniques, active and passive are described in [8]
		`snoop_emp -> gain_compromising_detail -> blackmail`	
Weaponization	Vulnerability Research	`find_known_vulnerabilities -> validate_vulnerabilities_using_ testbeds -> add_exploits`	
		`simulate_target_environment -> find_zero_day_vulnerabilities -> add_exploits`	Stuxnet uses 4 zero day vulnerabilities. Highly skilled security researchers are believed to have developed these exploits [30]
Delivery	Replication through Removable Media	`infected_USB_inserted -> autorun.inf_file_vulnerabillity -> install_library_file`	Earlier versions of Stuxnet exploited autorun.inf files vulnerability; Added commands that user inadvertently selected causing Stuxnet to be installed on host machine [32]
		`infected_USB_inserted -> win_LNK_vulnerabillity -> install_library_file`	Recent versions of Stuxnet exploited LNK vulnerability to auto-install malware on system as soon as USB is connected [32]
Exploitation	Propagation through LAN and network shares	`identify_network_accessible_windows- _system -> exploit_printer_spooler- _vulnerability -> escalate_privileges-> propagate_to_PCN`	Kriaa et al. [16] suggests three methods via which Stuxnet virus escalates privileges and reaches its intended target. It utilizes several zero-day exploits like printer spooler vulnerability, windows server service vulnerability etc. for lateral movement
		`identify_network_accessible_windows- _system -> exploit_windows_server- _service_vulnerability -> escalate_privileges -> propagate_to_PCN`	
		`find_winCC_environment -> siemens_credentials -> SQL_injection -> propagate_to_PCN`	
	Propagation through removable media	`removable_media -> stuxet_detects_drive -> clone_to_drive -> propagate_to_PCN`	Stuxnet can spread into systems not connected to the internet, at the time of maintainence, through removable media
	Propagation through WinCC/STEP7 project files	`infect_config_files -> file_access -> load_dll -> infectious_routines -> propagate_to_PCN`	Kriaa et al. [16] state that infected files, which when opened by a user can run execute malicious routines

(continued)

Table 1. (*continued*)

Cyber kill chain stage	APT attack technique	Attack processes	Remarks/References
Installation	Stealth and Infection	`security_products -> inject_payload -> fingerprint_target -> deploy_PLC_rootkit -> intercept_PLC_communication -> inject_PLC_payload`	Stuxnet scans for the anti-virus/anti-malware software present in host system. Based on the version, target process of code injection is determined [12]. It fingerprints for the target PLC in one of the 3 ways [21]. On successfully reaching the target, it installs the PLC rootkit and intercepts PLC communication. [12]
CnC	P2P Communication	`install_RPC_server -> wait1 -> update_malware1`	Stuxnet receives updates either via a P2P network mechanism or a via a direct TCP connection to a remote server [16]
	Remote Server Communication	`corrupt_IE -> bypass_firewall -> TCP_connection -> wait2 -> update_malware2`	
Action on Objective	Compromise Simatic 300 series controller function	`collect_data -> rouge_code -> falsified_data -> cascade_centrifuges1`	Kriaa et al. [16] state that stuxnet virus targets one of two simatic controller models(300 and 400 series). [21] confirms this and highlight the difference in the two attack mechanisms
	Compromise Simatic 400 series controller function	`record_I/O -> man-in-middle-attack -> cascade_centrifuges2`	

attack processes. An attack process is a sequence of atomic attack steps. For example, the attack technique of "Open source intelligence" is given by an attack process – `ping_sweep -> identify_ports_services -> asset_discovery`, where `ping_sweep`, `identify_ports_services` and `asset_discovery` are three atomic attack steps. An attack technique is successful if any of its attack process(es) is successfully executed, where the successful execution of an attack process amounts to the successful execution of all its attack steps and in a sequence. Here `a ->a'` symbol signifies the causal relationship between atomic attack steps, where the successive attack step `a'` is executed only after the successful execution of the previous step `a`. To successfully launch an APT attack, an attacker must successfully execute all the APT stages, beginning with the reconnaissance stage and in order from the reconnaissance stage to end at the actions on objectives stage.

Below, we describe the generic ECKC model.

Notations. We use 2^G to indicate the power of a set G and $PO(G)$ for the set of all partial ordered set over G. A partial function is denoted as $f : V \nrightarrow V'$, where V and V' are the domain and the codomain. The disjoint union of two sets B and B' is denoted by $B \sqcup B'$.

Step. A step s denotes an atomic event. It represents an attacker's action. We assume the universe of all steps is given by S, where $S = IS \sqcup TS$, where is $\in$ IS is an instantaneous step and ts $\in$ TS is a timed step. A *instantaneous step* describes attacker success that follows a Bernoulli probability distribution with parameter p. A *timed step*, ts represents attack success on executing the attack that follow an exponential probability distribution with rate $\lambda \in \mathbb{R}_{>0}$. The cumulative distribution function for this distribution is: $f(x) = 1 - exp^{-\lambda \cdot x}$, for any $x \in \mathbb{R}$

Attack Process. An attack process $P_j, j \in \mathbb{N}$ is a partial ordered set (W, $\rhd$) $\in$ PO(S), where W $\subseteq$ S is a set of atomic steps and $\rhd \subseteq$ W $\times$ W constrains the order in which the attack steps needs to be performed. A function $\triangle : 2^S \twoheadrightarrow$ {True, False} maps the attack processes to true/false, such that the attack process $P_j \in 2^S$ is true, if the attacker is able to accomplish an APT technique by successful execution and chaining of the attack steps, else otherwise. We assume that the attack processes are minimal.

APT Attack Technique. An APT attack technique $T_i, i \in \mathbb{N}$ describes a possible way of performing an APT stage.

APT Stage. The set of APT stages is given by St = {R, W, D, E, I, CC, AO}, where R stands for reconnaissance, W stands for weaponization, D stands for delivery, E stands for exploitation, I stands for installation, CC stands for command and control and AO stands for actions on objectives.

ECKC Model. An ECKC model is a partially ordered set (St, $\rhd$), where St is the set of APT stages and $\rhd$ is the partial ordering relationship between the stages. Each stage consists of i number of APT attack techniques $T_1 \ldots T_i$, where the value of i may vary between the stages. Note, an attack step can be shared between several attack techniques. Furthermore, each T_i consists of j attack processes $P_1 \ldots P_j$, where the value of j may vary between the APT attack techniques. We say an attack technique is succcessful if any of its associated attack process is true. We say an attack stage is successful if any of its associated attack technique is true.

2.2   Step 2: Analytic Model with Stochastic Timed Automata

In Step 2, we derive a system model from the ECKC model. The system model is a network of stochastic timed automata. It consists of one or more concurrent processes, local and global variables, and channels. The system model processes are defined in the form of a list of instantiated stochastic timed automata templates. Below we specify an STA template for timed step, instantaneous step, attack technique, APT stage, and the ECKC model. A network of STAs is thus the parallel composition of these instantiations.

Stochastic timed automata (STA, [11]), see Fig. 5, are state transition diagrams that allow modeling real-time systems. Unlike the popular time automata models [5], STAs are given stochastic semantics that enables them to model soft-real time constraints such as delays and probabilistic choices. A stochastic time automaton is a model consisting of control states and transitions between these control states. On the control states and edges, one can specify constraints that come in the form of guard edges and invariants at control states that may be used to block or force specific transitions at certain times. These constraints and invariants are specified in terms of clocks, which increase linearly over time but maybe reset when a transition is taken. Furthermore, STAs consists of 1) a sojourn time probability density function; 2) a probability mass function over the enabled transitions. Thus, STAs define a purely stochastic process: from a state, we first randomly choose a delay among all possible delays, then we will randomly choose an edge among all enabled edges. Multiple STAs can be combined using synchronization on transitions, where some edges waiting for a signal $a?$ can only be taken simultaneously with a transition in another STA emitting the corresponding signal $a!$. Below, we describe each template.

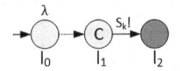

Fig. 5. STA template of timed step.

Timed Step. Figure 5, shows the STA template for the timed step ts. It consists of three locations with l_0 being the initial location. The parameter λ governs the execution time of the attacker, after which the automaton emits an output signal S_k, signifying its success and allowing other automaton waiting to synchronize on this channel. The location l_1 is committed, indicated by the label C, i.e. if any process is in a committed location, the next transition must involve an edge from one of the committed locations.

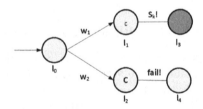

Fig. 6. STA template of instantaneous step.

Instantaneous Step. Figure 6, shows the STA template for the instantaneous step is. From the initial location l_0, the take transition to l_1 and l_2, depending on the probability distribution. It is expressed as a constant non-negative integer expression denoting the probabilistic likelihood of the branch being executed. The probability of a particular branch is determined as a ratio of its weight over the sum of weights of all branches emanating from the same branch node.

Attack Technique. Figure 7, shows the STA template for an attack technique. The template emits T_i, signifying that the APT attack technique T_i is successful if it receives a success $(S_1, S_2, \ldots S_k)$ from all k atomic steps comprising the attack technique in an order. Otherwise, the STA remains in a sink location.

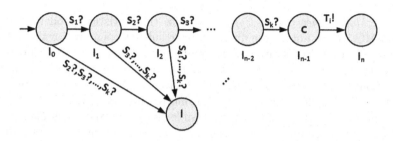

Fig. 7. STA template for an attack technique.

Attack Stage. Figure 8, shows the STA template for an attack stage st. The template emits St_i, signifying that an APT attack stage St_i is successful if it receives a success of $T_1, T_2, \ldots T_i$ from any of the i attack techniques comprising an attack stage.

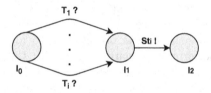

Fig. 8. STA template for an attack stage.

ECKC Model Template. Figure 9, shows the STA template for the ECKC model. It consists of a series of APT stages. It transmits a success signal once it receives the success signal St_i from each APT attack stage and in an order with first stage being reconnaissance and subsequent stages as described in the earlier section.

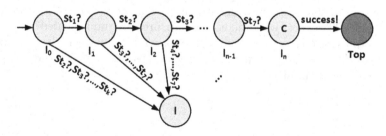

Fig. 9. STA template modelling the different attack stages success leading to the APT success.

Encoding of Metrics of Interest. To perform the statistical model checking, we specify the properties of interest in Uppaal-SMC query language [10]. We encode the query of "Probability of APT attack within 8800 h" as:

P[<8800] (`Top_template. Top`)

where `Top` is a location in the instantiated ECKC process `Top_template`.

Statistical Model Checking in Uppaal. We use the statistical model-checker of Uppaal-SMC [10] to obtain the quantitative results. Depending on the context, we instantiate each ECKC framework template to define the system processes. The instantiation logic is based on the system parameters and contextual synchronization requirements of the different interacting processes. The Uppaal tool provides few syntactic checks before allowing to simulate a model. It also provides a "Simulator", to examine the possible dynamic executions of a system during early design (or modeling) stages. The Uppaal tool also comes inbuilt with a "Verifier", that is used check safety and liveness properties by on-the-fly exploration of the state-space of a system in terms of symbolic states represented by constraints.

3 Case Study

To demonstrate the practical applicability of the ECKC model and statistical model-checking in practice, we have applied this method to the Stuxnet case study described in the previous section. Using statistical model checking, we compare the different scenarios. The objective is to identify the appropriate countermeasures by performing scenario-analysis. In this paper, we take two scenarios: the "as-is scenario", when no detection measures are implemented and the "what-if scenario", when detection measures are implemented. For each of these scenarios, we take below two cases.

- As-Is scenarios. The "As-Is" scenario asks two security questions:
  - Given the attack scenario and system parameters, what is the probability of an APT attack?
  - Given the attack scenario and system parameters, what is the probability of an APT attack, when a few attack steps are disabled?
- What-If scenarios. The What-If scenario asks two security questions:
  - Given the attack scenario and system parameters, what is the probability of an APT attack, when detection measures are implemented?
  - Given the attack scenario and system parameters, what is the probability of an APT attack, when a few attack steps are disabled and detection measures are in place?

Table 2. Parameters for basic attack steps used in the Stuxnet case study. Here MTTA is mean time to attack.

Attack step	MTTA	Instantanous success probability	Attack step	MTTA	Instantanous success probability
ping_sweep	2 days	–	clone_to_drive	–	0.9
identify_ports_services	1 day	–	infect_config_files	–	0.8
asset_discovery	1 day	–	file_access	1 day	–
snoop_emp	1 day	–	load_dll	4 h	–
phishing_mail	1 day	–	infectious_routines	12 h	–
gain_compromising_detail	2 days	–	security_products	1 day	–
blackmail	5 days	–	inject_payload	–	0.7
find_known_vulnerabilities	30 days	–	fingerprint_target	1 day	–
validate_vulnerabilities_ using_testbeds	15 days	–	deploy_PLC_rootkit	–	0.8
add_exploits	1 day	–	intercept_PLC_ communication	12 h	–
simulate_target_environment	20 days	–	inject_PLC_payload	–	0.8
find_zero_day_vulnerabilities	200 days	–	RPC_server	12 h	–
infected_USB_inserted	40 days	–	wait1	12 h	–
exploit_autorun.inf_file_ vulnerabillity	–	0.8	update1	–	0.9
install_library_file	4 h	–	corrupt_IE	12 h	–
exploit_win_LNK_vulnerabillity	–	0.9	bypass_firewall	–	0.7
identify_network_accessible_ windows_system	–	0.8	TCP_connection	1 h	–
exploit_printer_spooler_ vulnerability	–	0.6	wait2	12 h	–
exploit_windows_server_ service_vulnerability	–	0.6	update_malware2	–	0.9
escalate_privileges	–	0.8	collect_data	42 days	–
propagate_to_pcn	50 days	–	rogue_code	1 h	–
find_winCC_environment	–	0.4	falsified_data	6 h	–
siemens_credentials	–	0.75	cascade_centrifuges1	–	0.7
sql_injection	–	0.6	record_I/O	3 days	–
removable_media	30 days	–	man-in-middle	3 days	–
stuxet_detects_drive	–	0.9	cascade_centrifuges2	–	0.7

For the what-if scenario, to include detection measures, we modified the atomic attack step template. We assume that an attacker at beginning may be detected with a probability of $P_d = 0.4$. An undetected attacker may continue executing the attack with a given execution rate or detected with a given rate of detection. An attacker on detection aborts the attack. We assume that the detection rate is 0.0020833 (Mean time to detection is 20 days).

The experiment was performed on a 2.50 GHz Intel(R) Core(TM) CPU i7-6500 with 8 GB RAM under Windows. The UPPAAL SMC tool [11] was used to verify the properties. The statistical parameters chosen were the confidence interval $\alpha = 0.05$ and probability uncertainty = 0.01. For details on confidence intervals and probability uncertainties, readers are advised to refer [10].

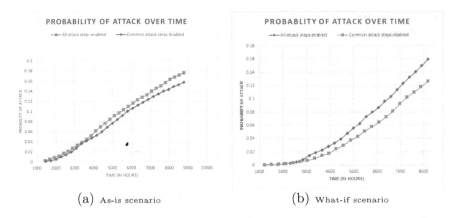

Fig. 10. Scenario analysis of Stuxnet computer virus.

To perform scenario analysis, we need to parameterize the templates with continuous probabilities (modeling the rate of execution/detection) and discrete probabilities (modeling the attacker's success). In APT scenarios, due to the public unavailability of the data mentioned above, we performed structured brainstorming to showcase our framework. In practical scenarios, the input data is based on practitioner experience. In Table 2, we tabulate the system parameters. The execution rate is the inverse of "Mean time to attack". Note that we have used exponential distribution; however, our framework and tool permit custom distributions. To validate our models, we fixed the mission time of 1 h and obtained the probability of APT success at the end of each stage. The cumulative probability of an APT attack is the product of probability at each stage, which we verified in our tool.

In Fig. 10(a), we plot the as-is scenarios. The probability of an APT attack within a mission time of 8800 h is 0.175. To select appropriate countermeasures that can reduce the impact of APT attacks, we iteratively disable few attack steps. As we see in Table 1, few attack stages such as Delivery consists of a technique where each of its attack processes shares common attack steps, for example, in this case, the infected_USB_inserted. If we disable any of these attack step(s), the attacker, being unsuccessful in the attack technique(s), cannot proceed to the successive stage. An interesting case would be to disable such attack steps that do not hinder the attacker from reaching one goal by following alternative attack processes. To see how the disabling of such attack steps make a difference in the attack values, we disable the attack steps of snoop_emp and identify_network_accessible_windows_system. We see in this case the probability of an APT attack within a mission time is 8800 h is 0.15. From this result, we infer that social engineering attacks are a considerable threat, and the emphasis should be on training the employees and raising their security awareness. We also see to prevent APT attacks; one should focus on mitigating the existing system vulnerabilities.

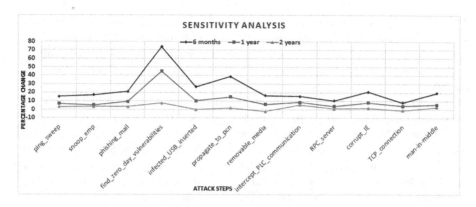

Fig. 11. Sensitivity analysis.

In Fig. 3, we plot the what-if scenarios. Here, we implement the detection measures as described in previous paragraphs. We see that in this case, the probability of an APT attack in 8800 h is 0.15, in conformance with our intuition. Similar to the previous case, we disable the same attack steps to note the difference in probability values given the detection measures are implemented. In this case, the probability of an APT attack in 8800 h reduces to 0.12. One can similarly perform many what-if analysis, for example, one can compare what is probability in the mission time of 1 year taking each stage at a time. In the same line, one can decorate the STA templates with cost structures. Doing so, one can answer more security questions, for example, What is the expected damage in one year? Which cost-effective countermeasures one can implement to reduce the probability of an attack? etc.

To account for variability in data values and know which attack steps contribute most to the uncertainty of the overall results, we perform a sensitivity analysis. Here, we modify the MTTA of all atomic steps one at a time by halving it. In Fig. 11, we see that the attack step, `find_zero_day_vulnerability` and `propagate_to_PCN` are highly sensitive, i.e., a small change in their input values lead to large difference in probability of success. Hence, these steps from modeling point require better attention and characterization. For obtaining the results in this paper, with the error bound discussed in previous paragraphs, the time required is in the order of seconds.

4   Conclusion

Traditional defensive approaches that focus on the vulnerability element of risk is not sufficient in the protection against APT attacks. Attack models could prove beneficial to understand better how APTs on a tactical level perform attacks. This paper provided a two-layer model combing the popular industry model of cyber-kill chain with stochastic timed automata. Our model can describe the APT attack in a systematic manner taking into account temporal dependencies.

The analysis is done using state-of-the-art model checking techniques to perform scenario analysis and time-dynamic analysis. Our paper thus describes APT attacks in a practitioner friendly manner with powerful mathematical semantics enabling the representation of important APT characteristics of multi-stage and concurrency.

Future work is to extend the model with defenses. As given in the original paper on cyber-kill chain [15], for each stage one can deploy several defense mechanisms. With defenses included in our model, we want to answer many other security questions on optimal defenses. Our model is based on flexible stochastic timed automata templates, incorporating cost structures requiring small addition in STAs. In a similar line, we plan to enrich our model with security policies; for example, an account is deactivated after five failed login attempts, etc. The second line of work involves making the framework tool-supported.

References

1. Capec: Common attack pattern enumeration and classification http://capec.mitre.org/
2. Mitre att&ck
3. Agha, G., Palmskog, K.: A survey of statistical model checking. ACM Trans. Model. Comput. Simul. **28**(1), 6:1–6:39 (2018)
4. Alshamrani, A., Myneni, S., Chowdhary, A., Huang, D.: A survey on advanced persistent threats: techniques, solutions, challenges, and research opportunities. IEEE Commun. Surv. Tutorials **21**(2), 1851–1877 (2019)
5. Alur, R., Dill, D.L.: A theory of timed automata. Theor. Comput. Sci. **126**(2), 183–235 (1994)
6. Arnold, F., Belinfante, A., Van der Berg, F., Guck, D., Stoelinga, M.: DFTCALC: a tool for efficient fault tree analysis. In: Bitsch, F., Guiochet, J., Kaâniche, M. (eds.) SAFECOMP 2013. LNCS, vol. 8153, pp. 293–301. Springer, Heidelberg (2013). https://doi.org/10.1007/978-3-642-40793-2_27
7. Arnold, F., Guck, D., Kumar, R., Stoelinga, M.: Sequential and parallel attack tree modelling. In: Koornneef, F., van Gulijk, C. (eds.) SAFECOMP 2015. LNCS, vol. 9338, pp. 291–299. Springer, Cham (2015). https://doi.org/10.1007/978-3-319-24249-1_25
8. Assante, M.J., Lee, R.: The industrial control system cyber kill chain, October 2015. https://www.sans.org/reading-room/whitepapers/ICS/industrial-control-system-cyber-kill-chain-36297/
9. Clio, S., et al.: Cyber kill chain based threat taxonomy and its application on cyber common operational picture. In: International Conference on Cyber Situational Awareness, Data Analytics And Assessment, pp. 1–8. IEEE (2018)
10. David, A., Larsen, K.G., Legay, A., Mikucionis, M., Poulsen, D.B.: Uppaal SMC tutorial. Int. J. Softw. Tools Technol. Transf. **17**(4), 397–415 (2015)
11. David, A., et al.: Statistical model checking for networks of priced timed automata. In: Fahrenberg, U., Tripakis, S. (eds.) FORMATS 2011. LNCS, vol. 6919, pp. 80–96. Springer, Heidelberg (2011). https://doi.org/10.1007/978-3-642-24310-3_7
12. Falliere, N., Murchu, L.O., Chien, E.: W32 stuxnet dossier. White paper, Symantec Corp., Security Response, vol. 5, no. 6, p. 29 (2011)

13. Giura, P., Wang, W.: A context-based detection framework for advanced persistent threats. In: 2012 ASE International Conference on Cyber Security, pp. 69–74. IEEE Computer Society (2012)
14. Holm, H., Sommestad, T., Ekstedt, M., NordströM, L.: CySeMoL: a tool for cyber security analysis of enterprises. In: 22nd International Conference and Exhibition on Electricity Distribution (CIRED 2013), pp. 1–4. Institute of Engineering and Technology (2013)
15. Hutchins, E.M., Cloppert, M.J., Amin, R.M.: Intelligence-driven computer network defense informed by analysis of adversary campaigns and intrusion kill chains, vol. 1, pp. 80–106 (2011)
16. Kriaa, S., Bouissou, M., Piètre-Cambacédès, L.: Modeling the stuxnet attack with BDMP: towards more formal risk assessments. In: 2012 7th International Conference on Risks and Security of Internet and Systems, pp. 1–8. IEEE (2012)
17. Kumar, R.: A model-based safety-security risk analysis framework for interconnected critical infrastructures. ICCIP 2020. IAICT, vol. 596, pp. 283–306. Springer, Cham (2020). https://doi.org/10.1007/978-3-030-62840-6_14
18. Kumar, R., Ruijters, E., Stoelinga, M.: Quantitative attack tree analysis via priced timed automata. In: Sankaranarayanan, S., Vicario, E. (eds.) FORMATS 2015. LNCS, vol. 9268, pp. 156–171. Springer, Cham (2015). https://doi.org/10.1007/978-3-319-22975-1_11
19. Kumar, R., Stoelinga, M.: Quantitative security and safety analysis with attack-fault trees. In: 2017 IEEE 18th International Symposium on High Assurance Systems Engineering (HASE), pp. 25–32 (2017)
20. Kumar, R.: Truth or dare: quantitative security risk analysis via attack trees. Ph.D. thesis, University of Twente, Netherlands, October 2018
21. Langner, R.: Stuxnet: dissecting a cyberwarfare weapon. IEEE Secur. Privacy 9(3), 49–51 (2011)
22. LeMay, E., Ford, M.D., Keefe, K., Sanders, W.H., Muehrcke, C.: Model-based security metrics using adversary view security evaluation (ADVISE). In: 8th International Conference on Quantitative Evaluation of Systems, QEST, pp. 191–200. IEEE Computer Society (2011)
23. Li, F., Lai, A., DDL: Evidence of advanced persistent threat: a case study of malware for political espionage. In: 6th International Conference on Malicious and Unwanted Software, MALWARE, pp. 102–109. IEEE Computer Society (2011)
24. Long, J.: Stuxnet: A digital staff ride, March 2019. https://mwi.usma.edu/stuxnet-digital-staff-ride/
25. Lund, M.S., Solhaug, B., Stølen, K.: The CORAS Risk Modelling Language, pp. 47–72. Springer, Berlin Heidelberg (2011). https://doi.org/10.1007/978-3-642-12323-8_4
26. Piètre-Cambacédès, L., Bouissou, M.: Beyond attack trees: dynamic security modeling with boolean logic driven Markov processes (BDMP). In: 2010 European Dependable Computing Conference, pp. 199–208 (2010)
27. Pols, P.: The unified kill chain: designing a unified kill chain for analyzing, comparing and defending against cyber attacks, Cyber Security Academy (2017). https://www.csacademy.nl/images/scripties/2018/Paul-Pols---The-Unified-Kill-Chain.pdf
28. Ross, R.: Managing enterprise security risk with nist standards 40(8), 88–91 (2007)
29. Shojaie, B., Federrath, H., Saberi, I.: Evaluating the effectiveness of ISO 27001: 2013 based on annex A, pp. 259–264 (2014)

30. Virvilis, N., Gritzalis, D.: The big four - what we did wrong in advanced persistent threat detection? In: 2013 International Conference on Availability, Reliability and Security, pp. 248–254 (2013)
31. Wideł, W., Audinot, M., Fila, B., Pinchinat, S.: Beyond 2014: formal methods for attack tree-based security modeling, vol. 52, no. 4 (2019)
32. Wolf, M.: Chapter 8 - cyber-physical systems. In: High-Performance Embedded Computing 2 edn. pp. 391–413 (2014)
33. Zhao, G., Xu, K., Xu, L., Wu, B.: Detecting APT malware infections based on malicious DNS and traffic analysis. IEEE Access **3**, 1132–1142 (2015)
34. Zhao, W., Wang, P., Zhang, F.: Extended petri net-based advanced persistent threat analysis model. In: Wong, W.E., Zhu, T. (eds.) Computer Engineering and Networking. LNEE, vol. 277, pp. 1297–1305. Springer, Cham (2014). https://doi.org/10.1007/978-3-319-01766-2_147

An Analysis of the Use of CVEs by IoT Malware

Raphaël Khoury[1]([✉]), Benjamin Vignau[1], Sylvain Hallé[1],
Abdelwahab Hamou-Lhadj[2], and Asma Razgallah[1]

[1] Department of Computer Science and Mathematics,
Université du Québec à Chicoutimi, Saguenay, Québec, Canada
{raphael.khoury,benjamin.vignau,asma.razgallah1}@uqac.ca,
shalle@acm.org
[2] Department of Electrical and Computer Engineering, Concordia University,
Montreal, Canada
wahab.hamou-lhadj@concordia.ca

Abstract. In recent years, IoT malware has become a significant threat to the IoT infrastructure, to the point where it even hinders the deployment of this promising technology. A distinctive aspect of this threat is its reliance on vulnerabilities as an infection vector. Many of these vulnerabilities are CVEs (Common Vulnerability Enumeration) selected from the National Vulnerability Database (NVD). In this study, we investigate the use of CVEs by IoT malware, with the ultimate aim of predicting which CVEs are more likely to be targeted by malware developers. Our results show that the CVEs exploited by IoT malware developers are sufficiently distinguished from those CVEs that IoT developers refrain from using to permit effective automated prediction. We detail these differences, develop other observations about the use of vulnerabilities by IoT malware and compile data on this topic that may be useful to security researchers.

Keywords: IoT malware · CVE Internet of Things · Malware

1 Introduction

The last ten years have seen an exponential rise in the use of IoT devices: mechanical or digital devices that are connected to a network and can send and receive information without interaction from a user [46]. Unfortunately, this growth has been matched with a corresponding growth in IoT malware, i.e. malware that has been specifically designed to target IoT connected devices. The fact that it is often difficult to update the firmware in such devices makes them a particularly inviting target for malware developers.

Previous research [58] showed that while IoT malware seems to be developed in isolation from malware targeting other device platforms, IoT malware developers borrow freely from each other, re-using code as well as broad features such

© Springer Nature Switzerland AG 2021
G. Nicolescu et al. (Eds.): FPS 2020, LNCS 12637, pp. 47–62, 2021.
https://doi.org/10.1007/978-3-030-70881-8_4

as infection strategies. A particularly important aspect of the latter is the use of CVEs as an infection vector. CVEs (for Common Vulnerabilities and Exposures) are software vulnerabilities that are documented and given a unique ID for future reference. The National Vulnerability Database (NVD), a database of all CVEs, is publicly available and maintained by the National Institute of Standards and Technology [43].

In this paper, we investigate the use CVEs as an infection vector by IoT malware. We examine how this infection strategy compares to other strategies employed by IoT malware designers to achieve their nefarious aims, as well as how CVEs are chosen for exploitation. Answers to these questions will allow developers and system managers to better protect their devices against the scourge of IoT malware, for instance by prioritizing CVEs that are more likely to be exploited.

In particular, we attempt to answer the following 3 research questions.

RQ1: What trends are detectable in the use of CVEs by IoT malware?
We first attempt to determine how the use of CVEs as an infection vector compares to other infection strategies employed by IoT malware developers. In particular, investigate if the use of CVEs has increased over time; if the certain classes of IoT malware are more likely to employ CVEs, and if vulnerabilities are more likely to be exploited if they are indexed by the NVD.

RQ2: What types of CVEs are targeted by IoT developers?
Next, we determine how malware developers choose the CVE entries that are incorporated in their code. We find that CVEs that are chosen by malware developers differs from the broader NVD in several respects, notably w.r.t. impact, complexity, type and date.

RQ3: Can we predict which CVEs will be used by a given malware?
Finally, drawing upon the insights gleaned in answering RQ2, we attempt to predict which CVEs are more likely to be exploited in the future using a machine learning process.

The main contribution of this paper is provide answers to the above questions. In addition, we list every CVE exploited by IoT malware during a ten year horizon, and compile other information about the exploitation of vulnerabilities by IoT malware that may be useful to security researchers.

The remainder of this paper is organized as follows: Sect. 2 presents background about the dataset we utilized. Sections 3, 4, and 5 address RQs 1, 2 and 3 respectively. Section 6 discusses threats to the validity of our conclusions, followed by related works in Sect. 7. Concluding remarks are given in Sect. 8.

2   Description of the Data

The National Vulnerability Database (NVD) is a freely available database of vulnerabilities, maintained by the National Institute of Standards and Technology, an agency of the United States Department of Commerce [43]. Each entry, called a CVE, captures a single vulnerability, in a any system, and presents it in a standardized format. The NVD contains over 140 000 entries.

The NVD provides standardized information about each entry by way of the Common Vulnerability Scoring System (CVSS). Two versions of the CVSS are currently in use: Version 2 (V2) introduced in 2007 [32] and Versions 3, introduced in 2015 [18].

Amongst the information provided by the CVSS, the following are particularly relevant to the topic of this study:

Attack Vector. Indicates the context by which exploitation can occurs. In the V2 score, this metric ranges over the values 'local', 'adjacent network', and 'network'. The V3 scores adds a fourth value: 'physical'.

Access Complexity. This metric captures the presence of conditions beyond the control of the attacker that are nonetheless required to successfully exploit the vulnerability. It ranges over 'low', 'med' and 'high' in the V2 score, and over 'low' and 'high' in the V3 score.

User Interaction. Indicates if user interaction is required in order to successfully exploit the vulnerability. This value ranges over 'true' and 'false' in the V2 score, and over 'none' and 'required' in the V3 score.

Impact score (called impact sub-score in the version 2). A value in the 0–10 range that captures the impact that exploiting the vulnerability may have on the targeted organization.

Exploitability score (called exploitability sub-score in CVSS version 2). It consists in a value in the 0–10 range that captures how vulnerable the system is to attack.

Base score. A value in the 0–10 range that captures the severity of the vulnerability. It is derived from the Impact score and Exploitability score using a algorithmic method.

Each CVE possesses a timestamp of the date of publication of the vulnerability and a unique identifier in the format CVE-YYYY-#### where #### is a sequential number. Each CVE also associates a a list of products and vendors that are affected by it. Note that each CVE may be associated with multiple different products, from multiple different vendors.

3   Research Question 1

What trends are detectable in the use of CVEs by IoT malware? We begin by examining what patterns can be discerned in the use of CVEs as an exploitation vector by IoT malware, as opposed to other attack vectors such as credential attacks.

We examined 27 IoT malware, spanning the period 2008 to present. These include every IoT malware that has been studied in the academic literature during this time period. Of these, 13 do not exploit vulnerabilities as part of their infection strategy, opting for other infection mechanisms such as common credentials dictionaries. A single one, Aidra, uses only a single vulnerability not

Table 1. Recent IoT malware, their type and number of vulnerabilities exploited by each

Malware	Year of creation	Objective	No of CVE used	No of non-CVE vuln. used
Hydra	2008	D	0	0
Psybot	2009	D	0	1
Chuck Norris	2009	D	0	0
Tsunami	2010	D	0	0
Aidra	2012	D	0	1
Carna	2012	–	0	0
Bashlite	2014	D	0	0
Darlloz	2014	I	1	0
Spike	2014	D	0	0
TheMoon1	2014	–	0	0
Wifatch	2014	–	0	0
XOR	2014	D	0	0
Elknot	2015	D	0	0
Remaiten	2016	D	0	0
Hajime	2016	-	4	0
Mirai	2016	D	0	0
NewAidra	2016	D	0	0
LuaBot	2016	D	0	0
Amnesia	2017	D	1	0
BrickerBot	2017	S	0	0
IoTReaper	2017	D	9	4
Persirai	2017	D	2	0
Satori	2017	D	1	1
JenX	2018	D	3	0
TheMoon2	2018	P, S	4	0
VPNFilter	2018	S	14	3
Hide'n Seek	2018	S, I, M	10	3
Echobot	2019	D	73	19

recorded in the CVE database. An additional 6 rely exclusively on vulnerabilities reported in the CVE database while the final 4 rely both on reported and unreported vulnerabilities. For vulnerabilities not present in the CVE, it is not certain how the malware developer became aware of the vulnerability.

The data we gathered is summarized in Tables 1 and 4.

Table 1 records every malware studied, and identifies for each how many vulnerabilities it exploits as part of its attack strategy, distinguishing vulnerabilities for which there exists a CVE record from those for which there are not. Table 1 also records the main objective of each IoT malware. These objectives are taken from a survey by Vignau et al. [58] and range over Denial of service attacks (D), Physical destruction of the target devise (P), income generation (i.e. cryptomining) (I), Spying (S) and Malware dissemination (M).

A number of observations are immediately obvious from an inspection of this data. As can be seen in Table 1, early IoT rarely exploited vulnerabilities, and never exploited multiple vulnerabilities. Starting in 2016, the use of vulnerabilities became more common, and some malware started exploiting multiple vulnerabilities. This trend reached an apex with Echobot, a highly dynamic malware whose code is regularly updated with the inclusion of new exploits.

Vulnerabilities recorded in the NVD (those for which a CVE entry exists) outnumber unlisted vulnerabilities by a factor of 4, hinting that the NVD database is the preferred venue of malware developers to select exploitable vulnerabilities. However, in this respect, it is important to stress that some vulnerabilities only acquired a CVE entry after it appeared that IoT malware were exploiting these vulnerabilities [10]. A complete listing of every CVE exploited by each IoT that made use of recorded vulnerabilities is given in Table 2. The right-most column of the table identifies the references listing the vulnerabilities exploited by each malware.

It does not appear that the objective of the malware correlates with it's use of vulnerabilities as an infection vector, thought the limited size of the malware sample, as well as the fact that certain objectives are more common in later malware, makes a definitive determination difficult. In particular, spying and malware dissemination only occur in a single IoT malware each, both of them towards the end of the period of our study when the use of vulnerabilities had become more commonplace.

> **Finding 1:**
>
> IoT malware increasingly rely on exploiting vulnerabilities as part of their infection strategy. Recent malware is also much more likely to exploit multiple vulnerabilities. There is not enough evidence to conclude that malware with a specific objective is more likely to adopt this infection strategy. The NVD seems to be the preferred venue for malware developers to search for and find exploitable vulnerabilities.

4 Research Question 2

What types of CVEs are targeted by IoT malware developers?
In this section, we seek to determine if the CVEs targeted by IoT malware developers share distinctive characteristics that can help predict which CVEs are more likely to be targeted.

Table 2. CVEs exploited by each IoT botnet

Malware	Exploited CVEs	References
Darlloz	CVE-2012-1823	[3,8,48,59]
Hajime	CVE-2016-10372, CVE-2018-10561, CVE-2018-10562, CVE-2015-4464, CVE-2018-7445, CVE-2018-14847, CVE-2013-6023	[17,22,25,47, 57,65]
Amnesia	CVE-2013-6023	[19,63]
IoTReaper	CVE-2017-8225, CVE-2017-18377, CVE-2013-2678, CVE-2018-14933, CVE-2018-15716, CVE-2017-18378, CVE-2013-4980 CVE-2013-4981, CVE-2013-4982	[9,33,44,49, 52,64]
Persirai	CVE-2017-8225, CVE-2017-18377	[13,54]
Satori	CVE-2014-8361	[36,37,39]
JenX	CVE-2017-18368, CVE-2017-17215, CVE-2014-8361	[14,45]
TheMoon2	CVE-2018-1056, CVE-2018-14847, CVE-2018-10561, CVE-2018-10562	[2,26,53]
VPNFilter	CVE-2015-7261, CVE-2011-4723, CVE-2014-9583, CVE-2013-2678, CVE-2013-0229, CVE-2013-0230, CVE-2017-6361, CVE-2017-8877, CVE-2017-5521, CVE-2012-5958, CVE-2012-5959, CVE-2016-6277, CVE-2017-6549, CVE-2013-2679	[1,15,27,28, 50]
Hide'n Seek	CVE-2016-10401, CVE-2017-8225, CVE-2017-18377, CVE-2018-14933, CVE-2018-15716, CVE-2017-18378, CVE-2013-4980, CVE-2013-4981, CVE-2013-4982, CVE-2013-2678	[4,5,7,12,31, 55]
Echobot	CVE-2003-0050, CVE-2005-0116, CVE-2005-2773, CVE-2005-2847, CVE-2005-2848, CVE-2006-2237, CVE-2006-4000, CVE-2007-3010, CVE-2008-3922, CVE-2009-0545, CVE-2009-2288, CVE-2009-2765, CVE-2009-5156, CVE-2009-5157, CVE-2010-5330, CVE-2011-3587, CVE-2011-5010, CVE-2012-0262, CVE-2012-4869, CVE-2013-3568, CVE-2013-4863, CVE-2013-5758, CVE-2013-5759, CVE-2013-5912, CVE-2013-5948, CVE-2013-7471, CVE-2014-3914, CVE-2014-8361, CVE-2015-2208, CVE-2015-4051, CVE-2016-0752, CVE-2016-10760, CVE-2016-1555, CVE-2016-6255, CVE-2016-6277, CVE-2017-14127, CVE-2017-14135, CVE-2017-16602, CVE-2017-16608, CVE-2017-18377, CVE-2017-5173, CVE-2017-5174, CVE-2017-6316, CVE-2017-6884, CVE-2017-8221, CVE-2017-8222, CVE-2017-8223, CVE-2017-8224, CVE-2017-8225, CVE-2018-1056, CVE-2018-10561, CVE-2018-10562, CVE-2018-11138, CVE-2018-11510, CVE-2018-14847, CVE-2018-14933, CVE-2018-15887, CVE-2018-17173, CVE-2018-20841, CVE-2018-6961, CVE-2018-7297, CVE-2018-7841, CVE-2019-12780, CVE-2019-12989, CVE-2019-12991, CVE-2019-14927, CVE-2019-14931, CVE-2019-15107, CVE-2019-16072, CVE-2019-17270, CVE-2019-18396, CVE-2019-2725, CVE-2019-3929	[10,11,16,23, 24,40,42]

We found that 11 different malware made use of 99 CVEs a total 128 times (counting each use of a CVE by a different malware as distinct). Of these, 98 posses a CVSS V2 score and 64 possess a CVSS V3 score[1]. An analysis of this data indicates that the vulnerabilities targeted by IoT malware developers distinguish themselves in several ways.

Unsurprisingly, CVEs employed by IoT malware developers exclusively employ the 'Network' access vector, meaning that the vulnerable component is connected to the network stack. The alternative classifications are 'local', 'Adjacent Network' and 'Physical'.

The V2 scoring provides a 3-valued verdict as to the difficulty of exploiting each vulnerability. Performing a standard Khi-square test, we find with strong confidence ($p < .01$) that the selection of CVEs by malware creators is skewed towards easier CVEs. This result is even starker when considering the V3 scoring of this same element: only 3 out of 64 (4.7%) CVEs for which a V3 score of complexity is provided are rated as 'HIGH' difficulty, versus 8.6% in the NVD database in general.

In addition to selecting attacks of lower complexity, IoT malware designers seem to prefer vulnerabilities with higher impact scores, as recorded in the V2 and V3 impact score metric. The average V2 and V3 impact scores for vulnerabilities exploited by IoT malware are 8.17 and 5.6 respectively, higher that the corresponding averages of 6.0 and 4.4 for the NVD database as a whole. Performing a standard Z-test [21] confirms that attackers indeed select CVE with high scores, for both V2 and V3.

The exploited CVEs also skew heavily towards CVEs that do not require user interaction: 93.8% of the exploited CVEs for which a V2 ranking of user interaction is provided do not require it, versus 68.6% for the NVD in general. Once again, a standard Z-test confirm the statistical significance of this result. The same result holds when considering the V3 score for user interaction: 92.1% of exploited malware did not require explicit user interaction versus 36.9% for the broader NVD.

Each CVE entry identifies a single CWE (Common Weakness Identification), that pinpoints the type of vulnerability in question. Once again, a Khi-square test indicates that the distribution of vulnerability types is not random, but seems to be skewed towards specific CWE types. The top six CWE types most frequently targeted by IoT malware developers are CWE-20 (Improper Input Validation), CWE-94 (Improper Control of Generation of Code), CWE-78 (Improper Neutralization of Special Elements used in an OS Command), CWE-77 (Improper Neutralization of Special Elements used in a Command), CWE-119 (Improper Restriction of Operations within the Bounds of a Memory Buffer) and CWE-287 (Improper Authentication); together accounting for 67% of exploited vulnerabilities. Table 3 shows the top six most common CWE exploited by IoT malware, alongside with their frequency of occurrence among exploited CVEs and in the entire NVD database. Note that all six of these weaknesses are either input validation errors or authentication errors.

---

[1] The only CVE for which no information was available, CVE-2013-5759, is a duplicate of CVE-2013-5758.

Table 3. Most frequently exploited CWE

CWE	Proportion in IoT malware	Proportion in NVD
CWE-78	23.0%	8.6%
CWE-77	14.9%	2.5%
CWE-20	9.2%	1.1%
CWE-94	5.7%	0.5%
CWE-119	6.9%	12.5%
CWE-287	6.9%	2.1%

This result, however, should be qualified. Unlike the other information recorded in CVE entries, the proportion of CWE of each times varies widely from year to year, a factor we were unable to account for. Other limitations of the dataset are discussed in Sect. 6.

As can be seen in Table 4, some malware developers often look back several years in search of exploitable vulnerabilities. Notably, Echobot, discovered in June 2019, employed a vulnerability first uncovered in 2003. However, our analysis shows that most IoT malware tends towards the exploitation of recent vulnerabilities.

In order to investigate further how the vulnerabilities exploited by IoT malware relate to the time of publication of the corresponding CVE entries, we computed the timespan that separates the public divulgation of a vulnerability and it's incorporation in IoT malware, for every CVE for which this information was available.

Unfortunately, only partial data was available in this regard. A malware may be updated multiple times, making it difficult to determine exactly when a given vulnerability was incorporated into its code. In fact, only for Echobot were we able to find multiple descriptions of the CVEs it exploits along with the exploitation date, allowing us to assign different CVEs to different versions of the malware. Furthermore, as discussed above, some vulnerabilities only received a CVE entry after it was found that a malware exploited this vulnerability. These and other limitations of the data are discussed in the Sect. 6. Nonetheless, the data that is available seems sufficient to draw broad conclusions.

Table 4 details the timespan, in months, that separates the publication of a CVE in the NVD database from its introduction in a malware. IoT malware for which this information could not be ascertained with sufficient confidence are omitted from the table. The information is grouped into the intervals of months given in the left most column. The center column gives the total number CVEs whose age was contained in each interval at the moment of their introduction in a malware while the right-most column breaks down this number by malware, using the following key: E: Echobot, D: Darlloz, A: Amnesia, V: VPNFilter.

In a December 2019 blogpost [41], Ruchna Nigam suggested that Echobot may be aiming at a 'sweetspot' of vulnerability exploitation by selecting both very recent vulnerabilities, for which the patch may not have been applied yet,

Table 4. Number of months that separate the publication of CVEs from their exploitation by IoT malware.

Time interval (number of months)	Number of CVEs (total)	Number of CVEs by malware
≤5	12	E: 12
6–12	1	E: 1
13–24	12	D: 1 E: 7 M: 4
25–72	19	A: 1 S: 1 E: 10 V: 7
73+	9	V: 5 E: 4

as well as much older vulnerabilities, targeting systems that are not longer maintained. The data we gathered bears this analysis. Only 23% of the CVE for which we were able to obtain data were more than 6 months old, but less than 2 years old.

This infection strategy, however, seems unique to the concepts of Echobot, and every other IoT malware for which data was available seems to have picked vulnerabilities whose date of publication falls inside a fairly narrow range.

It is also noteworthy to see that multiple CVEs are exploited by several different IoT bots. Indeed, of the 98 CVEs in our corpus, 13 are exploited at least twice, 8 are exploited at least three times and 2 are exploited four times. This phenomenon is likely due to the large amount of code reused between IoT malware [58] and highlights the need for the prompt applications of security updates. Since the NVD database contains upwards of 6800 entries for software and firmware used by IoT devices, a CVE that has been exploited in the past is more than 8 times more likely to be exploited again in a different IoT malware.

> **Finding 2:**
>
> Malware developers are more likely to use CVE with high exploitability score, and low exploit difficulty. CWEs related to input validation errors or authentication errors are more likely to be targeted, with a small number of CWEs accounting for the plurality of exploited vulnerabilities. Malware developers tend to prefer recent CVEs, and are likely to reuse CVEs that have been targeted by other malware developers in the past.

5 Research Question 3

Drawing on the results of the previous section, we attempt to automatically ascertain which CVE are more likely to be targeted by IoT malware developers using a machine learning process. A successful classification will enable IoT developers and sysadmins to prioritize CVEs in the design and application of patches, proactively focusing on CVEs with a high likelihood of being incorporated into malware.

We performed a first filter over the NVD, eliminating any CVE whose associated products were not IoT devices. For this purpose, we compiled a list of any product that figures in any CVE exploited by any of the IoT malware in our dataset and excluded CVEs that did not include any product in the target list. At the end of this process, we had 6 300 entries.

For each of the remaining CVEs, we created a feature vector comprising the following datum of information: year of publication, CWE, Access Complexity (V2), Impact sub-score (V2), user interaction, exploitability Score (V2), and impact score. Each vector also indicated whether the CVE exclusively concerned products on the above mentioned list or additionally targeted products not listed. The two classes are 'selected', for the CVEs that malware designer elected to target, and 'unsued', for other IoT vulnerabilities.

We used undersampling to overcome the unbalance in the dataset, aggregating the 98 CVEs used throughout this study with 200 randomly selected entries. We used 70% of the data for training and 30% for testing.

Table 5. Classifier results

Algorithm	Correctly classified instances	Incorrectly classified instances	Precision	Recall
SVM	52 (81.25%)	12 (18.75%)	78.8%	83.9%
Random Forest	50 (78.1%)	14 (21.9%)	79.3%	74.2%
J48	53 (82.8%)	11 (17.2%)	83.3%	80.6%

The results are reported in Table 5.

These results indicate that the CVEs targeted by malware designers are sufficiently distinguished from those they avoid to allow automated detection with reasonable effectiveness. The J48 algorithm was particularly effective at predicting which CVEs will be selected while the other SVM was more effective at at ruling out CVEs unlikely to be targeted. It's clear that while the classification provides useful and actionable information, more research is needed before security researchers can confidently predict the future evolution of IoT malware.

Interestingly, we repeated the experiment with the elision of the 'year' datum in the feature vector and obtained similar results to those reported in Table 5. This indicates that the classification relies on core features of the CVEs, rather than on time spans that separates the publication of a CVEs from the creation of the malware studied.

Our use of undersampling to overcome the unbalance in the dataset is a threat to the validity of this result. This problem can be corrected as more data becomes available, a near certainty given the continued prevalence of IoT malware and the resourcefulness of IoT malware developers.

> **Finding 3:**
>
> The CVEs targeted by malware developers are sufficiently distinguished from those they avoid to allow automated detection with reasonable effectiveness, though more research is needed to refine the detection process.

6 Threats to Validity

We opted to include the entire corpus of vulnerabilities present in the NVD database in our analysis. A possible threat to validity derives from this decision, since the NVD database contains vulnerabilities dating back from as early as 2002, and it is likely that most malware developers disregard such dated vulnerabilities. That said, some bots do include vulnerabilities several years old, such Echobot, deployed in 2019, which exploited a 16 year old vulnerability. We consequently opted to include the entire dataset.

The incompleteness of the data is another threat to validity. As discussed above, the V2 and V3 rating are not present for every vulnerability. Amongst the vulnerabilities utilized by IoT malware developers, a single one, CVE-2013-5759, utilized by Echobot, did not have either rating. Furthermore, a small number of CVEs may be duplicates, a fact we ignored. For example, CVE-2019-18396 is a duplicate report of the same vulnerability reported by CVE-2017-14127.

The fact that the average impact score, difficulty of exploitation and the distribution of CWEs in the NVD varies from year to year is a threat to the validity of the results presents in Sect. 4 since the vulnerabilities exploited by IoT designers skew towards the more recent past. The differences we observed in the CVSS scores and CWEs of exploited CVEs may be caused in part by drift in the values over the years.

A treat to the validity of our results exists because some vulnerabilities received a CVE entry only after they began to be exploited by an IoT malware, especially Echobot (see for e.g. [10]). We were unable to identify these vulnerabilities with certainty, and this fact may have led us to understate the number of vulnerabilities without a corresponding NVD entry that are exploited by IoT malware (Sect. 3) and to overstate the propensity of malware designer to target recent vulnerabilities (Sect. 4).

As mentioned above, the unbalance present in the dataset, and our use of undersampling to overcome it, is a threat to the validity of the results reported in Sect. 5.

7 Related Works

Recently, Blinowski et al. [6] proposed a classification of vulnerabilities associated with IoT devices, extracted from the NVD database. They manually grouped vulnerability records into seven categories (Home, mobile devices, etc.). This classification was used later to train an SVM to predict the category of new vulnerabilities. Their approach achieves a precision and recall of 70%–80% for categories for which they have a large number of vulnerabilities, and of 50% accuracy or less for less-populated categories.

Li et al. [30] proposed a vulnerability mining algorithm to analyze and obtain essential characteristics of software vulnerability-based data mining techniques. Their algorithm was used on software vulnerabilities using the NVD dataset. When applied to detecting vulnerabilities in three projects, their approach achieved a recall of around 70% and precision of 60%.

Spanos and Angelis [51] presented a model that can automatically predict the characteristics of vulnerabilities. This is an important task since the specification of vulnerabilities is used to determine their severity, complexity, impact, and other characteristics, used by vulnerability scoring systems. Their model combines text processing and multi-target classification technique. They applied their model to a dataset of 99,000 vulnerability records from the NVD. The results vary depending on the vulnerability characteristic that is the subject of prediction and the algorithm used for classification, with an F-measure ranging between 42.88% and 67.91%.

Le et al. [29] proposed an approach to automatically assess software vulnerabilities with concept drift using software vulnerability descriptions. Their approach combines both character and word features. They applied their approach to the prediction of seven vulnerability characteristics. They experimented with more than 100,000 vulnerabilities from NVD and showed that their approach can predict vulnerability effectively without having to retrain the models, which suggest that their models can be used to overcome the problem of concept drift.

Wijayasekara et al. [61] focused on so-called hidden impact vulnerabilities, i.e. vulnerabilities that appeared long after the associated bugs have been made public. They develop a text mining classifier to identify hidden impact vulnerabilities from bug report databases. The authors extended this work in [60,62] by using information gain and genetic algorithms [60] and three different classifiers (NaïveBayes, Naive Bayes Multinomial, and C4.5 Decision Tree) [62].

Murtaza et al. [34] conducted an empirical study to understand the trends of software vulnerabilities over time, the common patterns of software vulnerabilities, and whether or not one can predict the type of vulnerability in a software application. They used NVD and their main source of data to mine six years of software vulnerabilities from 2009 to 2014. They found that the patterns of vulnerability events follow the first order Markov property, i.e., the next vulnerability can be predicted by the previous vulnerability. They also found that the next vulnerability can be predicted with approximately 90% precision and 80% recall, just by using the previous vulnerability. finally, they found that collectively mobile applications have higher vulnerabilities than traditional software applications.

Na et al. [35] proposed a classification method for categorizing CVE entries into vulnerability type using naïve Bayes classifiers. They showed that their approach can analyze CVE entries that are not yet classified. Frei et al. [20] conducted a study in which they examine the time of discovery of vulnerabilities, the time of disclosure of attacks, and the time of availability of patches. Their study uses mainly NVD data. They found that software vendors are slow to provide patches despite the fact that attacks that exploit zero-day vulnerabilities are an increasing trend. Neuhaus and Zimmermann [38] proposed an approach to automatically categorize CVE vulnerabilities into vulnerability types by using Latent Dirichlet Allocation (LDA).

Valente et al. [56] analyze various types of IoT devices and uncover the vulnerabilities they contain. They found 9 new CVEs that can be employed to perform new kinds of attacks including drone hijacking, remote sexual assault, or harassment. They classify the CVEs exploited by IoT malware in 4 categories depending on the interactions between the attackers and the IoT devices.

8   Conclusions

In this study we investigated the use of CVEs by IoT malware developers. We found that IoT malware increasingly relies upon the exploitation of vulnerabilities as an infection vector, and that the NVD seems to be the preferred source to obtain these vulnerabilities. We also found that the vulnerabilities selected by IoT malware differ from the broader NVD in several respects. Notably, IoT malware developers then to prefer vulnerabilities with lower than average exploitation complexity and higher than average impact. Targeted vulnerabilities are remotely exploitable and less likely to necessitate user interaction. Certain specific CWEs, reflecting input validation and authentication errors, are also more likely to be targeted. Indeed, the CVEs targeted by malware designer are sufficiently distinct to permit automated prediction using machine learning algorithms.

In addition, we compiled data about the use of vulnerabilities by IoT malware, which may be useful to security researchers in the future.

References

1. Vpnfilter-affected devices still riddled with 19 vulnerabilities
2. Netlab 360. GPON exploit in the wild (IV) - TheMoon botnet join in with a 0day(?) (2018). https://blog.netlab.360.com/gpon-exploit-in-the-wild-iv-themoon-botnet-join-in-with-a-0day/
3. Angrishi, K.: Turning internet of things (IoT) into internet of vulnerabilities (IoV): IoT botnets, February 2017
4. Arsene, L.: Hide and seek IoT botnet learns new tricks: Uses ADB over internet to exploit thousands of android devices, September 2018. https://labs.bitdefender.com/2018/09/hide-and-seek-iot-botnet-learns-new-tricks-uses-adb-over-internet-to-exploit-thousands-of-android-devices/
5. Avast. Let's play hide 'n seek with a botnet, December 2018. https://blog.avast.com/hide-n-seek-botnet-continues

6. Blinowski, G., Piotrowski, P.: CVE based classification of vulnerable IoT systems. In: Theory and Applications of Dependable Computer Systems (DepCoS-RELCOMEX 2020), pp.82–93 (2020)

7. Botezatu, B.: New hide 'n seek IoT botnet using custom-built peer-to-peer communication spotted in the wild, January 2018. https://labs.bitdefender.com/2018/01/new-hide-n-seek-iot-botnet-using-custom-built-peer-to-peer-communication-spotted-in-the-wild/,

8. Botticelli, B.: IoT honeypots: state of the art (2017). https://fr.slideshare.net/BiagioBotticelli/state-of-the-art-iot-honeypots

9. Brian, K.: Fear the reaper, or reaper madness? (2017). https://krebsonsecurity.com/2017/10/fear-the-reaper-or-reaper-madness/#more-41321

10. Cashdollar, L.: Latest ECHOBOT: 26 infection vectors (2019). https://www.blogs.akamai.com/sitr/2019/06/latest-echobot-26-infection-vectors.html

11. Cimpanu, C.: Le nouveau malware d'echobot est un concentré de vulnérabilités (2019). https://www.zdnet.fr/actualites/le-nouveau-malware-d-echobot-est-un-concentre-de-vulnerabilites-39886143.htm

12. Şendroiu, A., Diaconescu, V.: Hide 'n' seek: an adaptive peer-to-peer IoT botnet. Virus Bull. (2018)

13. New Jersey Cybersecurity and Communications Integration Cell. Persirai (2017). https://www.cyber.nj.gov/threat-profiles/botnet-variants/persirai

14. Davila, A.: JenX botnet: a new IoT botnet threatening all (2019). https://unit42.paloaltonetworks.com/home-small-office-wireless-routers-exploited-to-attack-gaming-servers/

15. Brumaghin, E., Talos Unit: VPNFilter III: more tools for the Swiss army knife of malware (2018). https://www.blog.talosintelligence.com/2018/09/vpnfilter-part-3.html

16. Eli, K., Maxim, Z., Raymond, P.: Echobot malware now up to 71 exploits, targeting SCADA (2019). https://www.f5.com/labs/articles/threat-intelligence/echobot-malware-now-up-to-71-exploits-targeting-scada

17. Radware Emergency Response Team: Hajime - friend or foe? (2017). https://security.radware.com/ddos-threats-attacks/hajime-iot-botnet/

18. FIRST. Common vulnerability scoring system version 3.1, June 2019

19. Frank, C., Nance, C., Jarocki, S., Pauli, W.E., Madison, S.D.: Protecting IoT from Mirai botnets; IoT device hardening. In: Proceedings of the Conference on Information Systems Applied Research, Austin, TX, USA, p. 1508 (2017)

20. Frei, S., May, M., Fiedler, U., Plattner, B.: Large-scale vulnerability analysis. In: Proceedings of the 2006 SIGCOMM Workshop on Large-Scale Attack Defense, LSAD 2006, pp. 131–138. Association for Computing Machinery, New York (2006)

21. Freund, J.E., Miller, I., Miller, M.: John E. Freund's Mathematical Statistics with Applications. Pearson Education. Prentice Hall (2004)

22. Herwig, S., Harvey, K., Hughey, G., Roberts, R., Levin, D.: Measurement and analysis of Hajime, a peer-to-peer IoT botnet. In: NDSS (2019)

23. Ilascu, I.: Echobot botnet spreads via 26 exploits, targets oracle, VMware apps (2019). https://www.bleepingcomputer.com/news/security/echobot-botnet-spreads-via-26-exploits-targets-oracle-vmware-apps/

24. Ilascu, I.: New echobot botnet variant uses over 50 exploits to propagate (2019). https://www.bleepingcomputer.com/news/security/new-echobot-botnet-variant-uses-over-50-exploits-to-propagate/

25. Van Der Wiel, J., Vicente, D., Yury, N., Zykov, K.: Hajime, the mysterious evolving botnet (2017). https://securelist.com/hajime-the-mysterious-evolving-botnet/78160/

26. BlackLotus Lab. A new phase of TheMoon (2019). https://blog.centurylink.com/a-new-phase-of-themoon/
27. Largent, W.: New VPNFilter malware targets at least 500k networking devices worldwide (2018). https://www.blog.talosintelligence.com/2018/05/VPNFilter.html
28. Largent, W.: VPNFilter update - VPNFilter exploits endpoints, targets new devices (2018). https://www.blog.talosintelligence.com/2018/06/vpnfilter-update.html
29. Le, T.H.M., Sabir, B., Ali Babar, M.: Automated software vulnerability assessment with concept drift. In: Proceedings of the 16th International Conference on Mining Software Repositories, MSR 2019, pp. 371–382. IEEE Press (2019)
30. Li, X., et al.: A mining approach to obtain the software vulnerability characteristics. In: 2017 Fifth International Conference on Advanced Cloud and Big Data (CBD), pp. 296–301 (2017)
31. MalwareTech. Tracking the hide and seek botnet, January 2019. https://www.malwaretech.com/2019/01/tracking-the-hide-and-seek-botnet.html
32. Mell, P., Scarfone, K., Romanosky, S.: A complete guide to the common vulnerability scoring system. Technical report, National Institute of Standards and Technology and Carnegie Mellon University (2007)
33. Moriuchi, P., Chohan, S.: Mirai-variant IoT botnet used to target financial sector in January 2018 (2018). https://go.recordedfuture.com/hubfs/reports/cta-2018-0405.pdf
34. Murtaza, S.S., Khreich, W., Hamou-Lhadj, A., Bener, A.B.: Mining trends and patterns of software vulnerabilities. J. Syst. Softw. **117**(C), 218–228 (2016)
35. Na, S., Kim, T., Kim, H.: A study on the classification of common vulnerabilities and exposures using Naïve Bayes. In: BWCCA 2016. LNDECT, vol. 2, pp. 657–662. Springer, Cham (2017). https://doi.org/10.1007/978-3-319-49106-6_65
36. Netlab360. Botnets never die, satori refuses to fade away (2018). https://www.blog.netlab.360.com/botnets-never-die-satori-refuses-to-fade-away-en/
37. Netlab360. Warning: Satori, a Mirai branch is spreading in worm style on port 37215 and 52869 (2018). https://www.blog.netlab.360.com/warning-satori-a-new-mirai-variant-is-spreading-in-worm-style-on-port-37215-and-52869-en/
38. Neuhaus, S., Zimmermann, T.: Security trend analysis with CVE topic models. In: 2010 IEEE 21st International Symposium on Software Reliability Engineering, pp. 111–120 (2010)
39. NewSkySecurity. Masuta: Satori creators' second botnet weaponizes a new router exploit (2018). https://blog.newskysecurity.com/masuta-satori-creators-second-botnet-weaponizes-a-new-router-exploit-2ddc51cc52a7
40. Nigam, R.: Mirai variant ECHOBOT resurfaces with 13 previously unexploited vulnerabilities (2019). https://unit42.paloaltonetworks.com/mirai-variant-echobot-resurfaces-with-13-previously-unexploited-vulnerabilities/
41. Nigam, R.: Mirai variant ECHOBOT resurfaces with 13 previously unexploited vulnerabilities, December 2019
42. Nigam, R.: New Mirai variant adds 8 new exploits, targets additional IoT devices (2019). https://unit42.paloaltonetworks.com/new-mirai-variant-adds-8-new-exploits-targets-additional-iot-devices/
43. NIST. National vulnerability database - general information, August 2020
44. Check Point. IotRoop botnet: the full investigation (2017). https://research.checkpoint.com/iotroop-botnet-full-investigation/
45. Radware: JenX botnet: a new IoT botnet threatening all (2018). https://security.radware.com/ddos-threats-attacks/threat-advisories-attack-reports/jenx/

46. Salah, K., Khan, M.: IoT security: review, blockchain solutions, and open challenges. Future Gener. Comput. Syst. **82**, 395–411 (2018)
47. Sam, E., Ioannis, P.: Hajime: analysis of a decentralized internet worm for IoT devices (2016). www.cs.umd.edu/class/fall2017/cmsc818O/papers/hajime-rapidity.pdf
48. Scott Sr., J., Summit, W.: Rise of the machines: the DYN attack was just a practice run, December 2016
49. FortiGuard SE: Reaper: the next evolution of IoT botnets, 16 November 2017. https://www.fortinet.com/blog/threat-research/reaper-the-next-evolution-of-iot-botnets.html
50. Sicato, S., Costa, J., Sharma, P.K., Loia, V., Park, J.H.: VPNFilter malware analysis on cyber threat in smart home network. Appl. Sci. **9**(13), 2763 (2019)
51. Spanos, G., Angelis, L.: A multi-target approach to estimate software vulnerability characteristics and severity scores. J. Syst. Softw. **146**, 152–166 (2018)
52. Trend Mirco System: New rapidly-growing IoT botnet - reaper (2018). https://success.trendmicro.com/solution/1118928-new-rapidly-growing-iot-botnet-reaper#collapseTwo
53. Tara, S. TheMoon rises again, with a botnet-as-a-service threat (2019). https://threatpost.com/themoon-botnet-as-a-service/141393/
54. TrendMicro: Persirai: new Internet of Things (IoT) botnet targets IP cameras (2017). https://blog.trendmicro.com/trendlabs-security-intelligence/persirai-new-internet-things-iot-botnet-targets-ip-cameras/
55. TrendMicro: "hide 'n seek" botnet uses peer-to-peer infrastructure to compromise IoT devices, January 2018. https://www.trendmicro.com/vinfo/es/security/news/internet-of-things/-hide-n-seek-botnet-uses-peer-to-peer-infrastructure-to-compromise-iot-devices
56. Valente, J., Wynn, M.A., Cardenas, A.A.: Stealing, spying, and abusing: consequences of attacks on Internet of Things devices. IEEE Secur. Priv. **17**(5), 10–21 (2019)
57. Velasquez, J.: Hajime botnet variant, December 2018
58. Vignau, B., Khoury, R., Hallé, S.: 10 years of IoT malware: a feature-based taxonomy. In 2019 IEEE 19th International Conference on Software Quality, Reliability and Security Companion (QRS-C), pp. 458–465, July 2019
59. Wang, A., Liang, R., Liu, X., Zhang, Y., Chen, K., Li, J.: An inside look at IoT malware. In: Chen, F., Luo, Y. (eds.) Industrial IoT 2017. LNICST, vol. 202, pp. 176–186. Springer, Cham (2017). https://doi.org/10.1007/978-3-319-60753-5_19
60. Wijayasekara, D., Manic, M., McQueen, M.: Information gain based dimensionality selection for classifying text documents. In: 2013 IEEE Congress on Evolutionary Computation, pp. 440–445 (2013)
61. Wijayasekara, D., Manic, M., Wright, J.L., McQueen, M.: Mining bug databases for unidentified software vulnerabilities. In: 2012 5th International Conference on Human System Interactions, pp. 89–96 (2012)
62. Wijayasekara, D., Manic, M., McQueen, M.: Vulnerability identification and classification via text mining bug databases. In: IECON 2014–40th Annual Conference of the IEEE Industrial Electronics Society, Dallas, TX, USA, pp. 3612–3618 (2014)
63. Xiao, C., Zheng, C., Unit 42: New IoT/Linux malware targets DVRs, forms botnet (2017). https://unit42.paloaltonetworks.com/unit42-new-iotlinux-malware-targets-dvrs-forms-botnet/
64. yegenshen: IoT_reaper: A rappid spreading new IoT botnet, October 2017
65. Costin, A., Zaddach, J.: IoT malware comprehensive survey, analysis framework and case studies. In: Black Hat (2018)

Prevention and Efficiency

A Priority-Based Domain Type Enforcement for Exception Management

Manel Smine[1]([✉]), David Espes[2], Nora Cuppens-Boulahia[3], Frédéric Cuppens[3], and Marc-Oliver Pahl[1]

[1] IMT Atlantique, Rennes, Cesson-Sévigné, France
{manel.smine,marc-oliver.pahl}@imt-atlantique.fr
[2] University of Western Brittany, Brest, Brest, France
david.espes@univ-brest.fr
[3] Polytechnique Montréal, Montreal, Canada
{nora.cuppens,frederic.cuppens}@polymtl.ca

Abstract. Network Function Virtualization (NFV) is introduced as a new methodology that offers several advantages such as the optimization of the resources and the improvement of network efficiency and performance. However, potential security issues are an important obstacle for a wide adoption of NFV. To reduce the risk of these security issues, the communication between the different components of the network service have to be controlled through the deployment of access control policies. Existing solutions allowing access control management on NFV services are suffering from at least one of the following limitations. First, the lack of generality by either requiring the modification of the NFV infrastructure or supporting only specific types of access control policies. Second, the unscalability when complex (i.e., policies containing exceptions and/or inconsistent rules) access control policies are to be deployed. To overcomes these limitations, in this paper, we propose a DTE-based access control model that can efficiently enforce complex policies. The experimental results show that, compared to similar existing solutions, our model reduces considerably (1) the complexity of the DTE specification to be deployed and (2) the impact in terms of network performance of the VNF in which policies are deployed.

Keywords: Network Function Virtualization (NFV) · Access control · Domain Type Enforcement (DTE) · Exception management

1 Introduction

The new technology Network Function Virtualization (NFV) was proposed to improve the flexibility of network service provisioning allowing to a better information sharing between their components. Particularly, NFV allows a cost-efficient transformation from hardware-based services towards software-defined services. Despite the aforementioned advantages, existing NFV infrastructures

G. Nicolescu et al. (Eds.): FPS 2020, LNCS 12637, pp. 65–81, 2021.
https://doi.org/10.1007/978-3-030-70881-8_5

are suffering from several security concerns [18]. The access control policy violation can cause serious security threats such as invasion of users' privacy and/or confidential data exposure [12]. A possible solution to reduce the risks of the aforementioned threats is to control the access to the different components of NFV services. Access control techniques have been used during the last few years to reduce exposure to unauthorized activities while providing access only for the entities that have been approved.

In the literature, few models are proposed to manage access within and between NFV services [10,15,21,23]. Unfortunately, these techniques suffer from at least one of the following limitations: (1) It is not clear how the transformation from the high-level policy towards a concrete deployable policy is performed [10,23]. (2) The lack of generality by either requiring the modification of the NFV infrastructure to allow access control policy enforcement within VNF services [15,17], or supporting only specific access control policy model [15]. To overcome the previous limitations, the authors of [21] propose a Domain Type Enforcement (DTE) based formal model, allowing to handle most kind of access control policy models such as RBAC [20], ORBAC [11] and ABAC [9]. The model provides a formal and efficient methods for deploying access control policies within NFV services without requiring the modification of the NFV infrastructure. However, when complex policies containing exceptions and/or inconsistent rules are considered, the model proposed in [21] relies on complex DTE specifications to enforce them. This makes the management of the enforced DTE specifications by security administrators challenging.

In this paper, we extend the proposed DTE-based access control model in [21] to allow a clean and efficient deployment of complex access control policies containing exceptions and/or conflict rules on NFV services. Our model allows a clean deployment in the sense that, compared to the high level security policy[1] to be deployed, it does not introduce additional low-level rules which allows security administrator to straightforwardly understand and update the deployed concrete level policy. Our model relies on a provably correct approach for exception management in DTE specification. The conducted empirical evaluations show that the priority-based DTE model we are proposing is more efficient for enforcing big and complex policies that contain exceptions.

The paper is organized as follows, Sect. 2 illustrates the problem addressed in this paper with a motivating example. Section 3 provides a comparison with related work. Section 4 provides some background knowledge. Section 5 gives some definitions for the policy deployment in DTE. Section 6 describes the proposed priority-based DTE model. The Sect. 7 reports the experimental results. Finally, Sect. 8 concludes our work and outlines future work.

2   Motivation

5G networks are relying more and more on complex NFV services involving many VNF. Typically, as the complexity of the NFV services increases, the

---

[1] Security policy that is expressed using access control policy models such as RBAC.

access control policies that should be deployed on them become more and more complex. They might introduce exception rules i.e., rules that exclude some specific cases of general rules that should always apply. For access control policy models that support mixed policy i.e., policies that contain both positive and negative authorizations, the management of exceptions can be straightforwardly accomplished through the ordering of rules or the segmentation of condition attributes [2]. Nevertheless, most promising access control models on NFV (e.g., [21,22]) are relying on DTE model. However, this latter supports only closed policies which leads to a very complex configuration when policies containing exceptions are considered. To illustrate, let us consider the two following rules:

- r_1: Any VNF providing web server functionalities and having a low security level (e.g., a web server suffering from vulnerabilities) should be prohibited from reading and deleting records from VNF providing highly sensitive database server.
- r_2: Any VNF providing web_server functionalities should be allowed to read, write and delete records from a VNF providing a database server.

The previous two rules ensure that any web server except those having low security level can read, write, and delete records from any database. In order to be transformed to a DTE specification, r_1 and r_2 should be rewritten into a closed policy, which give the following three rules:

- r_1^*: Any VNF providing a web server functionalities can write on VNFs providing a database server.
- r_2^*: Any VNF providing a web server functionalities except the ones that have low security level are allowed to read and delete from VNF providing a database server.
- r_3^*: Any VNF providing a web server functionalities and having low security level are allowed to read and delete records from any VNF providing a database server except the ones storing highly sensitive data.

Clearly, the previous transformation increases the number of rules and introduces new domains, such as, the domain containing the VNF providing a web server but do not having low security and the domain of the VNF providing a database server but do not containing highly sensitive data. We formally show in Sect. 5.2 that, as the number of exceptions increases, the numbers of rules and DTE domains of the DTE specification to be deployed increases exponentially, which affects considerably the performance of the access control model. In this paper, we extend the basic DTE model by adding the concept of priority. This will allow us to deploy access control policies in an NFV service without adding any additional rule or DTE domain.

3 Related Work

Several approaches have been proposed to model and enforce security policies on NFV architectures. Searching to enforce specific security properties over virtualized networks, in [5], Basile, et al. integrate a new software defined component in the NFV infrastructure allowing to handle users' high-level security policies and refine them into configurations for specific VNF. Unfortunately, it is not clear whether we can use the proposed model to do access control management because the authors do not specify which security properties are provided by their model. Hence, it is not clear if the proposed approach can be used to handle and refine access control policies. In [14], a user centric privacy preserving model named SECURED has been proposed by Montero, et al. It allows the specification and the deployment of security policies to protect the security of users when interacting with NFV-based services. However, because of its user-centric characteristic, this model cannot be used to secure the interaction between NFV. The authors of [10] propose an SDN based security orchestrator in which they improve ETSI NFV reference architecture and provide a global view for efficient and fast topology validation using an extensive trust management. However, it is not clear how the proposed model can handle and enforce access control policies. In [13], Leopoldo, et al. propose ACLFLOW – a security framework designed for both NFV and Software-Defined Networking (SDN). It allows to transform high-level ACL rules into OpenFlow filter rules that can be used to control the communication between NFV. Unfortunately, ACLFLOW is useless when more advanced access control policies such as Role Based Access Control (RBAC) policies have to be deployed.

Several researches have investigated the usage of RBAC model [20] to control the interaction between VNF. The authors of [3] have proposed an RBAC-based approach for controlling the configuration of Virtual Objects to secure their interaction with the NFV infrastructure. In order to overcome verification and authorization issues in NFV infrastructures, in [7], the authors conceive a management module allowing Role based Access Control and identity management by using SONATA – an NFV-based service platform that relies on OAuth 2 [8] and OpenID connect [19]. Unfortunately, because this latter dependencies, the proposed model is only useful to control HTTP-based communications. In [15], a security orchestrator called SECMANO is developed as an extension of the MANO NFV orchestrator in order to manage the security properties of network services. The authors extend the TOSCA model [6] with specific security attributes to express an RBAC-like access control policies to be deployed on NFV services. In addition, they propose an instantiation of SECMANO in [16,17]. Nevertheless, the previous model suffers from the following three limitations: (1) the proposed approach is not generic enough as the model can handle only policies that are described using the RBAC model, (2) it is not clear how the transformation from the high-level policy towards a concrete deployable policy is performed and (3) the proposed model requires the modification of the NFV infrastructure.

Seeking to overcome the disadvantages of the aforementioned models, some approaches proposed models for access control policy specification and enforcement on NFV services that are relying on DTE. In [21], the authors proposed an access control as a service model for NFV services that allows to specify high level access control requirements to be enforced over NFV services, transform a high level policy towards a domain type enforcement (DTE) specification, and defines an efficient enforcement method for the policy over NFV architecture. The proposed model has several advantages: (1) it can handle most kind of access control policy models. (2) it provides an efficient method for deploying access control policies at the concrete level without requiring the modification of the NFV infrastructure. Unfortunately, the model cannot handle a complex policies containing exceptions and/or inconsistent rules.

In the context of 5G, the authors of [22] propose RDAC – an approach that combines the best of RBAC and DTE to allow secure resource sharing among the different players involved in providing services over 5G networks. Unfortunately, due to their dependency on DTE, the approaches in [21,22] have inherited one of the major limitation of the DTE model. When mixed (i.e., policies that contain both positive and negative authorizations) and complex (i.e., policies containing exception and/or conflict rules) policies are considered, DTE-based models lead often to quite complex specifications that (a) makes adding, updating, or deleting specific rules a challenging task for security administrators, and (b) reduces considerably the efficiency of the NFV services when deployed on them.

To solve the aforementioned problem, this paper extends the DTE model by adding the concept of priority between rules. We show experimentally that the proposed priority-based DTE model allows to enforce mixed and complex access control policies on NFV services while overcoming the limitations (a) and (b).

4   Background

4.1   Domain Type Enforcement (DTE)

Domain Type Enforcement was proposed in [4] as a method of implementing integrity systems without relying on a trusted user. As with many access control schemes, DTE views a system as a collection of active entities (subjects) accessing a collection of passive entities (objects) based on rules defined in an attached security context. DTE is based on two key concepts: (1) Domain that represents a set of entities having the same access requirements and (2) Type that represents a set of objects having the same properties. It manages access control by controlling access from domains to types and manages flow control by controlling transitions from domains to other domains.

4.2   Exception

In access control policy, exceptions are used to grant (resp. revoke) permissions (resp. prohibitions) exceptionally. For this, the *exception* rule has to be defined with a higher priority than the *generic* rule, i.e., by placing the former rule before the latter. Two types of exceptions can be distinguished:

- **Full exception**: A full exception occurs when the *exception* rule is totally included in the *generic* rule. To illustrate, let us consider the two rules r_1 and r_2 defined in Sect. 2. The rule r_1 is totally included in the rule r_2 since any access query that matches the rule r_1 matches also the rule r_2.

– **Partial exception**: A partial exception occurs when there is an intersection between a permission and a prohibition rules. As an illustration, the rule r_1 and the rule r_3 form a partial exception.
  • r_3: A VNF providing web server functionalities used by the commercial department should be allowed to read, write, insert and delete records from any VNF providing a database server used by the same department. Together, r_1 and r_3 ensure that a web server used by the commercial department except those having low security level are allowed to read, write, insert and delete records from any database server used by the same department.

5   Issue Related to the Policy Deployment in DTE

In this section, we define a model for exception management in DTE-based access control policies. We start by formalizing high-level access control policy and exception. Then, in Sect. 5.2, we propose a method for transforming arbitrary access control policies containing exceptions to a DTE specifications. Later, we discuss the issues related to the proposed model.

5.1   Access Control Policy and Exception

Definition 1 (Access control policy). *An access control policy is composed of a set of access control rules $\{r_1, \cdots, r_i\}$. Each rule r_i comprises:*

  – *A subject S_i representing one or many entities that want to access the object.*
  – *An action A_i denoting operations that are to be performed by S_i on O_i.*
  – *An object O_i represents resources over which A_i is going to be performed.*
  – *A decision D_i indicating whether it is a permission or denial rule.*

Each rule r_i in the security policy will be represented as $r_i = \langle S_i, A_i, O_i, D_i \rangle$.

In our work, we focus on ordered-rule policy. That is, we suppose that the rules are evaluated from top to bottom in the order they appear in the policy. This can be formalized as following.

Definition 2 (Ordered-rule policy). *Given a policy $\mathcal{P} = \{r_i | i \in [1, n]\}$ where i is the index of appearance of the rule r_i in $\mathcal{P}$. $\mathcal{P}$ is an ordered policy if for all $i, j \in [1, n]$, $i > j$ implies that the rule r_i has higher priority than r_j.*

Definition 3 (Exception). *Given an ordered-policy $\mathcal{P} = \{r_i | i \in [1, n]\}$, where i is the index of appearance of the rule r_i in the policy $\mathcal{P}$. Two rules r_i and r_j of $\mathcal{P}$ form an exception if and only if the following conditions hold:*

(i) $i < j$
(ii) $\forall i, j : S_i \cap S_j \neq \emptyset \ \wedge \ O_i \cap O_j \neq \emptyset \ \wedge \ A_i \cap A_j \neq \emptyset \ \wedge \ D_i \neq D_j$

Proposition 1. *The Definition 3 models both full and partial exceptions.*

In the sequel, we use the term exception to represent a full or a partial exception. An exception represented by two rules r_1 and r_2 is denoted by $\mathcal{E}(r_1, r_2)$.

5.2 Exception Management in DTE

As mentioned before, DTE-based systems are relying on closed policies. Hence, in order to deploy a mixed policy in a DTE-based system, we have to transform the mixed policy to be deployed to a closed policy. That is, only positive authorizations should be considered and all negative authorizations should be eliminated from the initial mixed policy. However, since there might be exceptions in the policy to be deployed, we need to make sure that these exceptions will be correctly enforced by the closed policy.

Policy Transformation. In the following, we propose a method for transforming an exception represented by a negative and a positive authorizations towards a set of positive authorizations. Then, we prove its correctness.

Definition 4. *Given an exception $\mathcal{E}(r_1, r_2)$ such that $r_1 = \langle S_1, A_1, O_1, D_1 \rangle$ and $r_2 = \langle S_2, A_2, O_2, D_2 \rangle$. The exception is transformed towards a set of positive authorizations $\mathcal{E}^*$ as following:*

(i) if $D_1 = allow$ and $D_2 = deny$, $\mathcal{E}^* = \{r_1\}$
(ii) if $D_1 = deny$ and $D_2 = allow$, $\mathcal{E}^* = \{r_1^*, r_2^*, r_3^*\}$ such that:
  $- r_1^* = \langle S_1, A_1, O_2 \backslash O_1, allow \rangle$
  $- r_2^* = \langle S_2 \backslash S_1, A_1, O_2, allow \rangle$
  $- r_3^* = \langle S_2, A_2 \backslash A_1, O_2, allow \rangle$

The case (i) (resp. (ii)) defines the transformation of exceptions in which the positive (resp. negative) authorization rule has higher priority than negative (resp. positive) authorization rule.

　　To prove the correctness of the transformation defined in the previous definition, we first introduce the concept of access query in Definition 5 and define the correctness of exception transformation in Definitoin 6.

Definition 5 (Access Query). *An access query $\mathcal{AQ}$ is represented by the triplet $\langle S, A, O \rangle$ where S denotes the subject performing the query, A is the set of requested actions, and O denotes the object over which the query is performed.*

Definition 6. *Given an exception $\mathcal{E}(r_1, r_2)$ and its corresponding transformation $\mathcal{E}^*$ as described in Definition 4. The transformation is correct if and only if, for any access query AQ, the following conditions hold:*

– If $\mathcal{AQ}$ is allowed by $\mathcal{E}(r_1, r_2)$, then it is allowed by $\mathcal{E}^*$.
– If $\mathcal{AQ}$ is denied by $\mathcal{E}(r_1, r_2)$, then it is denied by $\mathcal{E}^*$.

Theorem 1. [2] *The exception transformation method proposed in Definition 4 is correct.*

---

[2] Due to the lack of space, the proofs of all theorems are provided in the following link https://partage.imt.fr/index.php/s/5HTQJRkXJBpyoEN.

The following algorithm presents a method allowing to transform a mixed policy towards a closed policy. It takes as an input the initial mixed policy to be deployed and produces a set of rules representing the closed policy that can be deployed in the DTE-system.

Input: $\mathcal{P}$ /* the policy to be deployed */

1 $closed\_policy = \emptyset$
2 $exceptions = \textbf{get\_exception}(P)$ /* getting the exceptions in $\mathcal{P}$ */
3 **foreach** $exception \in exceptions$ **do**
4 | $\mathcal{E}^* = \textbf{transform}(exception)$ /* Definition 4 */
5 | $new\_exception = \textbf{get\_exception}(\mathcal{E}^*, P)$
6 | $exceptions = exceptions \cup new\_exception$
7 | $closed\_policy = closed\_policy \cup \mathcal{E}^*$
8 **end**
9 **foreach** $rule \in \mathcal{P}$ **do**
10 | **if** $rule \notin exceptions$ and rule is "allow" **then**
11 | | $closed\_policy = closed\_policy \cup rule$
12 | **end**
13 **end**

Algorithm 1: Policy transformation algorithm

The first loop (lines 3 to 8) transforms all the exceptions in the initial policy as described in Definition 4. In the second loop (lines 9 to 13), we add to the closed policy all the positive authorization rules that have not been part of an exception.

The number of rules in the closed policy increases exponentially on the number of exception in the policy to be deployed as stated by the following theorem.

Theorem 2. *Let us consider an ordered policy* $\mathcal{P} = \{r_1, r_2, \cdots, r_n\}$. *Let us denote by* Ω_i *the set of rules in* $\mathcal{P}$ *that represent an exception of* r_i *(i.e.,* $\forall r_j \in \Omega_i : \mathcal{E}(r_j, r_i)$), *and by* $\mathcal{P}^*$ *the closed form of* $\mathcal{P}$. *In the worst case:*

$$\|\mathcal{P}^*\| = \sum_{i=1}^{n} \Theta_i \quad with \quad \Theta_i = \left\{ \begin{array}{ll} 3^{\|\Omega_i\|} & if \ D_i = allow \\ 0 & if \ D_i = deny \end{array} \right\}$$

where $\|x\|$ *and* D_i *denote respectively the cardinality of* x *and the decision of* r_i.

The approach we describe in this section allows to transform an arbitrary mixed policy towards a closed policy that can be straightforwardly deployed in a DTE-based access control system by considering each subject (resp. object) of a rule as DTE domain (resp. DTE type). Hence, the number of DTE types and domains will also grow exponentially in the number of exceptions in the policy to be deployed. This makes difficult for security administrators to understand, read, update and maintain the deployed DTE specifications. The previous results are experimentally validated by the conducted evaluations (see Sect. 7). For these reasons, to overcome this problem, we propose priority-based DTE model that will be described in the following section.

6   Priority-Based DTE

In our Priority-based DTE model, we extend the concept of DTE domain transition by adding two elements: a transition condition C and a priority P. The classic DTE transition and its extension are defined in the following definitions.

Definition 7 (DTE Transition). *A DTE transition T is represented by the triplet $\langle S_d, E, D_d \rangle$ where S_d and D_d represent respectively the source and destination domains of the DTE transition, and E represents one or many entry points that can be used to transit a process from S_d to D_d.*

Definition 8 (Extended DTE Transition). *The extended DTE transition is represented by the quintuplets $\langle S_d, C, E, P, D_d \rangle$ where S_d, E and D_d are the same elements used in the Definition 7 and C and P are the conditions and priority of the extended transition applicability.*

Semantically, the extended DTE transition states that if a process is running in the source domain S_d, satisfies the conditions C, and executes an entrypoint E then it will transit from S_d to the destination domain D_d.

The condition C we add to the previous Definition makes sure that only the processes that are going to write on db_high_t will transit to the destination domain db_high_d. The condition C allows us to define the concept of possible transition

Definition 9 (Possible Transition). *Given a transition $T = \langle S_d, C, E, D_d, P \rangle$. T is a possible transition for an access query AQ if and only if:*

- *The subject of AQ (the process performing the action) is running in S_d*
- *AQ satisfies the condition C*
- *The object O is in D_d*

Example 1. To illustrate the concept of possible transition, let's assume that we have two access queries AQ_1 and AQ_2 such that:

- $AQ_1 = \langle web\_server\_1, read, db\_server \rangle$ in which the web server 1 wants to read from a database server 1
- $AQ_2 = \langle web\_server\_2\_high, read, db\_server \rangle$ in which the web server 1 having high security level wants to read from the database server 2.

Let us suppose that the considered DTE specification contains:

- *web_server_d*: a domain containing VNFs providing a web server functionalities,
- *web_server_high_d*: a domain containing VNFs providing a web server functionalities and having high security level,

– *db_server_t*: a type associated to VNFs providing database functionalities

Hence, *web_server_1* belongs to *web_server_d*, *web_server_2_high* belongs to both *web_server_d* and *web_server_high_d*, and *db_server* belongs to *db_server_d* and is associated to the DTE type *db_server_t*.

Let us now suppose that we have the following two extended DTE transitions:

– $T_1 = \langle web\_server\_d, db\_server\_t : read, /bin/db\_reader, p_1, db\_server\_d \rangle$ that says that the transition of the process from the domain *web_server_d* to the domain *db_server_d* is possible if: (1) the process is running in *web_server_d*, (2) the process wants to read from a resource in *db_server_t* and (3) the process executes the entrypoint *"/bin/db_reader"*.
– $T_2 = \langle web\_server\_high\_d, db\_server\_t : read, /bin/db\_reader, p_2, db\_server\_d \rangle$ that says that the transition of the process from the domain *web_server_high_d* to the domain *db_server_d* is possible if: (1) the process is running in *web_server_high_d*, (2) the process wants to read from a resource in *db_server_t* and (3) the process executes the entrypoint *"/bin/db_reader"*.

According to the Definition 9, the two transitions T_1 and T_2 are possible for the access query AQ_1 since web_server1 belongs to both domains web_server_d and web_server_high_d and AQ_1 satisfies all the three requirements that are defined in Definition 9 while only the transition T_1 is possible for the access query AQ_2.

As we can see in the previous example, the access query AQ_1 have two possible transitions. So in order to define the prioritized one, we will use the priority that we introduce in the extended DTE transition (Definition 8) as following.

Definition 10 (Prioritized Transition). *Given an access query AQ and a set of AQ's possible transitions $T_1, \cdots, T_n$. The transition T_j $(j \in [1, n])$ is the prioritized transition for AQ if and only if $\forall (i \in [1, n])$ and $i \neq j : P_j > P_i$ where P_i is the priority of T_i.*

Informally, the previous Definition states that the prioritized transition for AQ is the possible transition that has the highest priority.

Policy Transformation Towards Priority-Based DTE Specification

In this section, we propose a method for transforming a mixed access control policy $\mathcal{P} = \{r_1, \cdots, r_n\}$ towards a priority-based DTE specification using on the transformation method that was proposed in [21]. Hence, in order to transform the policy to be deployed to a priority-based DTE specification, each rule $r_i = \langle S_i, A_i, O_i, D_i \rangle \in \mathcal{P}$ will be transformed according to the following cases:

Case 1: If r_i does not belong to any exception we will do the following steps:

– **step 1.1:** Define a domain S_i_d which will contain all entities in the system that have the same properties used to characterize the subject S_i.
– **step 1.2:** Define a domain O_i_d which will contain all entities in the system that have the same properties used to characterize the object O_i.

- **step 1.3:** Define a type O_i_t which will be associated with objects that share the same properties with the access query.
- **step 1.4:** Define a transition T_i that transit from S_i_d to O_i_d.
- **step 1.5:** If the decision of the access query D_i is allow so give to the process that is in O_i_d and coming from S_i_d the possibility to execute the actions A_i in O_i_t. If the decision D_i is deny there's nothing to do in this step.
- **step 1.6:** Set the priority P_i of the transition T_i to 0.

Case 2: If r_i belongs to an exception $\mathcal{E}(r_i, r_j)$, we perform the following steps:

- **step 2.1:** Use the steps 1.1 to 1.5 of Case 1 on r_i.
- **step 2.2:** Use the steps 1.1 to 1.5 of Case 1 on r_j.
- **step 2.3:** Set the priority P_i (resp. P_j) of the transition T_i (resp. T_j) defined in step 2.1 (resp. step 2.2) such that:
  - If the decisions D_i = allow and D_j = deny: $P_j > P_i > 0$
  - If the decisions D_i = deny and D_j = allow: $P_i > P_j > 0$

Example 2. To illustrate the previous transformation, let's take the following access control policy P that is composed of the following rules:

- $r_1 = \langle mail\_server, \{read, write\}, ftp\_server, allow \rangle$ which authorizes a mail server to read and write information from an ftp server.
- $r_2 = \langle web\_server\_low, \{write\}, ftp\_server, deny \rangle$ which denies any web server having low security level to write information on ftp server.
- $r_3 = \langle web\_server\_low, \{read\}, database\_server, deny \rangle$ which denies any web server having low security level to read from a database server.

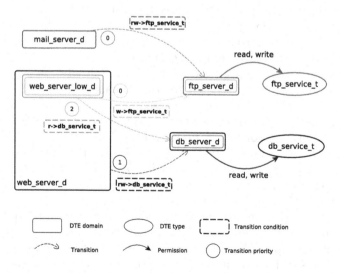

Fig. 1. Graphical representation of the DTE policy described in Example 2

– $r_4 = \langle web\_server, \{read, write\}, database\_server, allow\rangle$ which allows any web server to read and write on any database server.

The transformation of the policy P towards a priority-based DTE specification is illustrated in Fig. 1. The parts colored in green, yellow, blue and black represent respectively the transformation of the rule r_1, r_2, r_3 and r_4.

To illustrate the use of the DTE specification, let's take the example of the following access queries:

– $AQ_1 = \langle mail\_server1, read, ftp\_server1\rangle$ in which the mail server 1 wants to read from the ftp server 1.
– $AQ_2 = \langle web\_server2\_low, write, ftp\_server1\rangle$ in which the web server 2 having low security level wants to write on the ftp server 1.
– $AQ_3 = \langle web\_server2\_low, read, db\_server1\rangle$ in which the web server 2 having low security level wants to read from the database server 1.
– $AQ_4 = \langle web\_server2\_low, write, db\_server1\rangle$ in which the web server 2 having low security level wants to write on the database server 1.

When evaluating the access query AQ_1, the process executing AQ_1 will be initially in the domain $mail\_server\_d$ since the subject of AQ_1 ($mail\_server1$) belongs to $mail\_server\_d$. The latter have only one possible transition towards ftp_server_d which is allowed to read from objects in ftp_server_t including ftp_server_1. As result AQ_1 will be authorized.

When evaluating the access query AQ_2, the process executing AQ_2 will be initially in the domain $web\_server\_low\_d$ since the subject of AQ_2 (web_server2_low) belongs to the domain web_server_low_d and it belongs also to the domain web_server_d. Based on the Fig. 1, the domain $web\_server\_low\_d$ have two possible transitions. However, only one transition is possible for AQ_2 since only the condition "$w->ftp\_service\_t$" is satisfied. So following this transition, the process will transit to the domain $ftp\_service\_d$ and we know that all the access queries coming from $web\_server\_low\_d$ don't have any possible action on the type $ftp\_service\_t$. As result AQ_2 is denied.

To evaluate AQ_3, since the process is initially in the domain $web\_server\_low\_d$ and it belongs also to the domain web_server_d, so it will have two possible transitions (From $web\_server\_low\_d$ and web_server_d), so the two conditions "$r->db\_service\_t$" and "$rw->db\_service\_t$" are satisfied. Here we will apply the concept of priority defined in Definition 10. As result, the prioritized transition is colored in blue in which the process will transit from the domain $web\_server\_low\_d$ to the domain db_server_d. However, the access queries coming from $web\_server\_low\_d$ don't have any possible action on the type $db\_service\_t$. As result AQ_3 is denied

When evaluating the access query AQ_4, the process executing AQ_4 belongs to both domains $web\_server\_low\_d$ and web_server_d. On the other hand, it will have only one possible transition because only the condition "$rw->db\_service\_t$" is satisfied. So it will transit to the domain db_server_d. However, the access queries coming from web_server_d have the right to read and write on the type $db\_service\_t$. As a result AQ_4 is authorized.

7   Experimental Results

In this section, we experimentally evaluate the performance of our priority-based DTE model for deploying security policies on NFV services. For all conducted experiments, we used a (pseudo) randomly generated high-level policies that will be deployed on NFV services. The evaluations are conducted on a server running Linux with an Intel Xeon E5-2680 v4 Processor with 16 vCPU and 32 GB of RAM on which Openstack [1] is installed and used as an NFV infrastructure manager. We aim to compare the performance of our proposed model with the classic DTE-based access control model for NFV services proposed in [21] regarding the following characteristics:

– The number of required domains and types in the DTE specification as a function of the number of exceptions in the high-level policy to be deployed.
– The number of rules in the DTE specification as a function of the number of exceptions in the policy to be deployed.
– The time required for transforming the policy to be deployed towards a deployable DTE specification.
– The time needed to evaluate an access query as a number of exception in enforced policy.
– The impact on network performance.

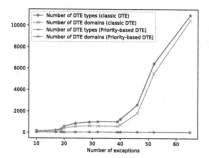

Fig. 2. The comparison of the growth of the number of required DTE domains and types in classic and priority-based DTE as a function of the number of exception in the policy

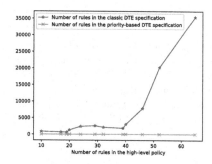

Fig. 3. The comparison of the number of rules in the classic DTE specification and in the priority-based DTE specification as a function of the number of rules in the policy to be deployed

Figure 2 compares the growth of the number of DTE domains and types for both classic and priority-based DTE as a function of the number of exceptions in the policy to be deployed. When the latter grows by a factor of 6 (from 10 to 60), the number of DTE domains and types grow by a factor of 2 for the priority-based DTE while growing by a factor of ≈ 192 in the case of classic DTE

[21]. Figure 3 compares the number of rules required by both the classic DTE and priority-based DTE specifications as a function of the number of rules in the policy to be deployed. When the latter increases from 10 to 60, the number of rules in the priority-based DTE increases by the same factor (factor of 6) while the number of rules required by the classic DTE grows by a factor of 230.

Figure 4 compares the time required for transforming a high-level policy towards a classic DTE and priority-based DTE specifications. In the case of priority-based DTE, the time of transformation is almost constant while growing by a factor of 10^5 in the case of classic DTE as the number of exceptions increases by only a factor of 10. This mainly due to the transformation of all exceptions of the policy (lines 3 to 8 of Algorithm 1). In fact, when an exception is transformed to a set of positive authorizations, these latter may introduce several new exceptions that need to be resolved.

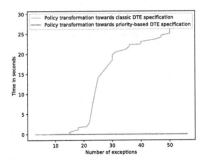
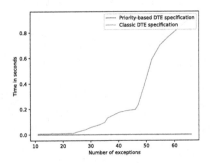

Fig. 4. The comparison of the time required to transform the policy towards classic DTE specification and priority-based DTE specification as a function of the number of exceptions in the high-level policy to be deployed

Fig. 5. The comparison of the access query evaluation time between the classic DTE specification and the priority-based DTE specification as a function of the number of exceptions in the policy to be deployed

Figure 5 compares the time needed by both classic DTE model in [21] and our priority-based DTE model for the evaluation of an access query. Compared to the model in [21], our model drastically reduces the time needed for evaluating an access query as the number of exceptions in the policy to be deployed increases. This due to the fact that, in the classic DTE specification, the number of domains and types grows exponentially relatively to the number of exceptions. As the evaluation of an access query requires matching the domains (resp. types) with the subject (resp. object) of access query. Therefore, the time required to evaluate an access query grows exponentially according to the number of exceptions.

Finally, we compare the impact in terms of network performance of the VNF. Figure 6a (resp. 6b) illustrates the growth of the round-trip time (RTT) of a network request when a classic DTE [21] (resp. our priority-based DTE) model

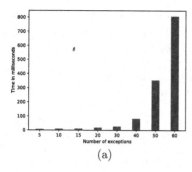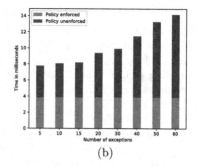

(a)   (b)

Fig. 6. The comparison of the growth of the round-trip time of a network request when (a) a classic DTE policy model is used and (b) a priority-based DTE policy model is used, as a function of the number of exceptions in the enforced policy

is used as a function of the number of exceptions in the deployed policy. When the classic DTE model is used, the RTT increases by a factor of 210 (from 3,84 to 801 milliseconds) while increasing by only a factor of 4 (from 3,8 to 14.2 milliseconds) when our priority-based DTE model is used. This is mainly due to the time required to evaluate access queries with both solutions.

8   Conclusion

In this paper we extend a DTE-based access control model proposed in [21] to allow an efficient deployment of complex access control policies containing exceptions and/or conflict rules on NFV services. We first studied the deployment of a policy on access control models based on a classic DTE. We have observed theoretically and experimentally that these models are not scalable when a complex policies (containing many exceptions) are considered. To overcome the previous limitation, we propose a provably correct priority-based DTE access control model. We experimentally show that our proposed model is by far more efficient than the existing solution [21] when dealing with high-level complex policies containing exceptions.

References

1. Openstack. https://www.openstack.org/software/. Accessed Sept 2020
2. Alfaro, J.G., Cuppens, F., Cuppens-Boulahia, N.: Management of exceptions on access control policies. In: Venter, H., Eloff, M., Labuschagne, L., Eloff, J., von Solms, R. (eds.) SEC 2007. IIFIP, vol. 232, pp. 97–108. Springer, Boston, MA (2007). https://doi.org/10.1007/978-0-387-72367-9_9
3. Alshehri, A., Sandhu, R.: Access control models for virtual object communication in cloud-enabled IoT. In: 2017 IEEE International Conference on Information Reuse and Integration (IRI), pp. 16–25. IEEE (2017)

4. Badger, L., Sterne, D.F., Sherman, D.L., Walker, K.M., Haghighat, S.A.: Practical domain and type enforcement for UNIX. In: Proceedings 1995 IEEE Symposium on Security and Privacy, pp. 66–77. IEEE (1995)

5. Basile, C., Lioy, A., Pitscheider, C., Valenza, F., Vallini, M.: A novel approach for integrating security policy enforcement with dynamic network virtualization. In: Proceedings of the 2015 1st IEEE Conference on Network Softwarization (NetSoft), pp. 1–5. IEEE (2015)

6. Binz, T., Breitenbücher, U., Kopp, O., Leymann, F.: TOSCA: portable automated deployment and management of cloud applications. In: Bouguettaya, A., Sheng, Q., Daniel, F. (eds.) Advanced Web Services, pp. 527–549. Springer, New York (2014). https://doi.org/10.1007/978-1-4614-7535-4_22

7. Guija, D., Siddiqui, M.S.: Identity and access control for micro-services based 5G NFV platforms. In: Proceedings of the 13th International Conference on Availability, Reliability and Security, pp. 1–10 (2018)

8. Hardt, D.: The OAuth 2.0 Authorization Framework. RFC 6749, October 2012. 10.17487/RFC6749. https://rfc-editor.org/rfc/rfc6749.txt

9. Hu, V.C., Kuhn, D.R., Ferraiolo, D.F., Voas, J.: Attribute-based access control. Computer 48(2), 85–88 (2015)

10. Jaeger, B.: Security orchestrator: introducing a security orchestrator in the context of the ETSI NFV reference architecture. In: 2015 IEEE Trustcom/BigDataSE/ISPA, vol. 1, pp. 1255–1260. IEEE (2015)

11. Kalam, A.A.E., et al.: Organization based access control. In: Proceedings POLICY 2003. IEEE 4th International Workshop on Policies for Distributed Systems and Networks, pp. 120–131. IEEE (2003)

12. Lal, S., Taleb, T., Dutta, A.: NFV: security threats and best practices. IEEE Commun. Mag. 55(8), 211–217 (2017)

13. Mauricio, L.A., Rubinstein, M.G., Duarte, O.C.M.: ACLFLOW: An NFV/SDN security framework for provisioning and managing access control lists. In: 2018 9th International Conference on the Network of the Future (NOF), pp. 44–51. IEEE (2018)

14. Montero, D., et al.: Virtualized security at the network edge: a user-centric approach. IEEE Commun. Mag. 53, 176–186 (2015)

15. Pattaranantakul, M., He, R., Meddahi, A., Zhang, Z.: SecMANO: towards network functions virtualization (NFV) based security management and orchestration. In: 2016 IEEE Trustcom/BigDataSE/ISPA, pp. 598–605. IEEE (2016)

16. Pattaranantakul, M., He, R., Zhang, Z., Meddahi, A., Wang, P.: Leveraging network functions virtualization orchestrators to achieve software-defined access control in the clouds. IEEE Trans. Dependable Secure Comput. (2018)

17. Pattaranantakul, M., Tseng, Y., He, R., Zhang, Z., Meddahi, A.: A first step towards security extension for NFV orchestrator. In: Proceedings of the ACM International Workshop on Security in Software Defined Networks & Network Function Virtualization, pp. 25–30 (2017)

18. Reynaud, F., Aguessy, F.X., Bettan, O., Bouet, M., Conan, V.: Attacks against network functions virtualization and software-defined networking: state-of-the-art. In: 2016 IEEE NetSoft Conference and Workshops (NetSoft), pp. 471–476. IEEE (2016)

19. Sakimura, N., Bradley, J., Jones, M.B., de Medeiros, B., Mortimore, C.: OpenID connect core 1.0. https://openid.net/specs/openid-connect-core-1_0.html

20. Sandhu, R.S., Coyne, E.J., Feinstein, H.L., Youman, C.E.: Role-based access control models. Computer 29(2), 38–47 (1996)

21. Smine, M., Espes, D., Cuppens-Boulahia, N., Cuppens, F.: Network functions virtualization access control as a service. In: Singhal, A., Vaidya, J. (eds.) DBSec 2020. LNCS, vol. 12122, pp. 100–117. Springer, Cham (2020). https://doi.org/10.1007/978-3-030-49669-2_6
22. Suarez, L., Espes, D., Cuppens, F., Cuppens-Boulahia, N.: Formalization of a security access control model for the 5g system (2020)
23. Thanh, T.Q., Covaci, S., Corici, M., Magedanz, T.: Access control management and orchestration in NFV environment. In: 2017 IFIP Networking Conference (IFIP Networking) and Workshops, pp. 1–2. IEEE (2017)

Developer-Proof Prevention of SQL Injections

Judicaël Courant[(✉)][iD]

Orange Cyberdefense, Lyon, France
Judicael.Courant@orangecyberdefense.com

Abstract. SQL queries, when written by unskilled or hurried developers for web applications, are prone to SQL injections. We propose an alternative approach for querying SQL databases that does not suffer from this flaw. Our approach is based on abstract syntax trees, lets developers build dynamic queries easily, and is easier to set up than an ORM tool. We provide a proof-of-concept in Java, but our approach can be extended to other languages.

Keywords: SQL injection · SQLi prevention · Dynamic queries · Code generation · Abstract syntax trees · Language-based security · Secure coding · Software security

1 Introduction

Can we prevent developers from writing programs vulnerable to SQL injections? Can we help them even if they do not care about security? These questions are of practical significance: SQL injections have been plaguing web applications for more than 20 years [17], yet they still rank first in application security flaws [18].

Here is a very simple example of vulnerable Java code:

```
q = "SELECT * FROM atable WHERE token = '" + tok + "'";
rs = connection.createStatement().executeQuery(q);
```

Listing 1: Example of vulnerable Java code

The code executes the following query, where the underlined placeholder is filled by the value of `tok`:

```
SELECT * FROM atable WHERE token = '_____'
```

The intent of the programmer is to retrieve all rows whose column `token` is equal to the value of `tok`. Unfortunately, if an attacker gave "x' OR 1=1 -- " as a value for `tok`, the following query would be executed:

© Springer Nature Switzerland AG 2021
G. Nicolescu et al. (Eds.): FPS 2020, LNCS 12637, pp. 82–99, 2021.
https://doi.org/10.1007/978-3-030-70881-8_6

```
SELECT * FROM atable WHERE token = 'x' OR 1 = 1 -- '
```

The semantics of the query significantly differs from the intent of the programmer: the WHERE clause is now the disjunction of two Boolean expressions, the second one, 1 = 1, being a tautology.

Therefore, execution of the query now returns the whole table atable instead of some selected rows: if access to rows were supposedly restricted to users knowing the values of the token column, it is a severe vulnerability.

That is the essence of *SQL injections*: by supplying carefully crafted malicious data, the attacker could alter the SQL code generated by the programmer.

How should programmers write their code in order to ensure that it is immune to injections? Solutions exist: validating inputs, escaping harmful characters or using prepared statements [16].

Unfortunately, none of them alone covers the full spectrum of SQL injections and each of them is insecure if improperly used. Therefore, developers have to resort to a blend of these techniques. In order to make the right choice and write secure code, they have to be properly trained, and to be given enough time. In practice, they are not.

As a side-effect, source code security audits are complicated by this state of affairs: auditors have to inspect each and every query in order to make sure that it is immune to injection, which often involves tracking down the origin of each input. Source code analysis tools might help, but things can get quite involved, especially for second-order injections [8].

This article proposes a way to build queries that do not suffer from these limitations. Our contributions are the following:

- We reconsider using strings for building queries and propose that trees be used instead in Sect. 2. We show how the example of listing 1 could be rewritten using a library for representing SQL queries as trees.
- We show how trees can be translated to standard queries, using a blend of techniques that developers would actually use in Sect. 3.
- We review classical injection attacks in Sect. 4 and show, through examples, how our library prevents most of them.
- We implemented these ideas as a small Java library, available under a free software license [7]. We present it in Sect. 5. Our library not only *lets* developers write secure queries but also *prevents* them from writing vulnerable ones.
- Our approach fills a gap between detection method based on parse trees and more heavyweight DOM-based methods relying on static typing to provide more guarantees, which we discuss in Sect. 6.
- In conclusion, we suggest some possible future works that could help closing security limitations of existing ORM in Sect. 7.

2 From Strings to Trees

An interesting point of view over SQL injections is that they alter the syntax tree of the query. Figure 1 displays the expected shape of the syntax tree of the query built by listing 1 side-by-side with the actual tree built with the attacker-supplied value for tok. The WHERE clause of the actual tree is quite different from the expected shape: in the expected shape, the WHERE clause was an equality between two terms (a single atomic proposition), whereas in the actual tree, the WHERE clause is the logical disjunction of two propositions.

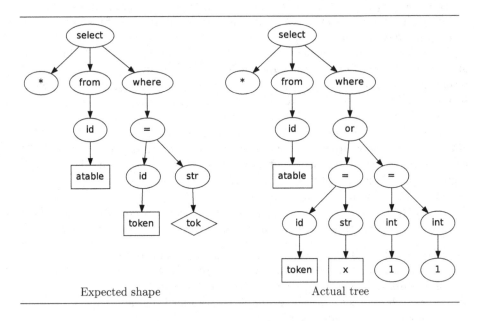

Expected shape   Actual tree

Fig. 1. Expected shape versus actual tree for listing 1

This situation is typical of a mismatch between what the programmer intended and what they actually programmed: the intent was to replace a leaf in a syntax tree, and string concatenation is the wrong way to do it.

Notice that generation of SQL queries is only a special case of code generation, which is a standard phase in compilers. Code generation is hardly ever done just by concatenating strings: most often, compilers use a large range of intermediate representations, mostly trees. Only at the end of the process is the last representation translated to strings. Therefore, we suggest to represent queries as trees.

We provide a small library for representing SQL syntax trees [7]. Actually, it provides an *internal* Domain Specific Language (DSL) that lets the user represent trees using a prefix notation (hence a somewhat Lispian taste).

Our initial example given in listing 1 can be rewritten with this internal DSL as shown in listing 2.

```
q = select(star, from(id("atable")),
                where(eq(id("token"), str(tok))));
rs = q.execute(connection)
```

Listing 2: Initial example, rewritten using our library

In that code, select, from, id, where, eq, and str are static methods for building a tree. id and str build a tree respectively denoting an identifier and a string literal from a String, the other ones build a tree from one or more subtrees, and star is a constant leaf. As displayed in Fig. 2, when the attacker supplies the same malicious value as previously, the shape of the tree is preserved.

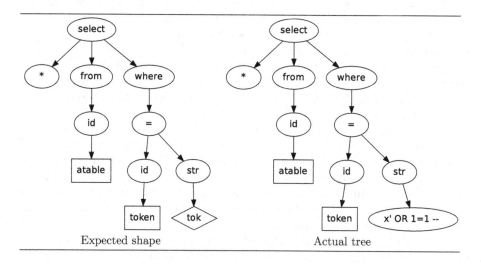

Fig. 2. Expected shape versus actual tree for listing 2

If there were some direct way to communicate the abstract syntax tree to the database we want to query, no injection could happen since, regardless of the value supplied for tok, the resulting tree q will have the intended shape, as displayed in Fig. 2.

Unfortunately, as of 2020, the usual way to send a query to a database is to send a character string. Therefore, we have to compile the syntax tree to a string representing our query.

3   Compiling Trees to Strings

In this section, we explain how we translate a syntax tree to a string that can be sent to an SQL database.

3.1   Principle

In order to make sure our code is immune to SQL injections, we have to make sure that the translation is faithful, in the following sense: if a tree t is compiled into a string $c(t)s$ and that this string is again parsed into a tree $p(c(t))$, then $p(c(t)) = t$.

The main difficulty here lies in the translation of the leafs of the trees, more precisely of identifiers and string literals.

As for string literals, we consider three options:

– Validating the value.
– Escaping dangerous characters.
– Using prepared statements

We reject the first option as it would be too dramatic a restriction. For instance, the string literal "L'île de Montréal" would be rejected since it contains the dangerous quote character. Yet it is a valid toponym in French. Likewise, the common Irish surname "O'Brian" would be rejected too.

Escaping dangerous characters is not an easy exercise as each database implementation escapes them in a slightly different way. We could use the library from the ESAPI project [24], but that would make our implementation depend on a non-standard library.

Fortunately, databases have a feature that provides a workaround for avoiding SQL injections at string literals: prepared statements. A *prepared statement* or *parameterized query* is a SQL query taking the form of a *template* in which some values are left unspecified: instead, they are replaced by placeholders, denoted by question marks in Java. The template and the actual values of the parameters are send separately to the database. The database driver encodes the parameters, so they cannot cause any injection.

That solution cannot apply when the input is supposed to be an identifier (a column name or a table name) though, since placeholders in prepared statements can only denote *values*, not *identifiers*. Therefore, another option must be considered. Restricting the set of accepted identifiers is much more reasonable than restricting the set of accepted literal strings. Thus, we ensure that the argument given to id is a valid identifier: we check that it is a non-empty sequence of alphanumeric characters starting with a letter and that it does not belong to the set of SQL keywords. We use an extensive list of 914 SQL keywords [22] in order to forbid not only keywords *officially* reserved in the SQL:2016 standard, but also some others reserved in *common* SQL databases. However, as for all blacklist approaches, it is not future-proof: if the SQL dialect understood by the database evolves, this list has to be updated.

3.2   Examples

Let us first see how the translation from trees to strings prevents injection for listing 2. Suppose an attacker passes "x' OR 1=1 -- " as a value for tok. Then the query is the tree denoted by the following expression:

```
select(star, from(id("atable")),
            where(eq(id("token"), str("x' OR 1=1 -- "))));
```

As explained in the previous section, the query is translated into a parameterized statement in which all literal strings (subtrees labeled by str) are turned into parameters:

```
SELECT * FROM atable WHERE token = ?
```

and the literal string "x' OR 1=1 -- " is used as the value for the parameter. As explained in the previous section, no injection occurs: the database indeed looks for rows whose field token is equal to the literal string given by the attacker, whatever special characters it may contain.

As noted by [11] and [12], prepared statements alone cannot prevent injections. For example, prepared statements cannot prevent injection at a column name or table name, since placeholder in prepared statements can only denote values, not identifiers. Consider for instance the following query:

```
SELECT pubcol
FROM _____ WHERE timestamp > 1234
```

where the underlined part is supposed to be replaced by some user-supplied table name. The intent is that the user can read some public column of any table for which timestamp is large enough. An attacker could provide a malicious value in order to build the following query:

```
SELECT pubcol
FROM (SELECT seccol FROM atable) -- WHERE timestamp > 1234
```

Thus, bypassing the restriction over timestamp (as the WHERE clause has been turned into a comment) and over the columns.

Using our library, such a query would be coded as

```
select(id(pubcol), from(id(t)),
        where(gt(id("timestamp"), num(1234))))
```

Since the library checks that t is a valid identifier, the attack would only raise an exception. Of course, that does not excuse developers from validating user input, unless all columns named pubcol in all tables are supposed to be readable by all users.

4   SQL Injections Prevented by Our Approach

Classifications of SQL injection attacks can be found in [11] and [20]. In [11], known injections attacks are presented and classified along two axis: *mechanism* and *intent*. In this section, we first discuss the mechanisms, then study how known attacks apply in our settings, and finally we discuss how much our setting restricts the goals an attacker could achieve.

4.1   Attack Mechanisms

Mechanisms in [11], are the channels through which an attacker can inject malicious inputs. The main mechanisms are user inputs, cookies, server variables, and *second-order injections* (occurring when a payload is stored on the web server and used later on by the application to build a query). Assessing second-order injections is particularly challenging for static analysis approaches such as taint analysis [19]. However, in our approach, the mechanism axis is quite irrelevant since we do not distinguish between trusted and untrusted inputs: all inputs are untrusted.

4.2   Known Attacks

Known attacks, as listed in [11] and [20], have the following impact in our setting:

- *Tautologies, Union Query, Piggy-Backed Queries, Alternate Encodings, End of Line Comment,* and *OPENROWSET Result Retrieval* all require the attacker to change the shape of the syntax tree of the query. *Inference* attacks (blind injections and timing attacks) also seem to require such a change. Therefore, they are prevented.
- *Illegal/Logically Incorrect Queries* are used by an attacker to gain information about the type and structure of the database. In order to mitigate such a risk, our library limits the details an attacker could learn by returning only a generic error containing no information in case an exception is raised by the database driver. Moreover, the attack surface is much reduced for the attacker. For instance, the attack proposed in [11] attempts to discover table names, by injecting some value. The attack fails in our setting for two reasons: since injecting values cannot provoke such errors, injection should happen at an identifier rather than at a value; moreover, a non-trivial expression is injected, which changes the shape of the syntax tree of the query. In order to succeed, an attacker would have to turn to more elaborated attacks at least.
- *Stored Procedure* attacks are a whole class of distinct attacks. Whereas all other attacks consist in sending a malicious payload to the application in order to get it to construct an unintended SQL query, attacks on stored procedures consist in having the application pass a malicious payload to the stored procedure, in order to get the stored procedure to construct an unintended SQL query.

As for stored procedure, listing 3 displays the authentication procedure proposed in [11]: A SQL query is dynamically constructed by concatenating strings, including the arguments @username and @password, which are supplied by the user of the stored procedure. Authentication would be bypassed by passing a value such as "admin' --" (if an admin account exists), and a database shutdown would be piggy-backed by passing the value " '; SHUTDOWN; --", as suggested by the authors. Actually, the full spectrum of SQL injection attacks can potentially happen in the context of stored procedure.

```
CREATE PROCEDURE DBO.isAuthenticated
@userName varchar2, @pass varchar2, @pin int
AS
EXEC("SELECT accounts FROM users
WHERE login='" +@userName+ "' and pass='" +@password+
"' and pin=" +@pin);
GO
```

Listing 3: Vulnerable stored procedure

Our library does not prevent an attack against such a procedure, since it has no way to distinguish benign values from malicious ones by itself. Of course, a programmer using our library could validate user-supplied arguments before sending them to this procedure.

Arguably, counter-measures should be put in place in the database itself. Therefore, we consider that these stored procedure attacks are out of the scope of our approach. Possible counter-measures are:

- The designers of stored procedures should clearly specify which inputs are valid inputs and which are invalid.
- Developers of stored procedures should not trust inputs coming from the application: inputs should be validated in the procedure itself. As an additional benefit, that would prevent at once all vulnerable usages of corrected procedures, from all database users or clients.
- As much as possible, developers of stored procedures should refrain from building dynamic queries. The code above had no real reason to build a dynamic query. The static version, as displayed listing 4, is immune to injection, simpler, shorter, and more readable.
- And of course, if the SQL dialect or the language used to define stored procedure is expressive enough to manipulate trees, our approach could be ported to that language. For instance, PostgreSQL allows stored procedures to be written in the Python language, and trees can easily be manipulated in Python.

We note that [4] mentions an additional kind of injection regarding LIKE queries. Consider a query such as

```
CREATE PROCEDURE DBO.isAuthenticated
@userName varchar2, @pass varchar2, @pin int
AS
SELECT accounts FROM users
WHERE login = @userName AND pass = @password;
GO
```

Listing 4: Secure version of listing 3

```
SELECT * FROM messages WHERE subject LIKE = '_____%'
```

where the parameter is supposed to be filled by the concatenation of a user-supplied string s and a percent sign: the intent is to find all messages whose subject starts with s. Using our library, that would be coded as follows:

```
select(star, from(id("messages"))),
      where(like(id("subject"), s + "%")))
```

Unfortunately, the database engine might behave quite differently depending on the contents of s. For instance, if s is the string "foo" and an index exists on column subject, then lookup takes time $O(\log n)$, where n is the number of rows of the table. On the other hand, if an attacker supplies the string "%foo", then the database can no longer take advantage of the index and lookup takes time $O(n)$. Such an injection is in fact an algorithmic complexity attack that could provoke a denial of service.

Interestingly, this attack does not change the abstract syntax tree of the query. Therefore, our library cannot prevent such an attack. The best counter-measure here seems to validate the value of s.

4.3   Attack Intents

Possible malicious intents for an attacker are listed in [11]. We discuss here how effective our approach is against these intents (excluding stored procedure attacks for the reasons previously given):

- *Identifying injectable parameters, performing database finger-printing, determining database schema* are not completely prevented by our approach in principle since illegal/logically incorrect queries attacks are still possible. They are severely restricted however: all the actual attacks presented in [11] would fail in our setting since they all inject at a place where a value is expected and they all inject expressions that change the shape of the syntax tree.
- *Performing denial of service* might still be possible, but seems limited to LIKE queries. For instance, tables cannot be dropped.

- *Extracting data, adding or modifying data, Bypassing authentication, executing remote commands,* and *performing privilege escalation* do not seem possible in our setting since they all require to change the shape of the abstract syntax tree.
- As for *evading detection,* our approach does not consider that aspect.

Thus our approach seems to severely restrict the goals an attacker can achieve.

5   Implementation

5.1   Features

Our approach is implemented in a small Java library [7]. The main features of our library are the following:

- It provides a small internal DSL for representing syntax trees.
- It provides a method to execute a query, represented as a tree, given a database connection.
- It is minimalistic: the shorter a code, the more likely its bugs and vulnerabilities can be corrected. Our library implements only a very small subset of SQL but it is so small (around 200 non-empty lines, not counting the list of the 900 reserved SQL keywords) that it can easily be adapted to other contexts.
- Database connection is achieved through the standard `Connection` class from the `java.sql` package. Thus issues regarding connections, drivers, and transactions do not have to be handled by our library.
- It is publicly available under a free software license [7].

5.2   Organization

Our implementation contains only seven classes. One is a custom exception class, and the six others are depicted in Fig. 3. The class `AST` is the central class of our implementation. We use it in order to represent the abstract syntax tree of a query and to execute it (using the only public method `execute`).

Our implementation can be considered as an instance of the Interpreter design pattern, as proposed in [10]. Indeed, the authors notice that the pattern can also be used for implementing a compiler. In our implementation, the class `CompiledStatement` plays the role of the context and the method `writeTo` plays the role of the interpretation method.

A `CompiledStatement` object is used to build parameterized queries. The most relevant attributes and methods of the `CompiledStatement` class are given in listing 5. Calls to `addToken` gradually accumulate lexical tokens (identifier, keywords and numeric tokens) into the text of the parameterized query, implemented as the buffer `tpl`. Calls to `addStringParam` accumulate string literals by adding question marks in the template and corresponding string values into the list of parameters `args`.

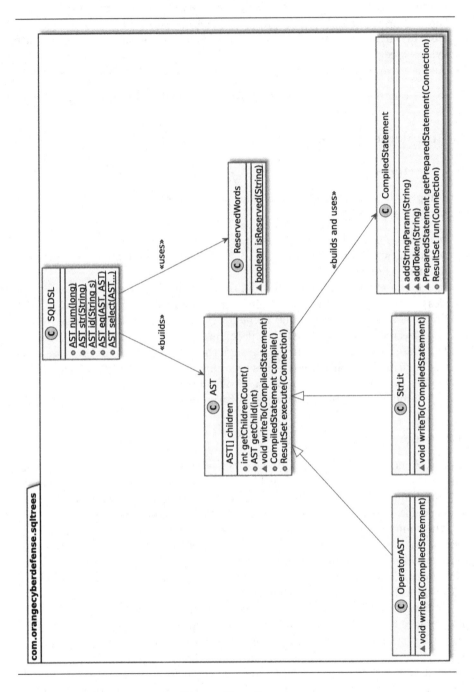

Fig. 3. Class diagram

Listing 6 displays the implementation of the **execute** method, from class **AST**, which you call in order to execute the query represented by the tree. The method **writeTo**, called by **compile**, is in charge of calling the methods **addToken** and/or **addStringParam** of b in order to build the actual **Compiledstatement**.

```java
private final StringBuffer tpl = new StringBuffer();
private final ArrayList<String> args = new ArrayList<String>();

void addStringParam(String s) {
    tpl.append("? ");
    args.add(s);
}

void addToken(String repr) {
    tpl.append(repr);
    tpl.append(" ");
}

PreparedStatement getPreparedStatement(Connection con)
  throws SQLException {
    PreparedStatement stmt = con.prepareStatement(tpl.toString());
    for(int i = 0; i < args.size(); i++) {
        stmt.setString(i+1, // numbering starts at 1
                    args.get(i));
    }
    return stmt;
}

public ResultSet run(Connection con) throws CompiledStatementError {
    try {
        return getPreparedStatement(con).executeQuery();
    } catch (SQLException e) {
        throw new CompiledStatementError();
    }
}
```

Listing 5: Main attributes and methods of CompiledStatement.java

5.3 Auditability

During a source code audit, in order to ensure that a code that uses the standard Java classes `java.sql.Statement` is not vulnerable to SQL injections, you have to make sure that all untrusted inputs are validated, escaped, or passed as parameters. The issue even arises in practice when developers use prepared

```
public CompiledStatement compile() {
    CompiledStatement b = new CompiledStatement();
    writeTo(b);
    return b;
}

public ResultSet execute(Connection con) throws CompiledStatementError {
    return compile().run(con);
}
```

Listing 6: Methods from class AST for executing a syntax tree

statements (see discussion about prepared statements in Sect. 6.1). Such an analysis can be quite involved and can be time-consuming (even when using evolved static analysis tools).

We would like to replace these analysis by a much simpler criterion: if the code does neither use java.sql.Statement nor java.sql.PreparedStatement, but only our library, it is immune to most SQL injections.

Therefore, we must not only ensure that a code using our library as intended is secure. We must also guarantee that our library cannot be used in some insecure, unexpected ways. We identify the following cases as being problematic:

- Unexpected ways to create instances of the classes we provide.
- Modification of objects after creation time.
- Creation of new classes inheriting from a class from our library.

In order to prevent such issues, inheritance is restricted as much as possible (by declaring classes final), all classes but CompiledStatement construct immutable objects, and the visibility of classes, attributes, and methods are restricted as much as possible.

For instance, in order to let developers debug their queries, we make the class CompiledStatement public and provide public methods that reveal the contents of objects of that class. However, we ensure that these methods cannot alter the contents. In contrast, the methods addStringParam and addToken, which mutate the content of a CompiledStatement have their visibility restricted to the package.

We must note however a limitation of encapsulation in Java: an application can access non-public fields or methods *via* reflection, if you run it without any security manager or if you grant the appropriate permission to the security manager (namely ReflectPermission("suppressAccessChecks")).

6 Related Works

Injection-related vulnerabilities have been largely studied. Related works are numerous, but mostly fall in one of the following two categories:

Prevention works trying to reduce the gap between the source programming language and the language used for queries in order to make it easier to write queries.

Detection works trying to detect (and possibly stop) actual exploitation of the vulnerabilities.

6.1 Prevention-Related Works

Validating User Inputs. Validating user-supplied inputs is generally recognized as a good idea. For instance, when a string of alphanumeric character is expected, a value containing a quote character can be rejected immediately. Unfortunately, although input validation is an inevitable part of secure coding, it is not enough to prevent injection. For instance, when a family name is expected, quote characters could not be rejected, without forbidding Irish surnames such as O'Brian.

Harmful Character Escaping. Features for sanitizing inputs, like those provided by OWASP's Enterprise Security API [24] work. However, programmers have to explicitly use them on each user input. If they fail to do so, that will not be detected, neither at compile time nor at run time. And one omission is enough to make an application vulnerable. Therefore, using input sanitization as the only method for preventing SQL injections is risky. Moreover, in case of a source code security audit, each query must be reviewed.

Therefore, the PHP community used a mechanism that would systematically escape user inputs: *magic quotes*. Unfortunately, magic quotes apply indiscriminately on all user inputs, irrespective of the database. Moreover, developers depend on the sysadmins in charge of the server as they are the only persons who can enable it. Finally, magic quotes raise more issues than they solve. Accordingly, they were eventually removed from PHP [5].

Prepared Statements. Prepared statements are the first defense option recommended by the OWASP project [16]. Unfortunately, they are only half a solution (see [11] and [12]) as they cannot protect against column or table injections.

Worse still, when improperly used, prepared statements are vulnerable to SQL injection attacks: since the template query is an ordinary string, nothing prevents developers from inserting unvalidated user inputs into the template part of the query.

Unfortunately, that happens in practice. Admittedly, when developers use prepared statements to search a database table on statically known criteria, their code is generally secure. But quite often, criteria are known only at execution time. Consider for example a product search for an online shop. In addition to the name of the product you are looking for, you may specify additional criteria (a maximum or minimum price, a category, etc.). Of course, the application must only consider criteria for which you gave a non empty value. Thus a SQL query has to be generated dynamically. Although it would be possible in theory to validate inputs, or to escape them, or to generate the right template together with the right list of parameters, it seems that, in practice, developers are much less rigorous. Criteria whose number and type are known at compile time are correctly passed as parameters, but the other ones tend to be appended to the template part. As a result, parameters known at compile-time cannot be injected, but the other ones are vulnerable if their contents have neither been validated nor escaped. We observed such a recurring anti-pattern in source code security audits.

Programming Language Extensions. SQLJ [23] and Embedded SQL [21] let you embed SQL queries in another programming language, such as Java, COBOL, Fortran, C or C++. A preprocessor then checks your queries and translate them into your programming language. Such a way to write queries is quite natural for developers. However, although you can pass arguments at run-time, the structure of your queries has to be known at compile-time. This approach is thus restricted to static queries.

Moreover, on the practical side, that approach raises integration problems regarding existing tools: most IDE do not handle code extended with SQL constructs (syntax highlighting, contextual help, error location, etc.) and you have to twist the build tools in order to make them preprocess code before compilation.

Object-Relational Mapping. Object-relational mapping can generate and execute SQL queries automatically. Tools like SQL DOM [14], Querydsl [3], and jOOQ [2] offer strong guarantees regarding execution *a la* "well-typed programs cannot go wrong" [15]: if the Java code compiles, then generated queries will be correct both regarding syntax and typing (no syntax error, no typing error). By contrast, our library does only guarantees that, if the abstract syntax tree is correct, then the generated query will be a syntactically correct representation of the tree.

ORM tools let you write more dynamic queries than embedded-SQL tools. Yet, these typed queries cannot provide access to all the SQL syntax. The situation is similar to the statically typed vs. untyped (or dynamically typed) dichotomy for programming languages: the statically typed approach is safer but less flexible than the untyped one. In order to compensate for this lack of flexibility, some ORM, such as [1] and [2], let developers write SQL queries as strings, which is a security risk if developers are not careful enough [9].

As a rule of thumb, adopting an ORM is a good decision at the very start of a project. Adopting it in on a legacy project is much more difficult from a software engineering point of view: ORM tools generally generate a data class for each table of the database. Developers then have to adapt their code to replace their homemade classes by the generated ones. In a project with tens or hundreds of tables and a large code base, this require good factoring skills and can be time-consuming. Therefore, for legacy projects in maintenance mode, switching to an ORM is often not an option. On the contrary, our approach requires little investment (you just have to understand how SQL syntax and our trees are related) and can be adopted gradually: you can replace each construction of `Statement` or `PreparedStatement` by a tree, one at a time.

6.2 Detection-Related Works

Static analysis techniques (such as *taint analysis*) can automatically analyze source code and detect some potential injection vulnerabilities at compile-time. However, leveraging such static analysis tools on legacy projects still looks difficult, because of the number of false positive that are initially raised and of skills needed to understand and correctly handle these alerts.

Several works such as [13] or [6,19] suggest to detect injection attempts dynamically, using methods that go beyond usual Web Application Firewalls. Like us, they regard trees as a relevant representation for queries.

For instance, [6] and [19] suggest that developers would insert marks in their queries in order to delimit user-input data. Such marks let the authors build two abstract syntax trees: on the one hand, a model of the query the developers expected, and the other hand, a model of the query they actually built. The two trees are compared: a mismatch is the sign of injection attempt.

Using that method, developers can generate arbitrarily complex and dynamic queries. However, the security of the method relies on the goodwill and care of developers, as for the input sanitization method, mentioned earlier.

The method proposed by [13] for avoiding XSS when generating HTML code does not suffer from this limitation, since the source language they consider (HOP, a Lisp-like programming language) lets you represent abstract syntax trees easily: you just have to write the abstract syntax of the HTML fragment you want to build as a tree. Therefore, you do not need to put any mark in order to extract a model: the tree you wrote *is* the model. Moreover the authors prove that their method is correct from a semantic point of view. Although the authors are concerned with HTML code generation whereas we are concerned with SQL code generation, our work is close to theirs. However, instead of generating code that is faithful to the tree, like we did (which means that dangerous characters have to be watched for), they chose to generate the HTML code without handling dangerous characters, and to parse the resulting text in order to detect a potential injection attempt.

7 Conclusion

Manipulating trees in Java is quite easy and is a simple, effective way to build dynamic queries that are immune to most injections. Tree structures are easily implemented as immutable structures. In functional programming, it is common knowledge that you can easily guarantee properties on such structures, once they are correctly encapsulated. More specifically, in our case, they help to ensure that developers will not build vulnerable queries.

Finally, we would like to extend this work in the following directions:

- From a theoretical point of view, we would like to compare our approach to [19]. Can we adapt the formal definition of injections given in that article and mathematically prove that our approach is secure?
- We could also provide libraries for other languages than Java. However, in languages with looser encapsulation facilities, it might be more difficult to ensure that such a library is developer-proof. We would like to study how language features help (or hinder) the development of such a library. We conjecture already that a strong static type system helps.
- We would like to extend our approach to other similar injections problems: XSS, LDAP injections, shell command injections, etc.
- Our library is only a proof of concept as it handles only a tiny subset of SQL at the moment. We would like to grow our implementation in order to make it usable in real projects. All contributions are of course very welcome!
- Our work has the potential to access all SQL syntax, which is more difficult for ORM tools. We would like to see whether direct accesses to SQL queries as strings provided by ORM could be replaced by accesses to our abstract syntax trees.

Acknowledgments. Claire Vacherot and the anonymous referees provided valuable feedback that helped improve the article.

References

1. Hibernate project. http://hibernate.org/
2. jOOQ website. https://www.jooq.org/
3. Querydsl website. http://www.querydsl.com/
4. Ahmad, K., Shekhar, J., Yadav, K.: Classification of SQL injection attacks. VSRD Tech. Non-Techn. J. **I**(4), 235–242 (2010)
5. Bergmann, S., Blankerts, A., Priebsch, S.: Why magic quotes are gone in PHP 7, August 2017. https://thephp.cc/news/2017/08/why-magic-quotes-are-gone-in-php7
6. Buehrer, G.T., Weide, B.W., Sivilotti, P.A.G.: Using parse tree validation to prevent SQL injection attacks. In: Proceedings of the International Workshop on Software Engineering and Middleware (SEM) at Joint FSE and ESEC, pp. 106–113 (2005)
7. Courant, J.: Sqltrees: a secure, developper-proof, java library for querying SQL databases (2020). https://github.com/Orange-Cyberdefense/sqltrees
8. Dahse, J., Holz, T.: Static detection of second-order vulnerabilities in web applications. In: Fu, K., Jung, J. (eds.) Proceedings of the 23rd USENIX Security Symposium, San Diego, CA, USA, 20–22 August 2014, pp. 989–1003. USENIX Association (2014). https://www.usenix.org/conference/usenixsecurity14/technical-sessions/presentation/dahse
9. Eder, L.: Never concatenate strings with jOOQ. jOOQ blog, March 2020. https://blog.jooq.org/2020/03/04/never-concatenate-strings-with-jooq/
10. Gamma, E., Helm, R., Johnson, R., Vlissides, J.: Design Patterns: Elements of Reusable Object-Oriented Software. Addison-Wesley Professional Computing Series, Pearson Education (1994)

11. Halfond, W.G., Viegas, J., Orso, A.: A classification of SQL-injection attacks and countermeasures. In: Proceedings of the International Symposium on Secure Software Engineering, Washington, D.C., USA, March 2006

12. Karwin, B.: SQL injection myths and fallacies (2012). https://www.percona.com/sites/default/files/WEBINAR-SQL-Injection-Myths.pdf

13. Luo, Z., Rezk, T., Serrano, M.: Automated code injection prevention for web applications. In: Mödersheim, S., Palamidessi, C. (eds.) TOSCA 2011. LNCS, vol. 6993, pp. 186–204. Springer, Heidelberg (2012). https://doi.org/10.1007/978-3-642-27375-9_11

14. McClure, R.A., Kruger, I.H.: SQL DOM: compile time checking of dynamic SQL statements. In: Proceedings. 27th International Conference on Software Engineering, ICSE 2005, pp. 88–96 (2005)

15. Milner, R.: A theory of type polymorphism in programming. J. Comput. Syst. Sci. **17**, 348–375 (1978)

16. OWASP project: SQL injection prevention cheat sheet (2020). https://cheatsheetseries.owasp.org/cheatsheets/SQL_Injection_Prevention_Cheat_Sheet.html

17. Puppy, R.F.: NT web technology vulnerabilities. Phrack Mag. **8**(54) (1998). http://phrack.org/issues/54/8.html

18. van der Stock, A., Glass, B., Smithline, N., Gigler, T.: OWASP Top 10 (2017). https://web.archive.org/web/20200406122129/owasp.org/www-pdf-archive/OWASP_Top_10-2017_(en).pdf.pdf

19. Su, Z., Wassermann, G.: The essence of command injection attacks in web applications. In: Morrisett, J.G., Jones, S.L.P. (eds.) Proceedings of the 33rd ACM SIGPLAN-SIGACT Symposium on Principles of Programming Languages, POPL 2006, Charleston, South Carolina, USA, pp. 372–382. ACM (2006). https://doi.org/10.1145/1111037.1111070

20. Sun, S.T., Wei, T.H., Liu, S., Lau, S.: Classification of SQL injection attacks. University of Columbia, Term Project (2007). https://courses.ece.ubc.ca/cpen442/term_project/reports/2007-fall/Classification_of_SQL_Injection_Attacks.pdf

21. Wikipedia, The Free Encyclopedia: Embedded SQL, March 2020

22. Wikipedia, The Free Encyclopedia: SQL Reserved Words, March 2020

23. Wikipedia, The Free Encyclopedia: SQLJ, March 2020

24. Wall, K., Seil, M.: The OWASP enterprise security API. https://web.archive.org/web/20200331100823/owasp.org/www-project-enterprise-security-api/

A Survey of Advanced Encryption for Database Security: Primitives, Schemes, and Attacks

Buvana Ganesh$^{(\boxtimes)}$ and Paolo Palmieri

School of Computer Science and IT, University College Cork, Cork, Ireland
{b.ganesh,p.palmieri}@cs.ucc.ie

Abstract. The use of traditional encryption techniques in Database Management Systems is limited, as encrypting data within the database can prevent basic functionalities such as ordering and searching. Advanced encryption techniques and trusted hardware, however, can enable standard functionalities to be achieved on encrypted databases, and a number of such schemes have been proposed in the recent literature. In this survey, different approaches towards database security through software/hardware components are explored and compared based on performance and security, and relevant attacks are discussed.

1 Introduction

Ross Anderson famously stated that "you cannot construct a database with scale, functionality and security because if you design a large system for ease of access it becomes insecure, while if you make it watertight it becomes impossible to use" [6]. While compromises between security and functionality are common in many technological domains, getting the right balance is critical in databases, which are a primary way to store complex information on digital systems. Two factors make research into database security more relevant than ever: first, the ever increasing amount of information that is being generated, collected and stored, most of which sensitive, partly due to advances in the Internet of Things and the diffusion of personal devices such as smartphones and wearables; secondly, the trend towards outsourcing information storage to the cloud, following the Database-as-a-Service (DBaaS) paradigm, which introduces additional privacy risks [4].

Traditional cryptographic techniques cannot be easily applied to databases, due to their inherent nature as a way to structure information. While cryptography can provide an "external" layer of security, where the information

Buvana Ganesh is supported by a PhD scholarship funded by the Science Foundation Ireland Centre for Research Training in Artificial Intelligence under Grant No. 18/CRT/6223.

G. Nicolescu et al. (Eds.): FPS 2020, LNCS 12637, pp. 100–120, 2021.
https://doi.org/10.1007/978-3-030-70881-8_7

is encrypted while at rest (for example through the use of file system or full disk encryption), this does not protect against any attack that targets a "live" database, for example via malicious queries. Trivially encrypting data within a database, instead, compromises the functionality of the database, as it prevents basic operations such as ordering, (partial) equality testing, search and many other. An alternative strategy to protect information is *differential privacy*, which adds noise to data but yields almost accurate results using statistical mechanisms, based on a privacy budget. Although corporations like Apple and Google favor this for ease of usage, it is not suitable for accurate search and retrieval, and is difficult to implement in dynamic (constantly changing) databases. On the other hand, research on advanced cryptographic mechanisms such as homomorphic or searchable encryption, combined with novel hardware security mechanisms, is increasingly pushing the boundaries of the security *vs.* functionality compromise in databases by allowing, for example, certain operations to be performed on encrypted data. Anderson's intuition remains true, and even the most advanced security schemes cannot entirely prevent leakage of information, which may allow an attacker to approximately reconstruct a database in less than linear time [27]. However, the adoption of these advanced mechanisms can undoubtedly enhance the security of database systems, while maintaining performance comparable to that of an unencrypted database.

In this paper, we discuss the novel cryptographic and security primitives that can be applied to databases (Sect. 3), and we survey the schemes in the literature that are employing these primitives for database security (Sect. 4). To the best of our knowledge, no previous survey covers secure databases with encryption and hardware. While a direct comparison of the schemes is challenging, due to the different levels of functionalities they provide, we categorise the schemes according to the security they claim to offer, and juxtapose their respective performances according to standard benchmark tests (Sect. 5). Finally, we discuss the main potential attacks in relation to the schemes, in order to gain valuable insight for the development of future schemes.

2   Terminology and Definitions

A database (DB) is an organised collection of data of any type, used for the storage, retrieval and management of information, which are performed through a database management system (DBMS). DBs are differentiated based on their structure and properties. Relational databases (RDB) are structured by predefined categories with a *Schema* of *Columns* and *Tables*. NoSQL databases are not as well-defined, and the data is malleable and eventually consistent, thus improving scalability and flexibility. Types include *Key-value*, *Graph*, *Wide Column* or *Document* oriented stores. NewSQL forms a class of RDBMS that seek to provide the same scalability of NoSQL and are distributed to enable faster distributed analytics. In terms of warehousing, Online Analytic Processing (OLAP) is utilized for large scale read-only multidimensional databases to create online comparative summaries of data. Online Transaction Processing (OLTP) helps in dynamic transactions and updates on smaller sizes of data with read and write access.

In the following, we refer to databases that are protected either cryptographically or through trusted hardware as encrypted databases (EDB), and their respective encrypted database management systems as EDBMS.

The aim of an EDB is to provide secure data outsourcing and sharing. When outsourced either to a cloud or third party, who performs computations on the database, the data should possess the necessary properties that enable such computations to be performed without decryption. These normally include search, retrieval, transactions and operations. The EDBMS should also enable access control and policies. A basic set of properties including full range of Queries, Storage, Memory management, Dynamic Updates, Access pattern hiding, etc. are to be considered for the construction. In EDBMS, generally, the client acts as user interface for identification, authentication, key generation and sometimes query processing. Proxies, if used, mainly help in the modification of queries received by the server dedicated to database storage-retrieval. Additional servers with various purposes such as key distribution, computation, etc. may be present.

2.1   Threats and Adversaries

Attacks on unencrypted databases are commonplace in the news causing significant losses every year. Common threats include privilege abuse, image leaks from virtual machines, SQL injections, and disk theft [28]. The main way to secure unencrypted DBs is through the use of policies and access control. *Query control* [55], for instance, uses policies to ensure the query is sufficiently targeted. However, only cryptographic security can make data provably secure, even in the case of attacks on the DBMS components. Currently, most industry DB solutions only rely on *Transparent Data Encryption* for securing data at rest, and *Transport Layer Security* for data in transit. This implies that any computation can be performed only after decryption. EDBs aim to provide increased security, and prevent log, memory and access pattern based attacks.

The security literature categorises adversaries based on their abilities. In the context of databases, *honest but curious* adversaries are administrators or service providers (SPs) with access to a part (or sometimes full) history of queries performed. Most schemes assume this and it is often referred to as the "Snapshot attack" [28]. Persistent passive attackers compromise the DBMS server and passively observe all its operations. *Malicious* administrators, users or servers are capable of modifying the contents of a DB to manipulate the output. They can carry out *chosen document, query* or *keyword* attacks based on prior knowledge, as discussed in Sect. 5.2. Databases can be attacked by internal or external entities with various levels of prior knowledge from *fully known document, partially known document, known document subset* to *distributional knowledge*. Based on the level of prior knowledge, it is possible to recover queries, plaintext or partial plaintext (see Sect. 5.2).

2.2   Provable Security

Different types of proofs are available to establish security, the most common being *game-based proofs*. Game-based proofs cover indistinguishability attacks such as *Known Plaintext Attack* (or Known Query Attack in DBs), *Chosen Plaintext Attack* (IND-CPA), Chosen Ciphertext Attack (IND-CCA). In this paper, we use the definitions provided in [35] for these classes of attacks. In game-based proofs two parties, the challenger and the adversary, play a cryptographic game. If the adversary cannot guess which of the two texts presented by the challenger is the right plaintext/ciphertext in polynomial time, then the encryption used is IND CPA/CCA secure respectively. This type is employed when one or more cryptosystems are used in a scheme.

Real/Ideal model also known as the simulation paradigm is a technique for provable security first described by Goldreich et al. in [24]. A protocol P securely computes a functionality if for every adversary A in the real model, there exists an adversary (a simulator) S in the ideal model, such that a real execution and an ideal execution of P is indistinguishable for the adversary. This is useful when input is provided by both honest and corrupt parties. Schemes which utilize privacy preserving data structures use such paradigms for proving security. Similarly, Universal Composability (UC-Secure) framework works with an environment, an ideal functionality and a simulator to prove security when composing different protocols [12].

3   Security Primitives

The primitives mentioned here are used for different applications and sometimes as standalones to provide security. But in order to achieve a number of basic database functionalities, the techniques used need to be used in a modular manner or modified. Leakage in encryptions is unavoidable, since the result of a query using that functionality would leak the same property about the data. Analytical queries for deriving data summaries such as *Equality, Order, Max, Min, Round, Sum, Average, Limit, Count, Like, Stemming*, and *Wildcard* require order-preserving, homomorphic and searchable encryptions. Boolean queries *And, Or, Not* require interoperability with conjunctive and disjunctive search support. In this section, we discuss the aforementioned mechanisms in relation to EDBs. We note, however, how most EDBs can execute only a subset of all possible queries, and therefore will use a selection, rather than all, of these schemes.

3.1   Property Preserving Encryptions (PPE)

Schemes in the class of Property Preserving Encryptions (PPE) enable functions such as Order, Search, Arithmetics, Equality, Distance, etc. to be performed in EDBs. Three main families of schemes are discussed below: homomorphic encryption; searchable encryptions; and order preserving/revealing encryptions.

Secure implementations of these functions are present in most of the surveyed schemes. While encryptions for other functions are available, such standalone methods usually imply significant leakages. For instance, Distance Recoverable Encryption were introduced by Wong et al. [62] for calculating k-nearest neighbors in EDBs, using asymmetric scalar-product-preserving encryption. Tex et al. [58] discuss case studies for encrypting SQL query logs using Xquery and use Distance preserving encryption with PPE.

Homomorphic Encryption (HE) – The property of an encryption that allows algebraic operations to be performed on ciphertext without decryption is called Homomorphic Encryption. A standard HE scheme comprises a minimum of 4 algorithms: Key Generation, Encryption, Decryption and Homomorphic Evaluation for the operations (often addition, $+$ and multiplication, $\cdot$). Based on the evaluations, a HE scheme can be *partially homomorphic* (PHE), supporting one of the two operations above, or *fully homomorphic* (FHE), supporting both operations. In order to improve performance, some schemes are *somewhat homomorphic* with just a limited set of operations before the noise makes the system unreliable. Also, as the encryptions are based on finite structures, in certain schemes homomorphic evaluation is possible only up to a modulus level, due to the increase in size of ciphertext, while others allow evaluations at all levels. Often, a leveled HE (LFHE) scheme is bootstrapped and extended to a fully homomorphic scheme.

Table 1. Types of homomorphic encryption

Scheme	Type	Underlying hard problem	Ops	Libraries
Paillier [44]	PHE	Composite Residuosity	$+$	Palisade, Paillier
DGHV [18]	SWHE	LWE	$+,\cdot$	–
FV/BFV [21]	LFHE	LWE	$+,\cdot$	SEAL, Palisade
BGV [11]	LFHE	LWE with no bootstrapping	$+,\cdot$	Helib
HEAAN [15]	LFHE	Approximate LWE	$+,\cdot$	HEANN, Palisade, SEAL, Helib

Since Gentry's FHE scheme in 2009, Post Quantum Public Key Encryption (PKE) HE are the most commonly used and are based on NP-hard problems like learning with errors (LWE) and its variants. Symmetric HE are more prone to attacks. Overall, HE schemes are susceptible to size pattern based attacks (Sect. 5.2).

In recent years, commercial interest in HE has increased, leading to many open source libraries, such as Microsoft Seal [54], IBM's HELib [29], IARPA's PALISADE [1]. The libraries support variants of HE schemes such as BFV [21], HEAAN [15], Paillier [44]. We summarize the schemes and their implementations in Table 1.

Searchable Encryptions (SE) – Searchable encryption, another PPE, is a type of functional encryption that allows Search on encrypted data. *Searchable Symmetric Encryption* (SSE) may have many or all of the search features, such as keyword, Boolean, and phrase search queries, as well as stemming, wildcard, and approximate-match searching. SSE provides provable security because of the predetermined leakage function, but requires a scan of the entire DB for every query, unless some Indexing is provided. SSE focuses on data outsourcing, where the data owner is the client. The client parses each input document and performs keyword extraction, followed by a probabilistic *setup algorithm* that outputs the EDB (to be hosted on the server) and the master Key. The *search protocol* requires the EDB, master key and the query (keyword) w as the input. To search for w, the client generates and sends a *trapdoor*, which the server uses to run the search and recover pointers to appropriate documents. *Dynamic SSE* introduced by Kamara et al. [34], are stateful and thus reduce leakage. The setup generates a state to be passed to the Search, Read or Write protocol. Dynamic schemes ensure forward or backward privacy, or both.

Boneh et al. proposed *Public Key Encryption with Keyword Search* (PEKS) based on public key infrastructure using bilinear pairing. The general structure is similar to SSE, but with PKE. The schemes can be for single keyword, conjunctive or subset search. Zhou et al. explain on the evolution of PEKS in their paper [65]. A *Private Information Retrieval* (PIR) protocol allows a query to retrieve an element from the DB without revealing the access patterns, relations between columns and their storage blocks. [33] and [31] are inspired by PIR. The schemes which form the basis for SSE systems are in Table 2.

Order Preserving Encryptions (OPE) – Range queries are critical for DBs and Order Preserving Encryptions provide this function. They are numeric and well ordered, therefore lead to significant leakage. Despite this, OPEs are widely studied as detailed in Table 3. Boldyreva et al.'s OPE scheme is the most commonly used due to its ease of implementation [9]. The algorithm constructs a deterministic *Random Order Preserving Function* (ROPF) on a domain of integers where the range is recursively bisected. This method reveals almost half of the bits in the ciphertext. Security for such encryptions is proved by Indistinguishability under Ordered Chosen Plaintext attacks (IND-OCPA) where an OPE leaks nothing but the order of the ciphertext. Other simulation-based security proofs are provided where IND-OCPA is considered insecure (Sect. 5.2).

Table 2. Searchable Symmetric Encryption (SSE) schemes

SSE - year	Feature	Operations
Song et al.'00 [56]	Embedding information in pseudorandom bit streams	Single word search
OSPIR OXT'13 [33]	Malicious, Oblivious PRF, Cross Tags (OXT) [14], IND CPA	Conjunctive, Boolean queries
ShadowCrypt'14 [30]	Efficiently searchable encryption with DOM	Standard Full text search
Mimesis Aegis'14 [38]	Efficiently deployable efficiently searchable encryption	Standard Full text search
Sophos'16 [10]	Pseudo-random functions and trapdoor permutations	L-Adaptively Secure forward private scheme
Pouliot et al.'16 [50]	Bloom Filters	Weighted Graph Matching attacks on EDESE
SisoSPIR'16 [31]	Oblivious Transfer, Secure node search. Real/Ideal	Distributed, Full SSE, Range queries
Saha et al.'19 [52]	Ring LWE, IND CPA	Conjunctive, Disjunctive and Threshold queries

Table 3. Order preserving/revealing encryptions (OPE) schemes

OPE	Feature	Security
Agrawal'09 [5]	Data Buckets transformed to Target distribution	Leaks more than Order
ROPF'09 [9]	ROPF with a hyper-geometric distribution. Modular ROPF by adding an integer modulo M	Leaks > half the bits
mOPE'13 [48]	Mutable - refreshes Cipher text using Merkle hashing	IND-OCPA
ORE'16 [39]	Left encryption: Domain's permutation and hashed key of plaintext. Right: encryptions of the comparison with every other value in the domain	Leaks d-bits of first differing block
Dyer et al.'17 [19]	Approximate Integer Common Divisor problem PKE	Window One-wayness
FHOPE'18 [40]	Appx Greatest Common Divisor based Symmetric Fully Homomorphic OPE	IND-HOCPA

3.2   Oblivious RAM

Initially introduced for secure multi-party computation, Oblivious Random Access Memory enables the oblivious execution of the RAM algorithm while hiding the access pattern from the server and memory. ORAM continuously reshuffles and re-encrypts (Symmetric or FHE) the data in blocks as they are accessed with fresh randomness using a position map with bandwidth and block size as parameters. The blocks are stored in binary search trees. *Path ORAM* [57] is the most used and practical version of ORAM. Here, when a block is read from the server, the entire path to the mapped leaf is read, the requested block is remapped to another leaf, and then the path that was just read is written back to the server. Garg et al. [23] use *TWORAM* with two rounds of oblivious exchange between client and server. It does not support inserts/deletes or hides result sizes. In ORAM based schemes, the message length from the server to the user, as the result of query execution, is proportional to the number of records matching the query, therefore causing leakage of the size pattern. Therefore ORAM-based schemes are vulnerable to size pattern-based attacks, e.g., count attack (Sect. 5.2).

3.3   Enclaves

Enclaves are software programs written into a trusted portion of the hardware for secure storage and computation of data. The hardware manufacturer becomes a trusted third party, with potential access to the keys and code. Some of the commercially available Trusted Execution Environments are Intel Software Guard Extensions (SGX) [16], ARM's TrustZone [3] to be used in devices like Raspberry Pi and AMD Secure Memory Encryption which is enabled at BIOS and uses a single key generated by the AMD Secure Processor at boot for transparent encryption. Our focus shall rest on SGX because of its usage in a majority of the Hardware based EDBs.

SGX is a set of new x86 instructions that enable code isolation within virtual containers. The attack models assume untrusted servers. The three main functionalities are: *Isolation, Sealing* and *Attestation*. SGX isolates enclave code and data in the Processor Reserved Memory (PRM). Cryptographic keys are owned by the trusted processor. SGX uses AES-GCM to encrypt with additional authenticated data for sealing. An enclave can derive a Seal Key, specific to the enclave identity, from the Root Seal Key and this can be used to encrypt/authenticate and store data in untrusted memory. A special signing key and instructions are used for attestation to ensure unforgeable reports Attestation can be done locally or remotely.

Enclaves occupy a fixed and limited part of the memory and so an application is built around the SGX. Intel becomes compulsory hardware to run SGX, which is the performance degrades around 4 times when a DBMS is run on the SGX.

4   Secure Database Schemes

In this section, we give a brief discursive description of current encrypted database schemes and their implementation, focusing on security and functionality. In previous work, Fuller et al. [22] provided a systematization of knowledge for cryptographically protected database search, but do not include hardware attacks. We divide the schemes into three categories – encrypted conventional databases, privacy-preserving data structure based schemes, and hardware-based schemes. The schemes were chosen for the survey based on novelty, relevance, extent of functionality and implementation.

For key management, most schemes assume that only the clients possess the master key. Proxies or trusted execution environments hold the encryption schemes for the particular components. For members of the organisation, access control is the primary way to ensure key distribution if the scheme supports multiple users. Also, the number of servers used in each model is normally not specified.

4.1   Encrypted Conventional Databases

CryptDB [49] is an DBMS that supports all of the standard SQL over encrypted data without requiring any client-side query processing, modifications to existing DBMS or legacy applications and offloads virtually all query processing to the server, using a proxy server to process encrypted queries. CryptDB uses the security of existing cryptosystems like AES-CBC/CMC, ROPF [9] and Paillier, forming an *Onion Layering Model* where encryptions and their respective keys are layered based on the type of queries. Therefore, CryptDB cannot perform Complex Join operations and lacks rich functionality though it primarily focuses on relational data. Although CryptDB shows good performance with TPC-C queries, it is 26% slower than performance on MySQL.

Monomi [59], based on the same Onion Layering model, delegates Queries between a trusted client and an untrusted server using a query planner and designer, based on the encryption and order of the Queries. The scheme is optimized based on Cost of Storage and Transaction, yet reserves as many tasks as possible for the server. This improves interoperability. But the data leaks order related properties in steady state and on querying and the adversary is assumed to have full access to the DB.

Arx [47] assumes the non-malicious non-curious CSP model with intrusion detection to prevent attackers from observing and logging queries over time, but fears "steal-and-run" attacks. Arx has the same building blocks structure along with *ArxAgg* for addition and two new DB indices, *ArxRange* for Range queries and *ArxEq* for equality queries, which uses treap like structure, whose nodes destroy and rebuild themselves for untraceability. Queries on these indices reveal only a limited per-query access pattern. Arx is built against leakage attacks based on frequency and order. Overheads are only about 6% to 15% more than on specific unencrypted data and deployed on MongoDB and similar databases to show functionality. Arx uses a two-round protocol to hide the relationship between the node values of the range query index and the DB rows holding that value to avoid snapshot attacks. Nevertheless, the leakage is sufficient to recover the values in the index using a variant of the bipartite matching attacks.

Seabed [45], built by Microsoft, uses Additively Symmetric Homomorphic Encryption (ASHE) for performing analytics on big data. The adversary is assumed to be with honest but curious. To prevent frequency attacks, Splayed ASHE (SPLASHE) uses deterministic encryption with padding for infrequent plaintext values, rather than a dedicated column in the schema. Seabed is built on Apache Spark. The performance-schema will leak a query histogram for only the frequently occurring values. However, a partial histogram could be reconstructed from the logs. With other leakage about frequent values from query patterns, damaging cross-column inference attacks can be performed [28]

DBMask [53] can efficiently handle large databases even when user dynamics change. The Proxy server acts as a mask for the data attribute based models with access control and cryptographic constructors like Attribute based Group Key Management (AB-GKM) are introduced for functionality in DBMask. No changes are made to the DBMS engine. An access tree is formed and thresholds are set with Shamir's Secret Sharing polynomials to derive group keys for querying. Privacy Preserving Numerical comparisons, key searches, joins are derivatives Hence, DBMask can perform access control and predicate matching at the time of query processing by adding predicates to the query being executed.

P-McDB [17] – Cui et al. proposed a dynamic SSE scheme for Privacy Preserving Multi Cloud DB which uses multiple clouds for storage and search, Index and witness and, re-randomize and shuffle. P-McDb is meant for multiple users and data cannot be re-encrypted on user revocation. In this system, the clouds are Honest but curious, capable of injecting malicious records. It supports partial searches of encrypted records. The communication between them could introduce more delays. The model is efficient enabling full search. The dual cloud system prevents inference attacks.

Encrypted NoSQL Databases – EncKV [64] uses Symmetric Searchable Encryption and ORE [39] to accomplish the primary task of the *Key Value Stores*. EncKV is tested on the Redis Cluster with the Amazon EC2 public cloud platform. *Graph Databases* for Encryption for Approximate Shortest Distance Queries (GRECS) [41] uses somewhat homomorphic and symmetric encryptions for secure Graph operations. GraphSE2 [37] provides scalable social search by decomposing queries and using interchangeable protocols, and demonstrate using Azure Cloud. Wiese et al. [61] present CloudDB guard adapting an Onion Layering model with PPE for *Wide Column Stores* and test their scheme on the Enron email dataset. The scheme presents optimised reading, writing and storage efficient schemes with low performance loss.

4.2 Privacy Preserving Data Structure Based Schemes

Structures such as B-trees, B+ trees are used in DBs for indexing purposes. Queries return observable states in memory, along with which parts of the DB are touched (called access patterns), frequency. To avoid this, EDBs often rely on modified data structures or mechanisms such as Inverted Index, Oblivious Index, Bloom filter trees, AVL Trees or SE based index, ORAM, etc.

Blind Seer [46] – Pappas et al. provide a framework (BLoom filter INDex SEarch of Encrypted Results) for developing secure and oblivious search using Bloom filter search trees, garbled circuits and HE. *Garbled circuits* (GC) [63] enable oblivious exchange of information between two parties. Bloom Filters are helpful in privately checking if an element belongs to a set, using hashes allowing no false negatives. A DB is permutated with a Pseudo-random Generator on a Random string XOR'ed with the Record which forms a *Bloom filter search tree*. The DB and Search tree are encrypted using an *additive homomorphism* in the server and sent to the Index server along with the public key. A Query gets transformed into a *Boolean Circuit*, which the index server securely computes, garbled and sent to the server, where the data is retrieved from the Search Tree and sent back. The transaction queries can be executed in constant time, but the periodic re-indexing that merges the temporary Bloom filter list to the tree on updations is expensive.

Blind Seer supports analytical Boolean queries and provides security against Access pattern leakage. Bloom filter search tree supports range queries without OPE. Blind Seer claims to be 1.2–3 times slower than MySQL.

Oblix [42] – Mishra et al. proposed a highly scalable Doubly *Oblivious Search Index* using SGX and Doubly Oblivious RAM. The client's access to the server's memory and to its own local memory are obliviously accessed and hence the double obliviousness. The attack model assumes a malicious attacker, performing any hardware attacks on the enclave and code modifications but the processor cannot be harmed. Oblix supports multi user access to data without revealing the other party's query results or changes. It creates Doubly Oblivious Sorted Multi-maps (DOSM) to store key-value pairs and Doubly Oblivious Data Structures (DODS) to store the EDB. The AVL binary trees are modified to rebalance only after a fixed number of nodes have been accessed in the previous phase, so the adversary can predict when rebalancing begins, and cache the nodes accessed. Oblix achieves protection against modification attacks and access pattern leakage for both Data and code via Merkle hash trees by using Intel SGX's built-in integrity tree and by employing a separate hash tree for data stored outside.

4.3   Trusted Hardware Based Schemes

TrustedDB [8] – Bajaj et al. were one of the first to propose an EDBMS based on Trusted hardware. TrustedDB is built on IBM 4764 series of secure co-processors (SCPU) with *Sensitive attributes* processed by SQLite and a com-modity Server for rich MySQL DBs. Query processing engines are run on both the server and SCPU. Private attributes can only be decrypted by the client or by the SCPU. The main CPU DBMS is an unmodified MySQL 14.12 engine, but can be substituted. An ample amount of changes are required to integrate the hardware to cooperate with each other.

CipherBase [7] is an extension of Microsoft SQL Server, designed to protect data against admins with root access privileges. Cipherbase integrates a custom designed FPGA to act as a secure DB processor for the *Trusted Module* (TM) a submodule for core operations over encrypted Data, alongside an Untrusted DB Server Module (UM), The Cipherbase query plan runtime system aids in shipping tuples encrypted with AES-ECB, AES-CBC or ROPF [9], from UM to TM then to decrypt, process, and re-encrypt these tuples in the TM, and ship results back. It provides end to end functionality. Computations runs an order of magnitude slower than regular processors.

ObliDB [20] is an enclave-based oblivious DB engine that efficiently runs gen-eral relational read workloads with an SGX implemented. ObliDB can store data with no obliviousness or indexed, or both combined. Based on the query's characteristics, like the amount of DB covered and choice of storage, the query planner chooses one of the available select algorithm for Select, Aggregate and Join queries. ObliDB uses Path-ORAM to cover the access patterns of the queries to avoid the disadvantages of CipherBase and TrustedDB. It is 2.6% slower than SparkSQL.

Stealthdb [60] creates three enclaves on the server: For client authentication, query pre-processing and operation. Based on the importance, columns are marked with an Encrypted or Unencrypted index. StealthDB with encrypted IDs incurs 4.2 times the overhead to PostgreSQL 9.6, for even large DBs.

EnclaveDB [51] is built with an enclave based on Hekaton, optimized for OLTP workloads where data fits in the available memory. The model assumes threats from any party controlling the DB server. It does not consider Access pattern attacks. The implementation uses AES-GCM, a high-performance AEAD scheme, and Oblivious transfers with Software Guard Extensions for security.

Table 4. Performance

EDBMS	Focus	Type	Benchmark	Code
CryptDB'11 [49]	S	RDBMS/NoSQL	TPC-C 31, TPC-H 4	[49]
Monomi'13 [59]	S/C	RDBMS/NoSQL	TPC-C 31, TPC-H 19	[59]
Arx'17 [47]	S	RDBMS/MongoDB	TPC-C 30	–
Seabed'16 [45]	S/C/H	Apache Spark	Ad Analytics, MDX API, TPC-DS 99	–
P-McDB'19 [17]	S	RDBMS, Cloud	TPC-H	–
DBMask'16 [53]	S/C	RDBMS	TPC-C, CRIS	–
Oblix'18 [42]	S	Search Index, Key-Value, Scalable	ZeroTrace, Google Key Transparency, Signal	–
Blind Seer [46]	S/C	Search Index	US Census and "Call of the wild" based	–
TrustedDB'13 [8]	TH	SQLite/MySQL	TPC-H	–
Cipherbase'13 [7]	TCH	MS SQL Server	TPC-C 31	–
ObliDB'17 [20]	TH	MongoDB	Big Data	[20]
StealthDB'17 [60]	TH	PostgreSQL	TPC-C 31	[60]
EnclaveDB'18 [51]	TH	Hekaton	TPC-C, TATP	–

Focus (Query Handling) - S: Server, C: Client, TH: Trusted Hardware

5   Discussion

In this section, we discuss and compare the schemes which we presented and categorized above. Section 5.1 discusses performances, compared based on run time and ability to execute queries in *benchmarks* including TPC-C, TPC-H, and TATP, Enron email dataset, Big Data [2]. Benchmarks simulate a complete computing environment to execute queries with varying degrees of complexity, centred around transactions, decision support systems, OLAP, etc. Table 4 lists the benchmarks relevant to each scheme.

Section 5.2 discusses the schemes from a security point of view, and identifies the main attacks. The security components included in each scheme are listed in Table 5.

Table 5. Security comparisons

EDBMS	Adv	Encryptions, ORAM	Hardware	Security
CryptDB	HbC	Paillier [44], AES, ROPF [9], mOPE [48]	–	IND CPA
Monomi	HbC	Paillier [44], ROPF [9], AES	–	IND-CPA
Seabed	HbC	Splayed Additively SHE	–	SS/ IND-CPA
DBMask	HbC	AB-GKM, AES, ROPF [9], Song SSE [56]	–	SS
P-MCDB	Mal	AES-ECB, Asghar OPE,	–	Real/Ideal
Arx	HbC	GC, AES, mOPE, ArxEq, ArxAgg	–	SS/IND-CPA
Blind Seer	Mal	GC, Bloom Filter Tree	–	SS
Oblix	Mal	Doubly Oblivious sorted multimaps/Data structures, D-ORAM	Enclave	Real/Ideal
TrustedDB	HbC	AES, RSA, SHA	SCPU	Hardware
Cipherbase	HbC	AES, Paillier, Column level, ROPF, ORAM	FPGA	IND-CPA
ObliDB	Mal	Path-ORAM	SGX	Real/Ideal
EnclaveDB	Mal	AES	SGX	IND-CPA/CTXT
StealthDB	HbC	AES GCM	SGX	SS

HbC: Honest but Curious, Mal: Malicious, SS: Semantic Security

5.1 Performance

The performance comparison presented here is based on the results included in the original papers. It would be outside the scope of this review, as well as technically challenging to reproduce the original results independently: the software based schemes considered have different basic components that are not easily integrated, while the hardware based schemes make use of equipment that is not readily available and whose configurations are hard to reconstruct. The code is available as open source only for the schemes mentioned in the Table 4, which is not sufficient for elaborate analysis. Comparisons in terms of complexity is usually done with respect to MySQL or other popular DBMS and are stated in the scheme descriptions.

Conventional EDB schemes like CryptDB, DBMask are feasible because of their modular structure and are faster as they resemble traditional DBs. These schemes, however, try to process full queries in the proxy or the server instead of delegating a portion to the client. This reduces the functionality. For example, a query with computation and comparison cannot be performed together as the encryptions do not allow this. In comparison, privacy-preserving data structure based systems are not immediately practical, due to their focus on obscuring the access pattern, including Oblix, Blind Seer, SisoSPIR. Here, every query has to search the entire DB to retrieve even one element.

Hardware-based solutions require utilities like SGX from all parties, which is not always ideal. Storage and Memory in SGX are not scalable over time. Moreover, making the hardware and the encryptions work together using an existing DBMS framework can be difficult, as stated in [8] and [7].

The distinct features of each scheme make them difficult to collectively compare and rank. A secure scheme may not be fully functional and vice versa. Each scheme has a different number of servers, presence or absence of proxies, integration of protocols, hardware, etc. Therefore, each of the three categories are compared using some standard parameters and benchmarks in Table 4.

Industry: Encrypted Databases have become commercialised for cloud computing platforms majorly and products are available for use, such as Bitglass Cloud Encryption, CipherCloud, McAfee MVISION Cloud from Skyhigh Networks, Microsoft Always Encrypted (SQL Server and Azure Plus enclaves), Netskope, Symantec CloudSOC, Google Encrypted BigQuery. A majority of the products feature secure search and retrieval using a combination of access control and established cryptosystems like AES-256. Schemes like Bitglass, also support Range Queries. However, advanced EDBs are still in research and experimental stages, e.g. Encrypted BigQuery.

5.2   Attacks and Security

EDBs support properties requiring ciphertext manipulation, thereby refusing IND-CCA. Hence most schemes prove security through Real/Ideal or IND-CPA though this does not guarantee the absence of leakage, which is discussed here as any piece of information that the user derives more than what the returned query result implies. It can occur online and offline. We classify leakage based on where it occurs: in the memory, or during computation.

Leakage from Memory – *Inference attacks*, termed IKK attack, proposed by Islam et al. [32] use frequency analysis on SSE with only access pattern disclosure and full document/partial query knowledge. Naveed et al. [43] performed inference attacks on EDBs and state that it is better to offload data to the client and perform queries locally. If the data distribution of a particular column is known, the column can be reconstructed in $O(N^4 \log N)$ queries where N is the number of entries. The attack is performed using frequency analysis on Static DB without any queries.

Another passive attack applicable for most schemes is the *Count attack*, where an adversary could recover queries by counting the number of matched records even if the encrypted records are semantically secure. The attacker with full knowledge of query distribution, sees how many records are returned in response to a query and identifies it if the number is unique, hence matching every returned record with that keyword [13].

Leakage from Computation – *Leakage abuse attacks* are common and cannot be eliminated in SE and PPE. In order to evaluate leakages from searchable encryptions, Curtmola et al. define a series of leakage levels which was then characterised by Cash et al. [13] as $\mathcal{L}_1$–$\mathcal{L}_4$, from least to most leakage. We present leakage levels and related attacks in Table 6.

Any snapshot of the system contains information about search tokens, past queries, workloads, and access patterns from logs in the byte level. With this knowledge, the attacker who compromised the disk can reconstruct queries that were used to modify the DB [28]. Prior knowledge of the plaintext at various degrees can lead to *Injection* of malicious records to reveal data or even without the knowledge, the record can simply alter the results of the analytics performed on the data. Only some schemes, like Oblix, can handle injections and malicious entities (Table 5).

By using just the *volume* of the range queries, databases can be reconstructed in at most $O(N^4 log N)$ time for N unique entries in the DB [26]. Lacharite et al. [36] consider Full and Approximate *Database Reconstruction* using range queries and access pattern leakage from just $O(N)$ queries. Grubbs et al. [27] perform ϵ-Approximate Database reconstruction (ADR) through access pattern leakage relating it closely to statistical learning theory and *no Query distribution Knowledge* with ϵ admissible error. On neglecting the extremities, ADR can be performed within $O(\epsilon^{-1} log(\epsilon^{-}1))$ time, which implies that the complexity is invariant of the number of items in the DB but focuses on the error ϵ.

Attacks on Hardware – Side channel attacks, as well as denial of service are applicable to the TEE as well [16]. The licensing allows Intel to force itself as an intermediary for their enclaves. The software used for isolating the memory to create the SGX can be made malicious using privilege escalation. Cache timing attacks observe the time differences between accessing a cached and uncached memory location Private caches can partially prevent this. Simple power analysis can correlate power consumption and type of query executed. Memory mapping attacks uses address retrieval for page tables. Some attacks can be solved by pairing with an ORAM or PIR.

5.3   Future Research Directions

As highlighted in our discussion, research gaps and open questions are evident in all three types of schemes: malicious attackers are often not defendable in the constructions; EDBs face issues with the dynamic updations; search features like wildcard, stemming, concatenation are not refined or available altogether. While SSEs focus on search, only schemes like SisoSPIR [31] give a near complete and secure framework.

Artificial intelligence and machine learning algorithms on DBs are gaining interest. In general, they require vectorization for efficient computation and tackling natural language processing problems. Secure matrix multiplication is necessary to deploy neural networks even after reducing the activation functions to polynomials like ML Confidential [25]. NewSQL DBs require privacy preserving matrix multiplication, while NoSQL structures demand array multiplication,

Table 6. Attacks based on leakage levels and the affected schemes [13]

Leakage	Attacks	Schemes
$\mathcal{L}_4$ - Full-text Substitution Cipher	Full DB Reconstruction	Song et al. [56]
$\mathcal{L}_3$ - PPE - Data Distribution (Occurrence leakage)	Inference, IKK [32], Count, Record Injection	Conventional EDB: CryptDB [49], Cipherbase [7], Monomi [59], Seabed [45]
$\mathcal{L}_2$ - DET, Appended PRF - Access, Size and Search Patterns	IKK, Count, Record Injection	Unencrypted Indexes - Blind seer [46], Arx [47], etc.
$\mathcal{L}_1$ - HE/ORAM - Communication Volume	Count	Encrypted Index/Result Length Hiding - Oblix [42], SisoSPIR [31]

graph operations as well. Also, for meaningful comparison between schemes, *leakage quantification* would prove very useful and would improve security of new schemes, as leakage is unavoidable.

6   Conclusions

In this survey, we highlight how several existing schemes are vulnerable to a number of known attacks. Finding the delicate compromise between performance and security, conforming to *Anderson's Law*, can only give a viable but imperfect solution. Our discussion points to future research directions, aimed on one hand to secure schemes in the shorter term, and on the other hand to improve the real-world applicability of more secure schemes in the long term.

This survey focuses in particular on the tools required to build an EDB, along with the pros and cons of using the different methods. When designing a future EDB, the aim can be to increase security, functionality or both. As the conventional systems are weaker in security because of PPE leakage, index based schemes are preferred, though they are not immediately viable. An index based scheme supporting access pattern hiding, updates, range queries, injection, etc, would represent a significant breakthrough.

References

1. PALISADE Lattice Cryptography Library (ver.1.9.2). http://palisade-crypto.org
2. TPC benchmarks. http://www.tpc.org/information/benchmarks.asp
3. ARM security technology building a secure system using TrustZone technology (rev. C). Technical report, ARM (2009)
4. Agrawal, D., El Abbadi, A., Emekçi, F., Metwally, A.: Database management as a service: challenges and opportunities. In: IEEE ICDE, pp. 1709–1716 (2009)

5. Agrawal, R., Kiernan, J., Srikant, R., Xu, Y.: Order-preserving encryption for numeric data. In: ACM SIGMOD International Conference on Management of Data, pp. 563–574 (2004)
6. Anderson, R.J.: Security Engineering: A Guide to Building Dependable Distributed Systems, 2nd edn. Wiley, Hoboken (2008)
7. Arasu, A., Eguro, K., Joglekar, M., Kaushik, R., Kossmann, D., Ramamurthy, R.: Transaction processing on confidential data using cipherbase. In: IEEE ICDE, pp. 435–446 (2015)
8. Bajaj, S., Sion, R.: TrustedDB: a trusted hardware-based database with privacy and data confidentiality. IEEE Trans. Knowl. Data Eng. **26**(3), 752–765 (2014)
9. Boldyreva, A., Chenette, N., Lee, Y., O'Neill, A.: Order-preserving symmetric encryption. In: Joux, A. (ed.) EUROCRYPT 2009. LNCS, vol. 5479, pp. 224–241. Springer, Heidelberg (2009). https://doi.org/10.1007/978-3-642-01001-9_13
10. Bost, R.: $\sum o\varphi o\varsigma$: forward secure searchable encryption. In: ACM SIGSAC CCS, pp. 1143–1154. ACM (2016)
11. Brakerski, Z., Gentry, C., Vaikuntanathan, V.: Fully homomorphic encryption without bootstrapping. Electron. Colloquium Comput. Complex **18**, 111 (2011)
12. Canetti, R.: Universally composable security: a new paradigm for cryptographic protocols. In: Foundations of Computer Science, FOCS 2001, pp. 136–145. IEEE (2001)
13. Cash, D., Grubbs, P., Perry, J., Ristenpart, T.: Leakage-abuse attacks against searchable encryption. In: ACM SIGSAC CCS, pp. 668–679. ACM (2015)
14. Cash, D., Jarecki, S., Jutla, C., Krawczyk, H., Roşu, M.-C., Steiner, M.: Highly-scalable searchable symmetric encryption with support for Boolean queries. In: Canetti, R., Garay, J.A. (eds.) CRYPTO 2013. LNCS, vol. 8042, pp. 353–373. Springer, Heidelberg (2013). https://doi.org/10.1007/978-3-642-40041-4_20
15. Cheon, J.H., Kim, A., Kim, M., Song, Y.: Homomorphic encryption for arithmetic of approximate numbers. In: Takagi, T., Peyrin, T. (eds.) ASIACRYPT 2017. LNCS, vol. 10624, pp. 409–437. Springer, Cham (2017). https://doi.org/10.1007/978-3-319-70694-8_15
16. Costan, V., Devadas, S.: Intel SGX explained. IACR Cryptology ePrint Archive 2016/86 (2016)
17. Cui, S., Song, X., Asghar, M.R., Galbraith, S.D., Russello, G.: Privacy-preserving searchable databases with controllable leakage. CoRR abs/1909.11624 (2019)
18. van Dijk, M., Gentry, C., Halevi, S., Vaikuntanathan, V.: Fully homomorphic encryption over the integers. In: Gilbert, H. (ed.) EUROCRYPT 2010. LNCS, vol. 6110, pp. 24–43. Springer, Heidelberg (2010). https://doi.org/10.1007/978-3-642-13190-5_2
19. Dyer, J., Dyer, M.E., Djemame, K.: Order-preserving encryption using approximate common divisors. Inf. Secur. Appl. **49**, 102391 (2019)
20. Eskandarian, S., Zaharia, M.: ObliDB: oblivious query processing for secure databases. PVLDB **13**(2), 169–183 (2019). https://github.com/SabaEskandarian/ObliDB
21. Fan, J., Vercauteren, F.: Somewhat practical fully homomorphic encryption. IACR Cryptology ePrint Archive 2012/144 (2012)
22. Fuller, B., et al.: SoK: cryptographically protected database search. In: IEEE Security & Privacy, pp. 172–191 (2017)
23. Garg, S., Mohassel, P., Papamanthou, C.: TWORAM: efficient oblivious RAM in two rounds with applications to searchable encryption. In: Robshaw, M., Katz, J. (eds.) CRYPTO 2016. LNCS, vol. 9816, pp. 563–592. Springer, Heidelberg (2016). https://doi.org/10.1007/978-3-662-53015-3_20

24. Goldreich, O., Micali, S., Wigderson, A.: How to play any mental game, or a completeness theorem for protocols with honest majority. In: Providing Sound Foundations for Cryptography: On the Work of Shafi Goldwasser and Silvio Micali, pp. 307–328. ACM (2019)

25. Graepel, T., Lauter, K., Naehrig, M.: ML confidential: machine learning on encrypted data. In: Kwon, T., Lee, M.-K., Kwon, D. (eds.) ICISC 2012. LNCS, vol. 7839, pp. 1–21. Springer, Heidelberg (2013). https://doi.org/10.1007/978-3-642-37682-5_1

26. Grubbs, P., Lacharité, M., Minaud, B., Paterson, K.: Pump up the volume: practical database reconstruction from volume leakage on range queries. In: ACM CCS, pp. 315–331 (2018)

27. Grubbs, P., Lacharite, M.S., Minaud, B., Paterson, K.G.: Learning to reconstruct: statistical learning theory and encrypted database attacks. In: IEEE Security & Privacy, pp. 1067–1083 (2019)

28. Grubbs, P., Ristenpart, T., Shmatikov, V.: Why your encrypted database is not secure. In: 16th Workshop on Hot Topics in Operating Systems, pp. 162–168 (2017)

29. Halevi, S., Shoup, V.: Algorithms in HElib. In: Garay, J.A., Gennaro, R. (eds.) CRYPTO 2014. LNCS, vol. 8616, pp. 554–571. Springer, Heidelberg (2014). https://doi.org/10.1007/978-3-662-44371-2_31

30. He, W., Akhawe, D., Jain, S., Shi, E., Song, D.X.: ShadowCrypt: encrypted web applications for everyone. In: ACM SIGSAC, pp. 1028–1039. ACM (2014)

31. Ishai, Y., Kushilevitz, E., Lu, S., Ostrovsky, R.: Private large-scale databases with distributed searchable symmetric encryption. In: Sako, K. (ed.) CT-RSA 2016. LNCS, vol. 9610, pp. 90–107. Springer, Cham (2016). https://doi.org/10.1007/978-3-319-29485-8_6

32. Islam, M.S., Kuzu, M., Kantarcioglu, M.: Access pattern disclosure on searchable encryption: ramification, attack and mitigation. In: NDSS. The Internet Society (2012)

33. Jarecki, S., Jutla, C.S., Krawczyk, H., Rosu, M., Steiner, M.: Outsourced symmetric private information retrieval. In: ACM SIGSAC CCS 2013, pp. 875–888. ACM (2013)

34. Kamara, S., Papamanthou, C., Roeder, T.: Dynamic searchable symmetric encryption. In: Yu, T., Danezis, G., Gligor, V.D. (eds.) the ACM CCS 2012, pp. 965–976. ACM (2012)

35. Katz, J., Lindell, Y.: Introduction to Modern Cryptography, 2nd edn. CRC Press, Boca Raton (2014)

36. Lacharité, M., Minaud, B., Paterson, K.G.: Improved reconstruction attacks on encrypted data using range query leakage. In: 2018 IEEE Security & Privacy, pp. 297–314 (2018)

37. Lai, S., Yuan, X., Sun, S., Liu, J.K., Liu, Y., Liu, D.: GraphSE^2: an encrypted graph database for privacy-preserving social search. In: ACM Security Asia CCS, pp. 41–54. ACM (2019)

38. Lau, B., Chung, S.P., Song, C., Jang, Y., Lee, W., Boldyreva, A.: Mimesis aegis: a mimicry privacy shield-a system's approach to data privacy on public cloud. In: 23rd USENIX Security Symposium. pp. 33–48. USENIX Association (2014)

39. Lewi, K., Wu, D.J.: Order-revealing encryption: new constructions, applications, and lower bounds. In: ACM SIGSAC- CCS 2016. ACM Press (2016)

40. Liu, G., Yang, G., Wang, H., Xiang, Y., Dai, H.: A novel secure scheme for supporting complex SQL queries over encrypted databases in cloud computing. Secur. Commun. Netw. **2018**(2), 1–15 (2018)

41. Meng, X., Kamara, S., Nissim, K., Kollios, G.: GRECS: graph encryption for approximate shortest distance queries. In: 22nd ACM SIGSAC. ACM (2015)
42. Mishra, P., Poddar, R., Chen, J., Chiesa, A., Popa, R.A.: Oblix: an efficient oblivious search index. In: 2018 IEEE Symposium on Security and Privacy, pp. 279–296 (2018)
43. Naveed, M., Kamara, S., Wright, C.V.: Inference attacks on property preserving encrypted databases. In: 22nd ACM SIGSAC-CCS 2015. ACM Press (2015)
44. Paillier, P.: Public-key cryptosystems based on composite degree residuosity classes. In: Stern, J. (ed.) EUROCRYPT 1999. LNCS, vol. 1592, pp. 223–238. Springer, Heidelberg (1999). https://doi.org/10.1007/3-540-48910-X_16
45. Papadimitriou, A., et al.: Big data analytics over encrypted datasets with seabed. In: 12th USENIX Symposium on OS Design and Implementation. USENIX Association (2016)
46. Pappas, V., et al.: Blind seer: a scalable private DBMS. In: 2014 IEEE Security & Privacy, pp. 359–374. IEEE (2014)
47. Poddar, R., Boelter, T., Popa, R.A.: Arx: an encrypted database using semantically secure encryption. Proc. VLDB Endow. **12**(11), 1664–1678 (2019)
48. Popa, R.A., Li, F.H., Zeldovich, N.: An ideal-security protocol for order-preserving encoding. In: 2013 IEEE Symposium on Security and Privacy, pp. 463–477 (2013)
49. Popa, R.A., Redfield, C.M.S., Zeldovich, N., Balakrishnan, H.: CryptDB: processing queries on an encrypted database. Commun. ACM **55**(9), 103–111 (2012). https://github.com/CryptDB/cryptdb
50. Pouliot, D., Wright, C.V.: The shadow nemesis: inference attacks on efficiently deployable, efficiently searchable encryption. In: ACM SIGSAC, pp. 1341–1352. ACM (2016)
51. Priebe, C., Vaswani, K., Costa, M.: EnclaveDB: a secure database using SGX. In: 2018 IEEE Symposium on Security and Privacy, pp. 264–278 (2018)
52. Saha, T.K., Rathee, M., Koshiba, T.: Efficient private database queries using ring-LWE somewhat homomorphic encryption. J. Inf. Secur. Appl. **49**, 102406 (2019)
53. Sarfraz, M.I., Nabeel, M., Cao, J., Bertino, E.: DBMask: fine-grained access control on encrypted relational databases. Trans. Data Priv. **9**(3), 187–214 (2016)
54. Microsoft SEAL: Microsoft Research (release 3.5), Redmond, WA (2020). https://github.com/Microsoft/SEAL
55. Shay, R., Blumenthal, U., Gadepally, V., Hamlin, A., Mitchell, J., Cunningham, R.: Don't even ask: database access control through query control. SIGMOD Rec. **47**(3), 17–22 (2018)
56. Song, D.X., Wagner, D.A., Perrig, A.: Practical techniques for searches on encrypted data. In: 2000 IEEE Symposium on Security and Privacy, pp. 44–55 (2000)
57. Stefanov, E., et al.: Path ORAM: an extremely simple oblivious RAM protocol. J. ACM **65**(4), 18:1–18:26 (2018)
58. Tex, C., Schäler, M., Böhm, K.: Towards meaningful distance-preserving encryption. In: 30th International Conference on Scientific and Statistical Database Management, SSDBM, pp. 2:1–2:12 (2018)
59. Tu, S., Kaashoek, M.F., Madden, S., Zeldovich, N.: Processing analytical queries over encrypted data. Proc. VLDB Endow. **6**, 289–300 (2013). https://github.com/stephentu/monomi-optimizer/
60. Vinayagamurthy, D., Gribov, A., Gorbunov, S.: StealthDB: a scalable encrypted database with full SQL query support. PoPETs **2019**(3), 370–388 (2019)
61. Wiese, L., Waage, T., Brenner, M.: CloudDBGuard: a framework for encrypted data storage in NoSQL wide column stores. Data Knowl. Eng. **126**, 101732 (2020)

62. Wong, W.K., Cheung, D.W., Kao, B., Mamoulis, N.: Secure kNN computation on encrypted databases. In: ACM SIGMOD 2009, pp. 139–152 (2009)
63. Yao, A.C.: Protocols for secure computations (extended abstract). In: 23rd Annual Symposium on Foundations of Computer Science, pp. 160–164. IEEE Computer Society (1982)
64. Yuan, X., Guo, Y., Wang, X., Wang, C., Li, B., Jia, X.: EncKV: an encrypted key-value store with rich queries. In: ACM Asia CCS, pp. 423–435 (2017)
65. Zhou, Y., Li, N., Tian, Y., An, D., Wang, L.: Public key encryption with keyword search in cloud: a survey. Entropy **22**(4), 421 (2020)

Fast Short and Fast Linear Cramer-Shoup

Pascal Lafourcade[1], Léo Robert[1(✉)], and Demba Sow[2]

[1] University Clermont Auvergne, LIMOS, CNRS UMR 6158, Aubière, France
{pascal.lafourcade,leo.robert}@uca.fr
[2] LACGAA, University Cheikh Anta Diop of Dakar, Dakar, Senegal
demba1.sow@ucad.edu.sn

Abstract. A linear Cramer-Shoup encryption scheme version was proposed by Shacham in 2007. Short Cramer-Shoup encryption scheme was designed by Abdalla et al. in 2014. This scheme is a variant of the Cramer-Shoup encryption scheme that has a smaller size. They proved that it is an IND-PCA secure encryption under DDH and the collision-resistance assumptions. We design a faster version of Short Cramer-Shoup encryption scheme denoted *Fast Short Cramer-Shoup* encryption. We also, proposed a faster version of linear Cramer-Shoup encryption called *Fast Linear Cramer-Shoup*. We prove that the Fast Short Cramer-Shoup is IND-PCA secure under DDH and the collision-resistance assumptions. We also, show that our linear encryption is CCA secure under the Linear assumption. Finally we run an evaluation of performances of our schemes.

Keywords: Short Cramer-Shoup · Linear Cramer-Shoup · Linear assumption · IND-CCA · IND-PCA

1 Introduction

Cramer-Shoup cryptosystem was introduced in 1998 by Cramer et al. in [5]. It is an encryption scheme based on ElGamal encryption that is IND-CCA secure. In [14], a linear version of Cramer-Shoup scheme was proposed. A short Cramer-Shoup scheme was also proposed in [1]. This scheme improves the performance of Cramer-Shoup scheme by reducing the number of generators in G and the number of parameters of the keys. This scheme is also IND-PCA secure which is lower security notion than IND-CCA and stronger than IND-CPA. But applied to small messages, IND-PCA implies IND-CCA.

Contributions. Our main aim is to improve the efficiency of Short and Linear Cramer-Shoup public key schemes. Our contributions are as follows:

- We design a cryptographic encryption scheme, called *Fast Short Cramer-Shoup*, based on the Generalized ElGamal encryption scheme [16]. We follow the spirit of Short Cramer-Shoup versions introduced in [1]. We modify the key generation and the decryption algorithm to be faster. We prove its security against Plaintext-Checking Attack (IND-PCA) under the Decisional Diffie-Hellman (DDH) and the collision-resistance assumptions.

© Springer Nature Switzerland AG 2021
G. Nicolescu et al. (Eds.): FPS 2020, LNCS 12637, pp. 121–136, 2021.
https://doi.org/10.1007/978-3-030-70881-8_8

- We also design a *Fast Linear Short Cramer-Shoup* scheme. We prove that our linear scheme is secure in the CCA sense if $\mathcal{HF}$ a secure **UOWHF** family and the Linear assumption hold in a group G.
- Finally, we implement all these schemes with GMP [10] to demonstrate that Fast Short Cramer-Shoup and Fast Linear Cramer-Shoup are significantly faster than Short Cramer-Shoup and Linear Cramer-Shoup respectively.

Related Works. ElGamal cryptosystem was proposed in 1984 by T. ElGamal in [9]. It was one of the first cryptosystems whose security was based on the problem of the discrete logarithm (DLP). ElGamal's scheme is IND-CPA secure under the Decisional Diffie-Hellman (DDH) hypothesis. Cramer-Shoup is a cryptosystem proposed by Cramer et al. in [5]. It is based on ElGamal's scheme and it is IND-CCA2 secure under the DDH assumption. Many versions based on Original Cramer-Shoup scheme [5] have been introduced. The original Cramer-Shoup's scheme presented in the eprint version [6], then the standard Cramer-Shoup's version published in CRYPTO'98 [5], the efficient Cramer-Shoup's version also proposed in [6] and finally Short Cramer-Shoup's version proposed in [1]. The main difference of Original and Standard Cramer-Shoup schemes is that the Standard scheme uses only one exponent z to compute the public parameter h instead of two exponents z_1 and z_2 in the Original scheme. In Sect. 4 of [6], the efficient variant of the Cramer-Shoup scheme is presented. Note that Original and Efficient Cramer-Shoup encryption algorithms are exactly the same. But theirs key generation and decryption algorithms are slightly different. In Efficient Cramer-Shoup, the key generation uses less elements and then less exponentiations. Short Cramer-Shoup scheme [1] is a variant of the above Cramer-Shoup scheme [5]. In Short Cramer-Shoup, key generation algorithm uses less generator and less elements in public and secret keys. Original, Standard and Efficient Cramer-Shoup schemes are IND-CCA secure under DDH but Short Cramer-Shoup scheme is IND-PCA secure under the DDH and the collision-resistance assumptions. In [8], Boneh et al. introduced the Decisional Linear Assumption (DLin) and proposed a linear scheme based on ElGamal. The linear ElGamal scheme is IND-CPA secure under the (DLin). In [14], Linear Cramer-Shoup scheme is presented. As Original Cramer-Shoup scheme, the Linear Cramer-Shoup scheme is IND-CCA secure under DDH. We improve both Short and Linear Cramer-Shoup schemes.

Outline. In Sect. 2, we recall public key encryption and the existing Cramer-Shoup schemes. In Sect. 3, we present our Fast Short Cramer-Shoup encryption scheme. In Sect. 4, we also propose a Fast Linear version of Cramer-Shoup. In Sect. 5, we show the results of our performance evaluations. The security proofs of our proposed schemes are available in [3].

2   Preliminaries

Boneh et al. [8] introduced a Decisional assumption, called Linear, intended to take the place of DDH in groups - in particular, bilinear groups [11] - where

DDH is easy. For this setting, the Linear problem has desirable properties, as they have shown: it is hard if DDH is hard, but, at least in generic groups [15], it remains hard even if DDH is easy. Let G be a cyclic multiplicative group of prime order p, and let g_1, g_2, and g_3 be arbitrary generators of G, we consider the following problem:

Linear Problem in G: Given $g_1, g_2, g_3, g_1^a, g_2^b, g_3^c \in G$ as input, output yes if $a + b = c$ and no otherwise. The advantage of an algorithm $\mathcal{A}$ in deciding the Linear problem in G is denoted by $\mathbf{Adv}_{\mathcal{A}}^{\text{linear}}$ and it is equal to:

$$|Pr[\mathcal{A}(g_1, g_2, g_3, g_1^a, g_2^b, g_3^{a+b}) = yes : g_1, g_2, g_3 \xleftarrow{\$} G, a, b \xleftarrow{\$} \mathbb{Z}_p]$$
$$-Pr[\mathcal{A}(g_1, g_2, g_3, g_1^a, g_2^b, \eta) = yes : g_1, g_2, g_3, \eta \xleftarrow{\$} G, a, b \xleftarrow{\$} \mathbb{Z}_p]|$$

with the probability taken over the uniform random choice of the parameters to $\mathcal{A}$ and over the coin tosses of $\mathcal{A}$. We say that an algorithm $\mathcal{A}(t, \epsilon)$-decides Linear in G if $\mathcal{A}$ runs in time at most t, and $\mathbf{Adv}_{\mathcal{A}}^{\text{linear}}$ is at least ϵ.

Definition 1. *We say that the (t, ϵ)-Decision Linear Assumption holds in G if no algorithm (t, ϵ)-decides the Decision Linear problem in G.*

The Linear problem is well defined in any group where DDH is well defined. It is mainly used in bilinear groups like in [4, 7, 13].

2.1 Original Cramer-Shoup Scheme

We recall the original Cramer-Shoup encryption scheme presented in the eprint version [6]. It is composed of a key generation algorithm, an encryption and a decryption algorithm. The decryption algorithm consists into two algorithms one for recovering from the ciphertext the plaintext and one to check the non-malleability of the ciphertext in order to ensure IND-CCA2 security. We define three functions: the setup function, denoted CS.KG(), the encryption function, denoted CS.Enc() and the decryption function, denoted CS.Dec().

CS.KG(1^λ): Select a group G of prime order q. Choose eight random elements: $g_1, g_2 \in G$ and $x_1, x_2, y_1, y_2, z_1, z_2 \in \mathbb{Z}_q$.
Compute in G: $c = g_1^{x_1} g_2^{x_2}$, $d = g_1^{y_1} g_2^{y_2}$ and $h = g_1^{z_1} g_2^{z_2}$. Choose a hash function H that hashes messages to elements of $\mathbb{Z}_q$. Return (pk, sk) where $pk = (g_1, g_2, c, d, h, H)$ and $sk = (x_1, x_2, y_1, y_2, z_1, z_2)$.

CS.Enc(pk, M): To encrypt message m with $pk = (g_1, g_2, c, d, h, H)$, choose a random element $r \in \mathbb{Z}_q$. Compute $u_1 = g_1^r, u_2 = g_2^r, e = h^r m, \alpha = H(u_1, u_2, e)$ and $v = c^r d^{r\alpha}$. Return the following ciphertext: (u_1, u_2, e, v).

CS.Dec(sk, ct): Knowing sk, decrypt a ciphertext (u_1, u_2, e, v). Compute $\alpha = H(u_1, u_2, e)$. Verify if $u_1^{x_1 + y_1\alpha} u_2^{x_2 + y_2\alpha} = v$. Output $m = e u_1^{-z_1} u_2^{-z_2}$ if the condition holds, otherwise output "reject".

Correctness
Verification: Since $u_1 = g_1^r$ and $u_2 = g_2^r$, we have: $u_1^{x_1 + y_1\alpha} u_2^{x_2 + y_2\alpha} = u_1^{x_1} u_2^{x_2} (u_1^{y_1} u_2^{y_2})^\alpha = (g_1^{x_1} g_2^{x_2})^r (g_1^{y_1} g_2^{y_2})^{r\alpha} = c^r d^{r\alpha} = v$.
Decryption: $e u_1^{-z_1} u_2^{-z_2} = h^r m g_1^{-rz_1} g_2^{-rz_2} = h^r m h^{-r} = m$.

2.2 Linear Cramer-Shoup Scheme

We recall the Linear Cramer-Shoup Encryption [14]. We define three functions: the setup function, denoted LCS.KG(), the encryption function, denoted LCS.Enc() and the decryption function, denoted LCS.Dec().

LCS.KG(1^λ): Choose random generators $g_1, g_2, g_3 \xleftarrow{\$} G$ and exponents $x_1, x_2, x_3, y_1, y_2, y_3, z_1, z_2, z_3 \xleftarrow{\$} \mathbb{Z}_p$ and set $c_1 \leftarrow g_1^{x_1} g_3^{x_3}$, $d_1 \leftarrow g_1^{y_1} g_3^{y_3}$, $h_1 \leftarrow g_1^{z_1} g_3^{z_3}$ $c_2 \leftarrow g_2^{x_2} g_3^{x_3}$, $d_2 \leftarrow g_2^{y_2} g_3^{y_3}$, $h_2 \leftarrow g_2^{z_2} g_3^{z_3}$. Choose a **UOWHF** $H \xleftarrow{\$} \mathcal{HF}$. The public key is $pk = (g_1, g_2, g_3, c_1, c_2, d_1, d_2, h_1, h_2)$; the secret key is $sk = (x_1, x_2, x_3, y_1, y_2, y_3, z_1, z_2, z_3)$.

LCS.Enc(pk, M): To encrypt a message $M \in G$, using $pk = (g_1, g_2, g_3, c_1, c_2, d_1, d_2, h_1, h_2)$. Choose random exponents $r_1, r_2 \xleftarrow{\$} \mathbb{Z}_p$, and set $u_1 \leftarrow g_1^{r_1}, u_2 \leftarrow g_2^{r_2}$, $u_3 \leftarrow g_3^{r_1+r_2}$ and $e \leftarrow M h_1^{r_1} h_2^{r_2}$; now compute $\alpha \leftarrow H(u_1, u_2, u_3, e)$ and finally, $v \leftarrow (c_1 d_1^\alpha)^{r_1}(c_2 d_2^\alpha)^{r_2}$. The ciphertext is $ct = (u_1, u_2, u_3, e, v)$.

LCS.Dec(sk, ct): Parse pk as $(g_1, g_2, g_3, c_1, c_2, d_1, d_2, h_1, h_2, H)$, the private key sk as $(x_1, x_2, x_3, y_1, y_2, y_3, z_1, z_2, z_3)$ and the ciphertext ct as (u_1, u_2, u_3, e, v). Compute $\alpha \leftarrow H(u_1, u_2, u_3, e)$ and test that $u_1^{x_1+\alpha y_1} u_2^{x_2+\alpha y_2} u_3^{x_3+\alpha y_3} \stackrel{?}{=} v$ holds. If it does not, output "**reject**".
Otherwise, compute and output $M \leftarrow e/(u_1^{z_1} u_2^{z_2} u_3^{z_3})$.

Correctness: If the keys and encryption are generated according to the algorithms above, the test in **LCS.Dec** is satisfied, since we have

$$
\begin{aligned}
v &= (c_1 d_1^\alpha)^{r_1}(c_2 d_2^\alpha)^{r_2} \\
&= (g_1^{x_1+\alpha y_1} g_3^{x_3+\alpha y_3})^{r_1} \cdot (g_2^{x_2+\alpha y_2} g_3^{x_3+\alpha y_3})^{r_2} \\
&= (g_1^{r_1})^{x_1+\alpha y_1} \cdot (g_2^{r_2})^{x_2+\alpha y_2} \cdot (g_3^{r_1+r_2})^{x_3+\alpha y_3} \\
&= u_1^{x_1+\alpha y_1} \cdot u_2^{x_2+\alpha y_2} \cdot u_3^{x_3+\alpha y_3}
\end{aligned}
$$

Next, decryption algorithm computes M as follows,

$$
\begin{aligned}
e/(u_1^{z_1} u_2^{z_2} u_3^{z_3}) &= e/(g_1^{r_1 z_1} g_2^{r_2 z_2} g_3^{(r_1+r_2)z_3}) \\
&= (e)/((g_1^{z_1} g_3^{z_3})^{r_1}(g_2^{z_2} g_3^{z_3})^{r_2}) \\
&= (M \cdot h_1^{r_1} h_2^{r_2}) \cdot (h_1^{r_1} h_2^{r_2}) \\
&= M.
\end{aligned}
$$

Security Proof of Linear Cramer-Shoup (LCS)

Theorem 1 [14]. *LCS scheme is IND-CCA secure if $\mathcal{HF}$ is a secure* **UOWHF** *family and if the Linear assumption holds in G.*

2.3   Short Cramer-Shoup Scheme

The Short Cramer-Shoup (SCS) encryption scheme [1] is a variant of the above Cramer-Shoup encryption scheme [5], but with one less element. It is defined as follows, in a cyclic group G of prime order p, with a generator g, together with a hash function H randomly drawn from a collision-resistant hash function family $\mathcal{HF}$ [12] from the set $\{0,1\}^* \times G^2$ to the set $G \backslash \{1\}$. We define three functions: the setup function, denoted SCS.KG(), the encryption function, denoted SCS.Enc() and the decryption function, denoted SCS.Dec(). We now describe how these functions work.

SCS.KG(1^λ): Pick five random elements $s, a, b, a', b' \in \mathbb{Z}_p$.
  Compute $h = g^s, c = g^a h^b, d = g^{a'} h^{b'}$.
  Return (pk, sk), where $pk = (g, h, c, d, H)$ and $sk = (s, a, b, a', b')$.
SCS.Enc(pk, m): To encrypt a message m with $pk = (g, h, c, d, H)$, choose random element $r \in \mathbb{Z}_p$. Compute $u = g^r, e = h^r m, \alpha = H(u, e)$ and $v = (c(d^\alpha))^r$. Output the ciphertext (u, e, v).
SCS.Dec$^\ell$(sk, ct): To decrypt a ciphertext (u, e, v) using sk, compute $\alpha = H(u, e)$. Then compute $m = eu^{-s}$ and check $v = u^{a+a'\alpha}(em^{-1})^{b+b'\alpha}$. Output m if the condition holds, otherwise output "reject".

Correctness
Decryption: $eu^{-s} = g^{sr} m g^{-sr} = m$, since $u = g^r$, $e = h^r m$ and $h = g^s$.
Verification: $u^{a+a'\alpha}(em^{-1})^{b+b'\alpha} = (g^r)^{a+a'\alpha}(g^{sr})^{b+b'\alpha} = (g^a h^a(g^{a'}h^{b'})^\alpha)^r = (c(d^\alpha))^r = v$.

Security Proof of Short Cramer-Shoup

Theorem 2 [1]. *The Short Cramer-Shoup (SCS) is IND-PCA under the DDH and the collision-resistance assumptions:*
$$Adv_{SCS}^{ind\text{-}pca}(t) \leq Adv_{\mathbb{G}}^{ddh}(t) + Succ_{\mathcal{H}}^{coll}(t) + 2(q_p+1)/p, \text{ where } q_p \text{ is the number}$$
of queries to the OPCA oracle.

3   Fast Short Cramer-Shoup

We define three functions: the setup function FSCS.KG(), the encryption function FSCS.Enc() and the decryption function FSCS.Dec().

FSCS.KG(1^λ): Select a cyclic group G of prime order p and a generator g. Pick two random elements $k, q \in \mathbb{Z}_p$ such that the size of q is half of the size of p, i.e., $log_2(q) = \frac{log_2(p)}{2}$. Compute $s', t \in \mathbb{Z}_p$ such that $kp = qs' + t$ and $s \equiv s'(mod\ p)$. Note that the size of t is smaller or equal to the size of q, i.e., $log_2(t) \leq log_2(q)$. Pick four random elements $a, b, a', b' \in \mathbb{Z}_p$. Compute $g_1 = g^s, h = g^t, c = g_1^a h^b, d = g_1^{a'} h^{b'}$. Choose a hash function H that hashes messages to elements of G. Return (pk, sk), where $pk = (g_1, h, c, d, H)$ and $sk = (q, a, b, a', b')$.

FSCS.Enc(pk, m): To encrypt a message m with $pk = (g_1, h, c, d, H)$, choose random element $r \in \mathbb{Z}_p$. Compute $u = g_1^r, e = h^r m, \alpha = H(u, e)$ and $v = (c(d^\alpha))^r$. Output the ciphertext $ct = (u, e, v)$.

FSCS.Dec(sk, ct): To decrypt a ciphertext ct with $sk = (q, a, b, a', b')$. Compute $\alpha = H(u, e)$. Compute $m = eu^q$ and verify if $v = u^{a+a'\alpha}(em^{-1})^{b+b'\alpha}$. Output m if the condition holds, otherwise output "reject".

Correctness

Decryption: $eu^q = g^{tr}mg^{srq} = mg^{r(sq+t)} = mg^{rkp} = m$, since $u = g^{sr}$, $e = h^r m$ and $h = g^t$.

Verification: $u^{a+a'\alpha}(em^{-1})^{b+b'\alpha} = (g^{sr})^{a+a'\alpha}(h^r)^{b+b'\alpha} = (g_1^a h^b(g_1^{a'} h^{b'})^\alpha)^r = (c(d^\alpha))^r = v$.

IND-PCA Security Proof of Fast Short Cramer-Shoup Scheme. We use the same notions and follows the same proof technique as in [1,2].

Theorem 3. *The Fast Short Cramer-Shoup (FSCS) is IND-PCA under the DDH and the collision-resistance assumptions:*
$$\mathbf{Adv}_{FSCS}^{ind\text{-}pca}(t) \leq \mathbf{Adv}_{\mathbb{G}}^{ddh}(t) + \mathbf{Succ}_{\mathcal{H}}^{coll}(t) + 2(q_p+1)/p, \text{ where } q_p \text{ is the number}$$
of queries to the OPCA oracle.

The full proof is given in [3] and follows the proof of [1].

4   Fast Linear Cramer-Shoup

We define three functions: the setup function, denoted FLCS.KG(), the encryption function, denoted FLCS.Enc() and the decryption function, denoted FLCS.Dec().

FLCS.KG(1^λ): Choose a random generator $g \xleftarrow{\$} G$ of order p and random elements $k_1, k_2, k_3, q_1, q_2, q_3, x_1, x_2, x_3, y_1, y_2, y_3 \xleftarrow{\$} \mathbb{Z}_p$ such that the size of q_i $(i \in \{1, 2, 3\})$ is half of the size of p, i.e., $log_2(q_i) = \frac{log_2(p)}{2}$. Compute $s_1, s_2, s_3, t_1, t_2, t_3 \in \mathbb{Z}_p$ such that $k_i p = q_i s_i + t_i$ and $0 < s_i < p$ $(i \in \{1, 2, 3\})$ and set $b_1 = g^{s_1}$, $b_2 = g^{s_2}$, $b_3 = g^{s_3}$, $c_1 \leftarrow b_1^{x_1} b_3^{x_3}$, $d_1 \leftarrow b_1^{y_1} b_3^{y_3}$, $h_1 \leftarrow g^{t_1+t_3}$, $c_2 \leftarrow b_2^{x_2} b_3^{x_3}$, $d_2 \leftarrow b_2^{y_2} b_3^{y_3}$, $h_2 \leftarrow g^{t_2+t_3}$. The public key is $pk = (b_1, b_2, b_3, c_1, c_2, d_1, d_2, h_1, h_2)$ and the secret key is $sk = (q_1, q_2, q_3, x_1, x_2, x_3, y_1, y_2, y_3)$.

FLCS.Enc(pk, M): To encrypt a message M using pk, choose random exponents $r_1, r_2 \xleftarrow{\$} \mathbb{Z}_p$, and set $u_1 \leftarrow b_1^{r_1}$, $u_2 \leftarrow b_2^{r_2}$, $u_3 \leftarrow b_3^{r_1+r_2}$ and $e \leftarrow Mh_1^{r_1} h_2^{r_2}$. Now compute $\alpha \leftarrow H(u_1, u_2, u_3, e)$ and finally, $v \leftarrow (c_1 d_1^\alpha)^{r_1}(c_2 d_2^\alpha)^{r_2}$. The ciphertext is $ct = (u_1, u_2, u_3, e, v) \in G^5$.

FLCS.Dec(pk, sk, ct): Parse the ciphertext ct as $(u_1, u_2, u_3, e, v) \in G^5$. Compute $\alpha \leftarrow H(u_1, u_2, u_3, e)$ and check $u_1^{x_1+\alpha y_1} u_2^{x_2+\alpha y_2} u_3^{x_3+\alpha y_3} \stackrel{?}{=} v$. If not, output "**reject**". Otherwise, compute and output $M \leftarrow e(u_1^{q_1} u_2^{q_2} u_3^{q_3})$.

Correctness. If the keys and encryption are generated according to the algorithms above, the test in **FLCS.Dec** is satisfied, since we then have

$$
\begin{aligned}
v &= (c_1 d_1^\alpha)^{r_1} (c_2 d_2^\alpha)^{r_2} \\
&= \left(g^{s_1 x_1 + s_3 x_3} g^{(s_1 y_1 + s_3 y_3)\alpha} \right)^{r_1} \cdot \left(g^{s_2 x_2 + s_3 x_3} g^{(s_2 y_2 + s_3 y_3)\alpha} \right)^{r_2} \\
&= \left(g^{s_1(x_1 + \alpha y_1)} \right)^{r_1} \cdot \left(g^{s_2(x_2 + \alpha y_2)} \right)^{r_2} \cdot \left(g^{s_3(x_3 + \alpha y_3)} \right)^{(r_1 + r_2)} \\
&= (b_1^{r_1})^{x_1 + \alpha y_1} \cdot (b_2^{r_2})^{x_2 + \alpha y_2} \cdot \left(b_3^{(r_1 + r_2)} \right)^{(x_3 + \alpha y_3)} \\
&= u_1^{x_1 + \alpha y_1} \cdot u_2^{x_2 + \alpha y_2} \cdot u_3^{x_3 + \alpha y_3}
\end{aligned}
$$

Next, decryption algorithm recovers the correct M,

$$
\begin{aligned}
e(u_1^{q_1} u_2^{q_2} u_3^{q_3}) &= M \cdot h_1^{r_1} h_2^{r_2} \cdot b_1^{r_1 q_1} \cdot b_2^{r_2 q_2} \cdot b_3^{r_3 q_3} \\
&= M \cdot g^{(t_1 + t_3) r_1} g^{(t_2 + t_3) r_2} g^{s_1 r_1 q_1} g^{s_2 r_2 q_2} g^{s_3 r_3 q_3} \\
&= M g^{r_1(t_1 + q_1 s_1)} \cdot g^{r_2(t_2 + q_2 s_2)} \cdot g^{r_3(t_3 + q_3 s_3)} \\
&= M g^{r_1 k_1 p} \cdot g^{r_2 k_2 p} \cdot g^{r_3 k_3 p} \\
&= M.
\end{aligned}
$$

Security proof of Fast Linear Cramer-Shoup (FLCS). We now show that the the FLCS scheme is CCA secure.

Theorem 4. *The FLCS scheme is secure in the CCA sense if $\mathcal{HF}$ a secure UOWHF family and the Linear assumption hold in G.*

The full proof is given in [3] and follows the proof of [14].

5   Performances Evaluation

We compare efficiency between our proposed schemes and existing ones. We first study the complexity and the performance of the short Cramer-Shoup variant, namely *Fast Short Cramer-Shoup* encryption scheme (Sect. 3) and *Short Cramer-Shoup* encryption scheme (Sect. 2.3). Next, we study the complexity and the performance of the linear construction, namely *Fast Linear Cramer-Shoup* encryption scheme (Sect. 4) with *Linear Cramer-Shoup* encryption scheme (Sect. 2.2).

In both cases (short and linear variants), we chose to compare them algorithm by algorithm. Hence, we study key generation, encryption and decryption algorithms apart. Note that the decryption algorithm is composed of two steps: a verification and the actual decryption (for retrieving the initial message). Thus, the full decryption algorithm is divided in two, each part corresponding to those specific phases (verification and actual decryption).

For all algorithms, we split the study in two approaches to conduct such comparison. The first one is relative to the theoretical complexity; we look the number of operations needed for each algorithm. The second one is an experimental study. For this, we have implemented the schemes using the C-library GMP [10] for computing the average execution time of algorithms. In all schemes, there are 1000 execution trials where new security parameters and messages are randomly generated for each execution. For a complete comparison though, the security parameters (such as prime number) and messages are the same for the schemes. The curves shown are the average execution time for a given size of security parameter (from $2^9 = 512$ to $2^{12} = 4096$ bits). Our proposed schemes are always represented by (black) circle points whereas standard schemes (Linear CS and Short CS) are represented by (blue) square points.

Table 1. Comparison of Short and Fast Short Cramer-Shoup for key parameters.

Public key parameters		
Number of	Short CS	Fast Short CS
Elements	4	4
Secret key parameters		
Elements	5	5

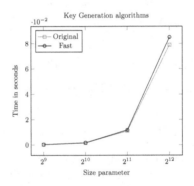

Fig. 1. Key generation comparison of Short and Fast Cramer-Shoup.

5.1 Short and Fast Short Cramer-Shoup

Key Generation Algorithms. We look for the differences between the key generation algorithm of *Fast Short CS* (Sect. 3) and *Short CS* protocol (Sect. 2.3). Table 1 shows that our scheme has the same number of parameters in the public and secret keys. Table 2 gives the number of parameters needed in this phase. The most noticeable difference lies in the number of modular exponentiations. Indeed, the short version uses only 5 of them while our uses 6. The additional exponent comes from the term $g_1 = g^s$; our construction implies to use this

Table 2. Comparison of Short and Fast Short Cramer-Shoup. We emphasize the minimum for each row with bold.

Key generation		
Number of	Short CS	Fast Short CS
Generator	1	1
Random	**5**	7
Multiplication	2	2
Exponentiation	**5**	6

Table 3. Comparison of Short and Fast Short Cramer-Shoup for encryption.

Encryption		
Number of	Short CS	Fast Short CS
Random	1	1
Multiplication	2	2
Exponentiation	4	4

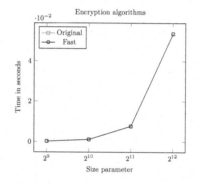

Fig. 2. Encryption comparison of Short and Fast Cramer-Shoup.

element instead of a simple generator (as in the standard version). This computation's difference can be observed in Fig. 1, as expected. We conclude that key generation is slightly slower for our proposed scheme. However, this inconvenient will be greatly rewarded during the decryption algorithm. Note that the key generation algorithm is ran only once per party thus the balance is in favour of the *Fast Short Cramer-Shoup* if several messages are sent/received with the same pair of key (i.e., the practical case).

Encryption Algorithms. We now study the encryption algorithm. Since both schemes use the same encryption algorithm, we have the same number of operations, as it is shown in Table 3. This matches with the average execution time given in Fig. 2.

Decryption Algorithms. Our contribution lies on a faster decryption algorithm. The average execution time is given in Fig. 3.

The decryption algorithms are composed of two distinct phases: a verification to check integrity of the message sent, and the actual decryption where the message is decrypted. Note that the full decryption algorithm from the short variant of Cramer-Shoup is reversed toward the standard Cramer-Shoup. The actual decryption is done first then the verification is computed from the message previously retrieved.

Table 4. Comparison of Short and Fast Short Cramer-Shoup for decryption.

Decryption		
Number of	Short CS	Fast Short CS
Inverse	1	**0**
Multiplication	1	1
Exponentiation	1	1

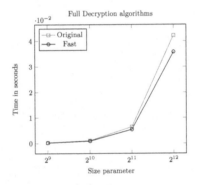

Fig. 3. Full decryption comparison of Short and Fast Cramer-Shoup.

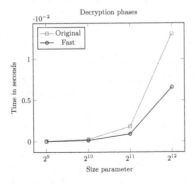

Fig. 4. Comparison of Short and Fast Cramer-Shoup for the actual decryption.

Actual Decryption. Our construction is dedicated to improve the actual decryption. There are two explanations for understanding the improvement of the average execution time (Fig. 4) during this phase. Firstly, The number of multiplication and modular exponentiation are the same, but the number of operations is reduced for the *Fast Short CS*. As depicted in Table 4, there is no inverse computation while the *Short CS* needs one. The second explanation lies on the modular exponentiation itself (from a purely computational point of view).

Indeed, despite the fact that both algorithms have the same computation there is a major difference, namely the size of the exponent. In the *Fast Short CS*, the exponent q has its size half of the security parameter leading to a faster modular exponentiation.

Verification Phase. Both schemes have the same verification computations thus we have the same average execution time as shown in Fig. 5 (Table 5).

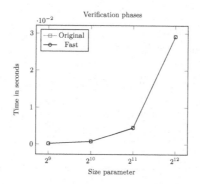

Fig. 5. Comparison of Short and Fast Cramer-Shoup for verification.

Table 5. Comparison of Short and Fast Short Cramer-Shoup for verification.

Verification		
Number of	Short CS	Fast Short CS
Inverse	1	1
Multiplication	2	2
Exponentiation	2	2

5.2 Linear and Fast Linear Cramer-Shoup

We study the complexity and average execution time of the algorithms of *Linear CS* and *Fast Linear CS*. We compare the key generation algorithms of *Linear CS* and *Fast Linear CS*. From Table 6, we can see that there is one less modular exponentiation in the standard scheme. However, the fast version has two exponentiations: $h_1 = g^{t_1+t_3}$ and $h_1 = g^{t_2+t_3}$, where elements t_i are computed as the rest of the euclidean division (recall that the equations are : $k_i p = q_i s_i + t_i$ for $i = 1, 2, 3$). We have $t_i \leq q_i$ where the size of q_i is the half of the size of p. Thus elements t_i have in average a size half of the size of q_i leading to smaller exponentiation of h_1 and h_2 in the fast version. In addition, the fast variant has two less multiplications than the standard scheme. The results of our experiences, presented in Fig. 6, confirm this slight improvement. As shown in Table 7 both schemes have the same number of key parameters.

Table 6. Key generation comparison of Linear and Fast Linear Cramer-Shoup.

Key Generation		
Number of	Linear CS	Fast Linear CS
Generator	3	**1**
Random	9	9
Multiplication	6	**4**
Exponentiation	12	13

Table 7. Key parameters comparison of Linear and Fast Linear Cramer-Shoup.

Public key parameters		
Number of	Linear CS	Fast Linear Fast CS
Elements	9	9
Secret key parameters		
Elements	9	9

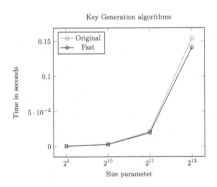

Fig. 6. Key generation comparison of Linear and Fast Linear Cramer-Shoup.

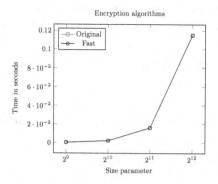

Fig. 7. Encryption comparison of Linear and Fast Linear Cramer-Shoup.

Table 8. Comparison of Linear and Fast Linear Cramer-Shoup for encryption.

Encryption		
Number of	Linear CS	Fast Linear CS
Random	2	2
Multiplication	5	5
Exponentiation	9	9

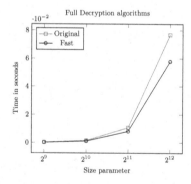

Fig. 8. Full Decryption comparison of Linear and Fast Linear Cramer-Shoup.

Table 9. Verification comparison of Linear and Fast Linear Cramer-Shoup.

Verification		
Number of	Linear CS	Fast Linear CS
Multiplication	2	2
Exponentiation	3	3

Encryption Algorithms. Both schemes use the same encryption algorithm thus the number of operations (Table 8) is the same so as the average execution time (Fig. 7).

Decryption Algorithms. We observe in Fig. 8 that our proposed scheme has a faster decryption algorithm.

Verification Phase. The verification is identical in both schemes. Hence they have same execution time. The results given in Table 9 and Fig. 9 corroborate it.

Actual Decryption. The construction of the *Fast Linear CS* aims at reducing the execution time of this phase. In Table 10, we observe that the number of multiplication and modular exponentiation are the same. However, there is no inverse computation in the fast version unlike the standard scheme. This is the first explanation for the result given in Fig. 10. This cannot be the only reason yet since the *Fast Linear CS* decryption is about twice as fast as the *Linear CS*. Indeed, the second explanation for such result concerns the modular explanation itself. Recall the decryption computations of the schemes: LCS: $M = e/(u_1^{z_1} u_2^{z_2} u_3^{z_3})$ and Fast LCS: $M = e(u_1^{q_1} u_2^{q_2} u_3^{q_3})$. The exponents z_1, z_2, z_3 of standard scheme are drawn from $\mathbb{Z}_p$ while the exponents q_1, q_2, q_3 of fast version have their size equal to the half of the security parameter. Hence, in average, the modular exponentiation costs less from the latter elements. This conclude the study of the actual decryption where our proposed scheme needs only half of the execution time of the standard scheme. Yet, this important gain

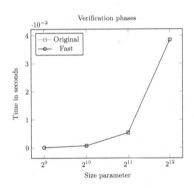

Fig. 9. Verification comparison of Linear and Fast Linear Cramer-Shoup.

Table 10. Comparison of Linear and Fast Linear Cramer-Shoup for decryption.

Decryption		
Number of	Linear CS	Fast Linear CS
Inverse	3	0
Multiplication	3	3
Exponentiation	3	3

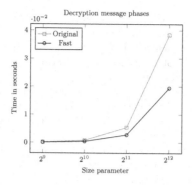

Fig. 10. Actual decryption comparison of Linear and Fast Linear Cramer-Shoup.

is relative to the full decryption algorithm where verification phase constitutes the majority of the execution time.

6   Conclusion

We designed two schemes to improve Short and Linear Cramer-Shoup schemes. We prove the same security as the original schemes for our faster schemes and under the same hypothesis. We also confirm experimentally the significant gain in our decryption algorithms.

Acknowledgement. This study was partially supported by the French ANR project ANR-18-CE39-0019 (MobiS5).

References

1. Abdalla, M., Benhamouda, F., Pointcheval, D.: Public-key encryption indistinguishable under plaintext-checkable attacks. Cryptology ePrint Archive, report 2014/609 (2014)
2. Abdalla, M., Benhamouda, F., Pointcheval, D.: Public-key encryption indistinguishable under plaintext-checkable attacks. In: Katz, J. (ed.) PKC 2015. LNCS, vol. 9020, pp. 332–352. Springer, Heidelberg (2015). https://doi.org/10.1007/978-3-662-46447-2_15
3. Anonymous. Full version our paper (2020). https://drive.google.com/file/d/1V-RwpHLK-sFCC00U-QNAgwFD-sjbLVGV/view?usp=sharing
4. Boneh, D., Franklin, M.: Identity-based encryption from the Weil pairing. SIAM J. Comput. **32**(3), 586–615 (2003)
5. Cramer, R., Shoup, V.: A practical public key cryptosystem provably secure against adaptive chosen ciphertext attack. In: Krawczyk, H. (ed.) CRYPTO 1998. LNCS, vol. 1462, pp. 13–25. Springer, Heidelberg (1998). https://doi.org/10.1007/BFb0055717
6. Cramer, R., Shoup, V.: A practical public key cryptosystem provably secure against adaptive chosen ciphertext attack. Cryptology ePrint Archive, report 1998/006, March 1998

7. Boneh, B.L.D., Shacham, H.: Short signatures from the Weil pairing. J. Cryptol. **17**(4), 297–319 (2004). https://doi.org/10.1007/s00145-004-0314-9

8. Boneh, D., Boyen, X., Shacham, H.: Short group signatures. In: Franklin, M. (ed.) CRYPTO 2004. LNCS, vol. 3152, pp. 41–55. Springer, Heidelberg (2004). https://doi.org/10.1007/978-3-540-28628-8_3

9. ElGamal, T.: A public key cryptosystem and a signature scheme based on discrete logarithms. In: Blakley, G.R., Chaum, D. (eds.) CRYPTO 1984. LNCS, vol. 196, pp. 10–18. Springer, Heidelberg (1985). https://doi.org/10.1007/3-540-39568-7_2. IT-31(4), 469–472

10. Granlund, T., The GMP Development Team: GNU MP: the GNU multiple precision arithmetic library, 6.2.0 edition (2020)

11. Joux, A., Nguyen, K.: Separating decision Diffie-Hellman from computational Diffie-Hellman in cryptographic groups. J. Cryptol. **16**(4), 239–47 (2003). https://doi.org/10.1007/s00145-003-0052-4

12. Naor, M., Yung, M.: Universal one-way hash functions and their cryptographic applications. ACM Press, May 1989

13. Paterson, K.: Cryptography from Pairings. 317 of London Mathematical Society Lecture Notes, pp. 215–251. Cambridge University Press (2005)

14. Shacham, H.: A cramer-shoup encryption scheme from the linear assumption and from progressively weaker linear variants. Cryptology ePrint Archive, report 2007/074 (2007)

15. Shoup, V.: Lower bounds for discrete logarithms and related problems. In: Fumy, W. (ed.) EUROCRYPT 1997. LNCS, vol. 1233, pp. 256–266. Springer, Heidelberg (1997). https://doi.org/10.1007/3-540-69053-0_18

16. Sow, D., Sow, D.: A new variant of EL Gamal's encryption and signatures schemes. JP J. Algebra Number Theory Appl. **20**(1), 21–39 (2011)

Anonymous Proof-of-Asset Transactions Using Designated Blind Signatures

Neetu Sharma[1], Rajeev Anand Sahu[2(✉)], Vishal Saraswat[3], and Joaquin Garcia-Alfaro[4]

[1] Pt. Ravishankar Shukla University, Raipur, India
rajeev.sahu@uni.lu
[2] University of Luxembourg, Esch-sur-Alzette, Luxembourg
[3] Robert Bosch Engineering and Business Solutions Pvt. Ltd., Bangalore, India
[4] Institut Polytechnique de Paris, Télécom SudParis, Evry, France

Abstract. We propose a scheme to preserve the anonymity of users in proof-of-asset transactions. We assume bitcoin-like cryptocurrency systems in which a user must prove the strength of its assets (i.e., solvency), prior conducting further transactions. The traditional way of addressing such a problem is the use of blind signatures, i.e., a kind of digital signature whose properties satisfy the anonymity of the signer. Our work focuses on the use of a designated verifier signature scheme that limits to only a single authorized party (within a group of signature requesters) to verify the correctness of the transaction.

Keywords: Blind signature schemes · Anonymity · Designated verification · Cryptocurrencies · Identity-based cryptography · Bilinear pairings

1 Introduction

Blind signature schemes [3] offer a practical way of handling privacy constraints in cryptocurrency transactions. A blind signature construction is essentially an interactive two-party protocol between the signer of a message and a (group of) signature requester(s). In this protocol the requester disguises the content of the message before sending it to the signer for authorization. Hence the signer actually signs a blinded message (i.e. produces a blind signature without knowing the actual content) which is later unblinded by the requester to realize signature on the actual message. However, the validity of the signature can be verified by anyone. Now there may be situations where the requester may want to designate the signature to an authorized recipient with requiring that the designated verifier cannot transfer the conviction of verification to others, for example a bidder requires this functionality in the electronic auction. This is the objective of DVS (Designated Verifier Signature) schemes [9,11].

In the realm of blockchain cryptocurrencies (i.e., bitcoin-like digital cash schemes), the aforementioned situation may appear in the so-called proof-of-asset transactions, in which users must prove their solvency prior getting access

© Springer Nature Switzerland AG 2021
G. Nicolescu et al. (Eds.): FPS 2020, LNCS 12637, pp. 137–146, 2021.
https://doi.org/10.1007/978-3-030-70881-8_9

to online services such as cryptocurrency exchange markets. In other words, situations in which users must prove that they control a given amount of assets (i.e., bitcoins) but without releasing the specific amount they owe. In addition, we assume situations in which the users want to uniquely designate who can verify those proof-of-asset transactions, e.g., to avoid that a leakage of the proof is used by other parties (i.e., advertisement services, gambling platforms, etc.).

We address the aforementioned challenges and present a designated verifier blind signature (DVS) construction using pairing-based cryptography. The security of our scheme relies on the hardness of the computational and the decisional bilinear Diffie-Hellman problem (cf. Appendix A and [13]). We analyze the security of the approach and perform an efficiency comparison w.r.t. the closest approach in the literature.

Paper Organization—Section 2 surveys related work. Section 3 provides some preliminaries. Section 4 presents our construction and discusses about the security and efficiency of our approach. Section 5 concludes the paper.

2 Related Work

Following seminal work by Chaum [3], Boldyreva [1] demonstrated and formalized the concept of blind signature schemes under the random oracle model and the computational Diffie-Hellman assumptions [13]. Work by Chow et al. [5] proved, as well, *unlinkability* properties of blind signatures. Camenisch et al. [2] proposed new constructions without random oracle constraints, without achieving proofs against strong unforgeability. Zhang and Kim [17], followed by Huang et al. [8], proposed identity-based blind signatures, achieving unlinkability. Zhang et al. [18] uncovered linkability attacks in [8] (signers being traced back under valid message-signature pairs). Pointcheval and Stern [10] settled fundamental security properties of blind signatures. Schröder et al. [12] offered fair guidelines for the security of blind signatures. They revisited the definition of unforgeability in [10] and proposed a new unforgeability definition to avoid adversaries repeating a message for more than one signature.

The public verifiability of a signature is undesirable when a signature shares sensitive information between the signer and the verifier. To deal with this situation, the signer requires to sign the document for a fixed receiver with control on its verification. For this purpose, the idea of undeniable signature [4] was suggested by Chaum and Van Antwerpen. Desmedt and Yung reported in [7] some weaknesses in the aforementioned approach. Jakobsson et al. [9] proposed a non-interactive designated verifier proof which enables the signer to produce transfer-resistant signatures for a designated verifier. In other words, the verifier does not possess the capability to transfer the proof of origin of the signature to third parties. Jakobsson et al. [9] also suggested the necessity of keeping the anonymity of signers. A concrete construction satisfying such constraints (i.e., impossibility of transfer to third parties and signer anonymity) was provided by Saeednia et al. in [11]. Identity-based versions inspired by the previous approach were presented by Susilo et al. in [14], and later by Zhang and Wen in [19]. Limitations in [19] include the lack of proofs for unverifiability, non-transferability and strongness, and the possibility of a signer with direct access to the original message to blind and unblind messages and signatures, hence not fulfilling the standard definition settled in [3,10,12]. The construction presented in this paper addresses such shortcomings.

Bitcoin-like transaction anonymity has been addressed by Yi et al. by proposing schemes with achieving blindness and unforgeability [16]. More recently, Wang et al. in [15] have proposed the application of designated verifier blind signatures for bitcoin proof-of-asset transactions. When a vendor requires to an anonymous buyer to provide a proof of solvency prior enabling an online service (e.g., a certain amount of bitcoins), the buyer provides a proof about it in a designated manner. Hence, only the specific vendor requesting solvency to the user can process the signature. The vendor cannot further use this proof with any other third party. Our new construction addresses the same problem, offering a more compact construction over pairings, improving the efficiency of the identity-based construction by Zhang and Wen in [19], and satisfying unverifiability, non-transferability and strongness properties (cf. Sect. 3 and citations thereof).

3   Preliminaries

Next, we provide formal definitions related to the construction of identity-based strong designated verifier blind signature (hereinafter, ID-SDVBS) schemes [19]. In such schemes, a signer with identity ID_S intends to send a signed message to a designated verifier with identity ID_V such that no one other than the designated verifier can verify the signature. The scheme consists of the five algorithms described next:

1. $params \leftarrow \mathsf{Setup}(\lambda)$: Executed by the Private Key Generator (PKG), taking a security parameter λ as input and producing, as output, the master secret s and the public parameters ($params$) of the system. The remaining algorithms listed below receive all the values of $params$ as implicit inputs.
2. $(P_{ID}, Q_{ID}) \leftarrow \mathsf{Key\ Extract}(ID)$: The PKG takes as input an identity ID and produces, as output, a public and private key pair (P_{ID}, Q_{ID}).
3. $\sigma \leftarrow \mathsf{DVBSig}(Q_{ID_S}, P_{ID_S}, P_{ID_V}, m)$: Signer and user run this interactive process. Inputs include the signer's public and private key (P_{ID_S}, Q_{ID_S}), the designated verifier's public key P_{ID_V} and a message m. Signer and user stop this process in polynomial time, producing either a signature σ of m, or false (in case an error happens).
4. $b \leftarrow \mathsf{DVBVer}(Q_{ID_V}, P_{ID_S}, m, \sigma)$: Run by the verifier, taking as inputs Q_{ID_V} (private key of the verifier), P_{ID_S} (public key of the signer), a message m and a signature σ. It returns a bit b which is 1 if the signature is valid (otherwise, it returns 0 if the signature is invalid).

5. $\widehat{\sigma} \leftarrow \mathsf{DVBSim}(P_{\mathsf{ID}_S}, Q_{\mathsf{ID}_V}, m)$: Run by the verifier, it takes as inputs Q_{ID_V} (verifier's private key), P_{ID_S} and P_{ID_V} (public keys of the signer and the designated verifier), and a message m. It generates a signature $\widehat{\sigma}$ as output.

In addition to correctness, unforgeability and blindness (cf. [13,19] for further details), we aim at satisfying additional security properties– unverifiability, non-transferability and strongness.

Definition 1 (Unverifiability). An ID-SDVBS scheme is said to be unverifiable if nobody, except the signer, can verify the signature without the knowledge of private key of the designated verifier. Please refer [13] for the definition of unverifiability based on the challenger-attacker security game.

Definition 2 (Non-transferability). An ID-SDVBS scheme is said to achieve non-transferability if the signature generated by the signer is computationally indistinguishable from that generated by the designated verifier, that is,

$$\sigma \leftarrow DVBSig(P_{\mathsf{ID}_V}, P_{\mathsf{ID}_S}, Q_{\mathsf{ID}_S}, m) \approx \widehat{\sigma} \leftarrow DVBSim(P_{\mathsf{ID}_S}, Q_{\mathsf{ID}_V}, m).$$

Definition 3 (Strongness). An ID-SDVBS scheme is said to be strong designated if given $\sigma \leftarrow \mathsf{DVBSig}(Q_{\mathsf{ID}_S}, P_{\mathsf{ID}_S}, P_{\mathsf{ID}_V}, m)$, anyone (say V^*) other than the designated verifier V can produce identically distributed transcripts (say $\widehat{\sigma}$) pretended to be generated from someone except the signer S (say S^*) that are indistinguishable from those of σ. That is,

$$\sigma \leftarrow \mathsf{DVBSig}(P_{\mathsf{ID}_V}, P_{\mathsf{ID}_S}, Q_{\mathsf{ID}_S}, m) \approx \widehat{\sigma} \leftarrow \mathsf{DVBSim}(P_{\mathsf{ID}_{S^*}}, Q_{\mathsf{ID}_{V^*}}, m).$$

4   Proposed Construction

Find below the algorithms of our construction (Setup, Key Extract, Designated Blind Signature DVBSig, Designated Verification DVBVer and Transcript Simulation DVBSim):

- $params \leftarrow \mathbf{Setup}(1^\lambda)$: In this algorithm, on input security parameter 1^λ PKG outputs the master private key $s \in \mathbb{Z}_q^*$ and the public parameters

$$params = (1^\lambda, G_1, G_2, q, e, H_1, H_2, P, P_{pub}),$$

where G_1 is an additive cyclic group of prime order q with generator P, G_2 is a multiplicative cyclic group of prime order q, and $H_1 : \{0,1\}^* \rightarrow G_1$, $H_2 : \{0,1\}^* \times G_1 \rightarrow \mathbb{Z}_q^*$ are two cryptographic secure collision resistant hash functions, and $P_{pub} = sP \in G_1$ is system's public key, $e : G_1 \times G_1 \rightarrow G_2$ is a bilinear map (cf. Appendix A).
- $(P_{\mathsf{ID}}, Q_{\mathsf{ID}}) \leftarrow \mathbf{Key\ Extract}(\mathsf{ID})$: Given a user's identity $\mathsf{ID}_i \in \{0,1\}^*$, the PKG computes its
  - Public key as: $P_{\mathsf{ID}_i} = H_1(\mathsf{ID}_i)$; and
  - Private key as: $Q_{\mathsf{ID}_i} = sP_{\mathsf{ID}_i}$.

- $(U', \sigma) \leftarrow$ **DVBSig**$(Q_{\mathsf{ID}_S}, P_{\mathsf{ID}_S}, P_{\mathsf{ID}_V}, m)$.

    Commitment Phase: The signer $\mathcal{S}$ selects a random $r \xleftarrow{\$} \mathbb{Z}_q^*$ and computes
    - $U = rP_{\mathsf{ID}_S} \in G_1$
    and sends U to the user as a commitment.

    Blinding Phase: The user selects blinding factors $x, y \xleftarrow{\$} \mathbb{Z}_q^*$ and computes
    - $U' = xU + xyP_{\mathsf{ID}_S}$;
    - $h = H_2(m, U') \in \mathbb{Z}_q^*$;
    - $h_1 = x^{-1}h + y$;
    and sends h_1 to the signer.

    Signing Phase: Upon receiving h_1, the signer computes
    - $V = (r + h_1)Q_{\mathsf{ID}_S} \in G_1$
    and sends V back to the user.

    Unblinding Phase: The user computes
    - $V' = xV$;
    - $\sigma = e(V', P_{\mathsf{ID}_V})$;
    and publishes $(U', \sigma) \in G_1 \times G_2$ as the strong designated verifier blind signature on
    m.

- $b \leftarrow$ **DVBVer**$(P_{\mathsf{ID}_S}, Q_{\mathsf{ID}_V}, m, (U', \sigma))$
    - To verify the signature (U', σ) on a message m,
    - the verifier $\mathcal{V}$ computes
        - $h = H_2(m, U') \in \mathbb{Z}_q^*$
    and accepts the signature if
        - $\sigma = e(U' + hP_{\mathsf{ID}_S}, Q_{\mathsf{ID}_V})$

- $(\widehat{U'}, \widehat{\sigma}) \leftarrow$ **DVBSim**$(Q_{\mathsf{ID}_V}, P_{\mathsf{ID}_S}, m)$
    The designated verifier $\mathcal{V}$ can produce the same signature $\widehat{\sigma}$ intended for itself, by performing this algorithm: chooses an integer $\widehat{r}, \widehat{x}, \widehat{y} \xleftarrow{\$} \mathbb{Z}_q^*$ and computes:
    - $\widehat{U} = \widehat{r}P_{\mathsf{ID}_S} \in G_1$;
    - $\widehat{U'} = \widehat{x}U + \widehat{x}\widehat{y}P_{\mathsf{ID}_S} \in G_1$;
    - $\widehat{h} = H_2(m, \widehat{U'}) \in \mathbb{Z}_q^*$;
    - $\widehat{h_1} = \widehat{x}^{-1}\widehat{h} + \widehat{y}$;
    - $\widehat{V} = (\widehat{r} + \widehat{h_1})P_{\mathsf{ID}_S} \in G_1$;
    - $\widehat{V'} = \widehat{x}\widehat{V}$; and
    - $\widehat{\sigma} = e(\widehat{V'}, Q_{\mathsf{ID}_V})$.

4.1 Security Analysis

Theorem 1 *(Correctness).* *The proposed ID-SDVBS scheme is correct i.e. the verification follows correctly.*

Proof: Let (U', σ) be a signature generated from our construction for message m signer ID_S and designated verifier ID_V, then the verification of the signature follows as:

$$
\begin{aligned}
e(U' + hP_{\mathsf{ID}_S}, Q_{\mathsf{ID}_V}) &= e(xU + xyP_{\mathsf{ID}_S} + hP_{\mathsf{ID}_S}, Q_{\mathsf{ID}_V}) \\
&= e(xU + xyP_{\mathsf{ID}_S} + hP_{\mathsf{ID}_S}, sP_{\mathsf{ID}_V}) \\
&= e(xrP_{\mathsf{ID}_S} + xyP_{\mathsf{ID}_S} + hP_{\mathsf{ID}_S}, sP_{\mathsf{ID}_V}) \\
&= e(x(rP_{\mathsf{ID}_S} + yP_{\mathsf{ID}_S} + x^{-1}hP_{\mathsf{ID}_S}), sP_{\mathsf{ID}_V}) \\
&= e(x(rQ_{\mathsf{ID}_S} + yQ_{\mathsf{ID}_S} + x^{-1}hQ_{\mathsf{ID}_S}), P_{\mathsf{ID}_V}) \\
&= e(x(r + (x^{-1}h + y))Q_{\mathsf{ID}_S}, P_{\mathsf{ID}_V}) \\
&= e(x(r + h_1)Q_{\mathsf{ID}_S}, P_{\mathsf{ID}_V}) \\
&= e(xV, P_{\mathsf{ID}_V}) \\
&= e(V', P_{\mathsf{ID}_V}) \\
&= \sigma.
\end{aligned}
$$

Next, we discuss the achievement of following security properties: unverifiability, non-transferability, strongness (cf. proofs and extended properties, such as unforgeability and blindness are available in the full version of this paper [13]).

Theorem 2 *(Unverifiability). Given a security parameter λ, if there exists a PPT adversary $\mathcal{A}(\lambda, t, \varepsilon, q_{H_1}, q_{H_2}, q_E, q_S, q_V)$ which breaks the designated unverifiability of the proposed ID-SDVBS scheme in time t with success probability ε, then there exists a PPT adversary $\mathcal{B}(\lambda, t', \varepsilon')$ which solves DBDHP with success probability at least*

$$
\varepsilon' \geq \left(1 - \frac{1}{q^2}\right)\left(1 - \frac{2}{q_{H_1}}\right)^{q_E + q_V}
$$
$$
\left(1 - \frac{2}{q_{H_1}(q_{H_1} - 1)}\right)^{q_S} \left(\frac{2}{q_{H_1}(q_{H_1} - 1)}\right)\varepsilon
$$

in time at most

$$
t' \leq (q_{H_1} + q_E + 3q_S + q_V)S_{G_1} + (q_S + q_V)P_e
$$
$$
+ q_S O_{G_1} + S_{G_1} + S_{G_2} + P_e + t
$$

where S_{G_1} (resp. S_{G_2}) is the time taken for one scalar multiplication in G_1 (resp. G_2), O_{G_1} (resp. O_{G_2}) is the time taken for one group operation in G_1 (resp. G_2), and P_e is the time taken for one pairing computation.

Proof: Available in the full version of this paper [13].

Theorem 3 *(Non-transferability). Given two signatures (U', σ) and $(\widehat{U'}, \widehat{\sigma})$, both generated with message m by, respectively, the signer and the designated verifier, they are indistinguishable.*

Proof: It can be observed that the claimed indistinguishability holds immediately as the following two distributions:

$$U = rP_{\mathsf{ID}_S};$$
$$U' = xU + xyP_{\mathsf{ID}_S};$$
$$h = H_2(m, U');$$
$$h_1 = x^{-1}h + y;$$
$$V = (r + h_1)Q_{ID_S};$$
$$V' = xV;$$
$$\sigma = e(V', P_{ID_V});$$

and

$$\widehat{U} = \widehat{r}P_{\mathsf{ID}_S};$$
$$\widehat{U'} = \widehat{x}U + \widehat{x}\widehat{y}P_{\mathsf{ID}_S};$$
$$\widehat{h} = H_2(m, \widehat{U'});$$
$$\widehat{h_1} = \widehat{x}^{-1}\widehat{h} + \widehat{y};$$
$$\widehat{V} = (\widehat{r} + \widehat{h_1})P_{\mathsf{ID}_S};$$
$$\widehat{V'} = \widehat{x}\widehat{V};$$
$$\widehat{\sigma} = e(\widehat{V'}, Q_{\mathsf{ID}_V});$$

are identical.

Theorem 4 *(Strongness).* *The proposed designated verifier blind signature achieves the property of strongness as defined in Sect. 3.*

Proof: Let $\sigma \leftarrow \mathsf{DVBSig}(Q_{\mathsf{ID}_S}, P_{\mathsf{ID}_S}, P_{\mathsf{ID}_V}, m)$. Then following the definition of strongness formalized in Sect. 3 it will be sufficient to show that the signature σ can be shown as $\sigma \leftarrow \mathsf{DVBSim}(P_{\mathsf{ID}_S^*}, Q_{\mathsf{ID}_V^*}, m)$ (where $P_{\mathsf{ID}_S^*}$ and $Q_{\mathsf{ID}_V^*}$ are defined as in the following).

$$\begin{aligned}
\sigma &= e(xrQ_{\mathsf{ID}_S} + xh_1Q_{\mathsf{ID}_S}, P_{\mathsf{ID}_V}) \\
&= e(xrQ_{\mathsf{ID}_S} + xh_1Q_{\mathsf{ID}_S}, mP_{\mathsf{ID}_V^*}) && \text{where } P_{\mathsf{ID}_V} = mP_{\mathsf{ID}_V^*} \\
&= e(xrmQ_{\mathsf{ID}_S} + xh_1mQ_{\mathsf{ID}_S}, P_{\mathsf{ID}_V^*}) \\
&= e(xrQ_{\mathsf{ID}_S^*} + xh_1Q_{\mathsf{ID}_S^*}, P_{\mathsf{ID}_V^*}) && \text{where } Q_{\mathsf{ID}_S^*} = mQ_{\mathsf{ID}_S}.
\end{aligned}$$

Remark: Here we provide sketch of the proof. For related description please refer to the full version of this paper [13].

4.2   Performance Estimation

Inspired by the performance analysis discussed by Debiao et al. in [6], we discuss next the expected computation time for the generation and verification of signatures using our approach.

We assume the same pairing used by Debiao et al., i.e., a Tate pairing, which is capable of achieving an equivalent of 1024-bit RSA security. It is defined over the supersingular elliptic curve $E = F_p : y^2 = x^3 + x$ with embedding degree 2 was used, where q is a 160-bit Solinas prime $q = 2^{159} + 2^{17} + 1$ and p a 512-bit prime satisfying $p + 1 = 12qr$. Accordingly, operation times are assumed as follows: 6.38 ms for each scalar multiplication; 5.31 ms for each exponentiation in G_2; 3.04 ms for each map-to-point hash execution; and 20.04 ms for each pairing computation. Other operations, such as the cost of an inverse operation over Z_q^*, are omitted in our analysis, since it takes less than 0.03 ms. Likewise, the operation time of performing one general hash function is also omitted, since it is expected to take less than 0.001 ms, hence negligible compared to the time taken by aforementioned (most costly) operations (cf. [6] and citations thereof for further details).

A careful analysis of our approach shows that each signature generation would require five scalar multiplications (i.e., 6.38 ms each), one map-to-point hash execution (i.e., 3.04 ms), and one pairing computation (i.e., 20.04 ms). In other words, our approach would require about 54.98 ms per signature generation. In terms of signature verification, our approach would require one scalar multiplication, one map-to-point hash execution and one pairing computation. Hence, leading to about 29.46 ms per signature verification. If we conduct now the same analysis to the closest approach in the literature, i.e., the identity-based construction by Zhang and Wen in [19], we would obtain about 67.74 ms per signature generation (i.e., five scalar multiplications, one map-to-point hash execution and one pairing computation) and 89.58 ms per signature verification (i.e., one scalar multiplications, one map-to-point hash execution and four pairing computations). Hence, and by using the performance analysis in [6], our construction offers higher efficiency while addressing the limitations in [19] (i.e., lack of *Blinding* and *Unblinding* procedures in their signature protocol, as well as lack of unverifiability, non-transferability and strongness properties).

5   Conclusion

We have presented a designated verifier signature scheme to enable anonymity in proof-of-asset transactions. It allows cryptocurrency users to prove their solvency in a privacy-friendly manner, while designating a single authorized party (from a group of signature requesters) to be able to verify the correctness of the transaction. The approach uses pairing-based cryptography. More precisely, an adaptive approach using an identity-based setting. The security of our construction has been proved using the hardness assumption of the decisional and computational bilinear Diffie-Hellman problem. We have also presented an early estimation of the computation cost of our approach, in terms of signature generation and signature verification. The estimation shows that the computational cost and operation time of the new scheme is significantly more efficient that previous efforts in the literature, while addressing the previous limitations.

A   Identity-Based Cryptography Preliminaries

A probabilistic polynomial time (PPT) algorithm is a probabilistic random algorithm that runs in time polynomial in the length of input. $y \xleftarrow{\$} A(x)$ denotes a randomized algorithm $A(x)$ with input x and output y. For X being a set $v \xleftarrow{\$} X$ stands for a random selection of v from X. A function $f : N \to [0, 1]$

is said to be negligible in n if for any polynomial p and for sufficiently large n, the relation $f(n) < 1/p(n)$ holds. Elements $g \in G$, where G is a set, denote the group $G = \langle g \rangle$ if g spans G.

Definition 4 (Bilinear Map). *Let G_1 and G_2 be two cyclic groups with a prime order q, where G_1 is additive and G_2 is multiplicative. Let P be the generator of G_1. Then a map $e : G_1 \times G_1 \to G_2$ is said to be a cryptographic bilinear map if it fulfils the below conditions.*

Bilinearity: *For all integers $x, y \in \mathbb{Z}_q^*$, $e(xA, yA) = e(A, A)^{xy}$, or equivalently, for all $A, B, C \in G_1$, $e(A + B, C) = e(A, C)e(B, C)$ and $e(A, B + C) = e(A, B)e(A, C)$.*
Non-Degeneracy: *The points $A, B \in G_1$ with $e(A, B) \neq 1$. As G_1 and G_2 are prime ordered groups this property is equivalent to have $g := e(A, A) \neq 1$, or in other words $g := e(A, A)$ is a generator of G_2.*
Computability: *The map $e(A, B) \in G_2$ can be computes efficiently for all $A, B \in G_1$.*

Further definitions, such as *Bilinear Map Parameter Generator, Bilinear Diffie-Hellman Problem, the Bilinear Diffie-Hellman problem (BDHP), BDHP Parameter Generator, Bilinear Diffie-Hellman Assumption, the Decisional BDHP,* and *the DBDHP Parameter Generator* are available in the full version of this paper [13].

References

1. Boldyreva, A.: Efficient threshold signature, multisignature and blind signature schemes based on the gap-diffie-hellman-group signature scheme. IACR ePrints **2002**, 118 (2002)
2. Camenisch, J., Koprowski, M., Warinschi, B.: Efficient blind signatures without random oracles. In: Blundo, C., Cimato, S. (eds.) SCN 2004. LNCS, vol. 3352, pp. 134–148. Springer, Heidelberg (2005). https://doi.org/10.1007/978-3-540-30598-9_10
3. Chaum, D.: Blind signatures for untraceable payments. In: Chaum, D., Rivest, R.L., Sherman, A.T. (eds.) Advances in Cryptology, pp. 199–203. Springer, Boston, MA (1983). https://doi.org/10.1007/978-1-4757-0602-4_18
4. Chaum, D., Van Antwerpen, H.: Undeniable signatures. Conference on the Theory and Application of Cryptology, pp. 212–216. Springer, Berlin (1989)
5. Chow, S.S.M., Hui, L.C.K., Yiu, S.M., Chow, K.P.: Two improved partially blind signature schemes from bilinear pairings. In: Boyd, C., González Nieto, J.M. (eds.) ACISP 2005. LNCS, vol. 3574, pp. 316–328. Springer, Heidelberg (2005). https://doi.org/10.1007/11506157_27
6. Debiao, H., Jianhua, C., Jin, H.: An id-based proxy signature schemes without bilinear pairings. Ann. Telecommun. **66**(11–12), 657–662 (2011)
7. Desmedt, Y., Yung, M.: Weaknesses of undeniable signature schemes. In: Davies, D.W. (ed.) EUROCRYPT 1991. LNCS, vol. 547, pp. 205–220. Springer, Heidelberg (1991). https://doi.org/10.1007/3-540-46416-6_19

8. Huang, Z., Chen, K., Wang, Y.: Efficient identity-based signatures and blind signatures. In: Desmedt, Y.G., Wang, H., Mu, Y., Li, Y. (eds.) CANS 2005. LNCS, vol. 3810, pp. 120–133. Springer, Heidelberg (2005). https://doi.org/10. 1007/11599371_11

9. Jakobsson, M., Sako, K., Impagliazzo, R.: Designated verifier proofs and their applications. In: Maurer, U. (ed.) EUROCRYPT 1996. LNCS, vol. 1070, pp. 143–154. Springer, Heidelberg (1996). https://doi.org/10.1007/3-540-68339-9_13

10. Pointcheval, D., Stern, J.: Security arguments for digital signatures and blind signatures. J. Cryptol. **13**(3), 361–396 (2000)

11. Saeednia, S., Kremer, S., Markowitch, O.: An efficient strong designated verifier signature scheme. In: Lim, J.-I., Lee, D.-H. (eds.) ICISC 2003. LNCS, vol. 2971, pp. 40–54. Springer, Heidelberg (2004). https://doi.org/10.1007/978-3-540-24691-6_4

12. Schröder, D., Unruh, D.: Security of blind signatures revisited. In: Fischlin, M., Buchmann, J., Manulis, M. (eds.) PKC 2012. LNCS, vol. 7293, pp. 662–679. Springer, Heidelberg (2012). https://doi.org/10.1007/978-3-642-30057-8_39

13. Sharma, N., Anand-Sahu, R., Saraswat, V., Garcia-Alfaro, J.: Anonymous proof-of-asset transactions using pairing-based designated blind signatures (Full Version), September 2020. http://arxiv.org/abs/2009.13978

14. Susilo, W., Zhang, F., Mu, Y.: Identity-based strong designated verifier signature schemes. In: Wang, H., Pieprzyk, J., Varadharajan, V. (eds.) ACISP 2004. LNCS, vol. 3108, pp. 313–324. Springer, Heidelberg (2004). https://doi.org/10.1007/978-3-540-27800-9_27

15. Wang, H., He, D., Ji, Y.: Designated-verifier proof of assets for bitcoin exchange using elliptic curve cryptography. Future Gener. Comput. Syst. **107**, 854–862 (2020)

16. Yi, X., Lam, K.-Y.: A new blind ECDSA scheme for bitcoin transaction anonymity. In: Proceedings of the 2019 ACM Asia Conference on Computer and Communications Security, pp. 613–620 (2019)

17. Zhang, F., Kim, K.: ID-based blind signature and ring signature from pairings. In: Zheng, Y. (ed.) ASIACRYPT 2002. LNCS, vol. 2501, pp. 533–547. Springer, Heidelberg (2002). https://doi.org/10.1007/3-540-36178-2_33

18. Zhang, J., Wei, T., Zhang, J.Y., Zou, W.: Linkability of a blind signature scheme and its improved scheme. In: Gavrilova, M.L., et al. (eds.) ICCSA 2006. LNCS, vol. 3983, pp. 262–270. Springer, Heidelberg (2006). https://doi.org/10.1007/11751632_28

19. Zhang, N., Wen, Q.: Provably secure blind id-based strong designated verifier signature scheme. In: CHINACOM'2007, pp. 323–327. IEEE (2007)

Privacy by Design

Modeling Attacks and Efficient Countermeasures on Interpose PUF

R. Raja Adhithan[1](✉) and N. Nalla Anandakumar[2]

[1] Hardware Security Research Lab, Society for Electronic Transactions and Security,
Chennai, India
r.rajaadhithan@gmail.com
[2] Department of Electrical and Computer Engineering, University of Florida,
Gainesville, USA
nallananth@gmail.com

Abstract. Physical unclonable function is a promising hardware security primitive that is more suitable for device authentication and key generation applications. However, it is found to be vulnerable to modeling attacks when an attacker has access to challenge and response pairs. In this paper, we examine the machine learning (ML) and deep learning (DL) based modeling attacks on Interpose PUF (IPUF) and also propose two efficient countermeasures based on obfuscating challenge that protects the IPUF against these modeling attacks. We begin by analyzing building blocks of IPUF such as Arbiter PUF (APUF) and XOR Arbiter PUF (XAPUF) against modeling attacks. Subsequently, we show that the IPUF is possible to attack by changing the input position configuration of switch elements in the APUF and reducing the number of arbiter chains in the XAPUF. Finally, we implement the proposed countermeasures on Nexys 4 FPGA boards and collect real measurements. Experimental results show that the implemented countermeasures can mitigate ML and DL modeling attacks significantly.

Keywords: Physical Unclonable Functions (PUFs) · Arbiter PUF · XOR Arbiter PUF · Interpose PUF · Obfuscation · Machine learning attacks

1 Introduction

With the rapid growth of the Internet of Things (IoT), securing communication is fundamentally important. Authentication is one of the methods for securing communications between IoT devices [15]. Typically, authentication methods mostly rely on classical cryptographic algorithms that handle the secret keys stored in non-volatile memories (NVMs). However, it has been shown that secret keys in NVMs are vulnerable to various kinds of attacks (e.g. Invasive attacks and side-channel attacks) and can be easily obtained or cloned. Further, maintaining such secrets in NVMs is difficult and expensive. To overcome these limitations,

© Springer Nature Switzerland AG 2021
G. Nicolescu et al. (Eds.): FPS 2020, LNCS 12637, pp. 149–162, 2021.
https://doi.org/10.1007/978-3-030-70881-8_10

silicon Physical unclonable function (PUFs) [10] has been proposed as a low-cost solution for secure authenticating IoT devices without additional cryptographic algorithms. PUF has been defined as a one-way function that extracts a unique electronic fingerprint from the intrinsic process variability of silicon devices by using a set of challenge-response pairs (CRPs). Moreover, PUFs are easy to challenge and whose responses are easy to measure, but very hard to clone, predict, or reproduce due to their physical structures.

PUF architectures can be broadly divided into two categories [28]: weak PUF and strong PUF. Weak PUFs have a limited number of CRPs, ideally increasing linearly with PUF size and they are more suited to limited applications such as key generation and component of Pseudo-Random Number Generators (PRNG). Different from weak PUFs, strong PUFs have a large set of challenge-response pairs (CRPs), ideally increasing exponentially with PUF size and can be used directly for authentication without additional cryptographic hardware. Arbiter PUF is one of the most popular and widely studied strong PUFs. However, it has been successfully attacked using machine learning techniques [18] by using linear adaptive mapping of CRPs. While researchers have proposed several techniques to improve its resistance to modeling attacks, for example, the APUF [10], XOR APUF [21], feed-forward arbiter PUF (FF-APUF) [12], double arbiter PUF (DAPUF) [13] and lightweight secure PUF (LSPUF) [14]. However, these have also been broken with a sufficient number of CRPs due to the lack of complexity in the challenge to response mapping. Recently, Nguyen et al. [16] proposed the Interpose PUF (IPUF) to the repertoire of robust PUFs, essentially consisting of two XOR APUFs. However, it has also been successfully attacked using machine learning [24] and deep learning [20] based modeling attacks. In this paper, we study the modeling attacks on IPUF and also provide efficient countermeasures based on obfuscates challenges that improves the resistance of the IPUF against modeling attacks. The main contributions of this paper can be summarized as follow:

- Two most widely studied modeling attacks are used to investigate the resistance of the IPUF to modeling attacks and show that the IPUF and its building blocks are vulnerable to classical ML and DL based modeling attacks by changing the input positions of switch elements in the APUF and the number of arbiter chains in the XAPUF.
- We propose two efficient countermeasure techniques and prove that the proposed countermeasures make the IPUF design resilient to classical ML and DL based modeling attacks by experiments.

The rest of the paper is explained as follows. Some of the well-known PUF modeling attacks and the corresponding countermeasures are briefly discussed in Sect. 2. The IPUF construction and its components are given in Sect. 3. Then modeling attacks on IPUF and its building blocks are discussed in Sect. 4. Countermeasures for thwarting modeling attacks on the IPUF are presented in Sect. 5. Finally, conclusions are drawn in Sect. 6.

2 Related Work

Machine Learning (ML) based modeling attacks are the most powerful attack for strong PUFs, where the adversary builds an accurate model of the PUF. In these attacks, the adversary intentionally collects a subset of all CRPs of the PUF to train the model and uses them to derive a numerical model that can accurately predict the responses of unknown challenges. We note that previous works have most often utilized ML based model as a way to attack the strong PUF architectures [6,7,18,19]. The model of a PUF instance is built based on CRPs or some side channel information by using Logistic Regression (LR) [19], Support Vector Machine (SVM) [11] and Evolution Strategies (ES) [6]. In order to resist ML-based modeling attacks, many defense mechanisms are proposed which can be broadly divided into CRP obfuscation [5,9,17,26,27], and non-linearity addition to the PUF structures [22,29]. In recent years, there has been an ongoing effort to model and protect PUFs against side-channel attacks such as power analysis [19] and fault injection [4]. In [16], the authors claimed that using the middle bit of the second XOR APUF as the interpose position, the IPUF is robust against classical ML-based modeling attack. However, it has also been successfully attacked using DL based modeling attack [20] (i.e., such as 64-bit challenge length and sizes of up to (4, 4)-IPUFs) and divide-and-conquer based ML attack [24] (such as 64-bit challenge length and sizes of up to (8, 8)-IPUFs). In this paper first, we study the modeling attacks on IPUF and also propose two countermeasure techniques based on obfuscating the IPUF challenges to increase the computation complexities of classical ML and DL based modeling attacks. The IPUF is constructed using APUFs and XAPUFs. Therefore, first a brief description of the APUF, XAPUF, and IPUF are presented which is then followed by the vulnerability analysis of them against classical ML and DL based modeling attacks.

3 Background: APUF, XAPUF and IPUF

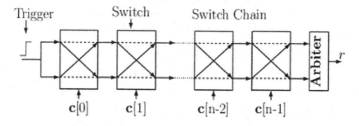

Fig. 1. Basic arbiter PUF structure [20]

An APUF is composed of two identically configured delay paths that are stimulated by a clock signal as shown in Fig. 1. It is composed of a sequence of switch components (i.e., pair of 2-to-1 multiplexers). Each one interconnects two input ports to two output ports with straight or crossed configurations depending on the applied challenge bit (0 or 1). The outputs ports of the last stage are connected to an arbiter, which determines which signal arrived first. Based on this result, the arbiter generates a single bit response (0 or 1). The estimation of the path delays of the APUF can be modeled by using the linear additive delay model [3]. The total delays of both paths of the APUF are modeled as the sum of the delays in each switch component depending on the challenge bits (i_1, $i_2....i_k$). The final delay difference between the upper and the lower path in a n-bit APUF can be described as follows:

$$\Delta = w[0]f[0] + ... + w[i]f[i] + ...w[n]f[n] = \langle w, f \rangle$$

where n is the number of challenge bits, f and w are known as a parity (feature) vector and weight, respectively. In this delay model, the unknown weight vector w depends on the process variation of the APUF instance. The parity vector f is derived from the challenge c defined as:

$$f[n] = 1, \ and \ f[l] = \prod_{i=l}^{n-1}(1 - 2c[i]), \quad for \ l = 0.....n - 1.$$

The final response bit is defined as follows: if $\Delta \geq 0$, the response bit is '1', otherwise, the response bit is '0'. Hence, accurately predicting the value of weight w is lead to the successful modeling of APUF. This can be achieved quite successfully by using several ML algorithms such as LR [19], SVM [11], and (ES) [6].

3.1 XAPUF

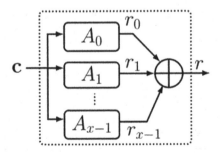

Fig. 2. Schematic diagram of XOR-Arbiter PUF

The schematic diagram of XAPUF is shown in Fig. 2. In a XAPUF, multiple APUF outputs (r_0, r_1..., r_{x-1}) are xor'ed to form a single response bit (r). This leads to an exponential increase in the number of CRPs. Thus, it is improving the

APUF modeling attack resistance. The mathematical model [19] of the XAPUF is expressed as:

$$response_{XAPUF} = sign \left(\prod_{i=1}^{n} w_i^{\rightarrow T} f_i^{\rightarrow} \right)$$

where f is the parity vector corresponding to the applied challenge (input) vector. In [18], the author mentioned that a modeling attack on x-XAPUF is infeasible if x is more than 6. Later in [23] shown that it was able to break for $x \leq 9$ by using LR algorithm. A combination of ML and SCA information-dependent ML based attack on x-XAPUF was reported in [19] for up to $x \leq 15$. The authors of [2] showed that the attack complexity increases only linearly with x for x-XAPUFs by taking advantage of its imperfect reliability characterization information.

3.2 Interpose PUF (IPUF)

The Interpose PUF (IPUF) [16] is one of the most recent strong PUF design constructed using two XAPUFs (i.e., (x, y)-XAPUFs). First, the x-XAPUF takes an n-bit challenge and generates a 1-bit response. Subsequently, the generated response is interposed in the middle bit position of the y-XAPUF (see in Fig. 3). The y-XAPUF takes an $(n + 1)$ bit challenge and generates a final response bit of the IPUF. This PUF design claims to mitigate the classical and reliability based ML attacks. In particular, the authors demonstrate that the (3, 3)-IPUF is satisfactorily resistant to classical ML-based modeling attack. However, the authors of [20] demonstrated that (4, 4)-IPUF has been successfully attacked using DL based modeling attack. More recently, (8, 8)-IPUF design has also been broken using divide-and-conquer based ML attack [24]. In this paper, we demonstrate that the original IPUF can be modeled using classical ML-based modeling attacks by changing the input positions of switch elements in the APUF

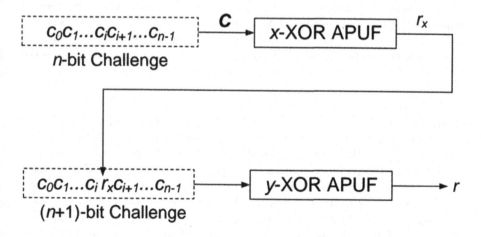

Fig. 3. Schematic diagram of Interpose PUF

and the number of arbiter chains in the XAPUF. Furthermore, we propose two countermeasure techniques to obfuscate the challenge of the IPUF which is to overcome the classical ML and DL based modeling attacks.

4   Analysis of Modeling Attack on IPUF and Its Components

In this section, we will take a closer look at the resistance of IPUF and its building blocks (i.e., APUF, XAPUF) towards ML and DL based modeling attacks. In the following, we first show that modeling attacks on APUF and XAPUF implementations by changing the input position configurations of APUF switch elements and also reducing the number of XAPUF chains. Then, we will take a closer look at their effectiveness when incorporating them in IPUF design against ML and DL based modeling attacks. In this connection, we collected a 100,00 CRPs from these PUF implementations on Xilinx Artix-7 FPGA to model a PUF by using the DL and ML technique (i.e., Logistic Regression).

4.1   Modeling Attacks on Arbiter PUF

The APUF is composed of two parallel delay lines with N number of switch elements (see Sect. 3). First, an input signal is supplied to the top and bottom selectors at the same time. The genetic idea behind APUF is to race the delay times between the two signals. The two signals propagate through various routes depending on the challenge bits. We have noticed that two ways of APUF constructions have been reported in literature [8,25] based on input position/section configuration of multiplexers, namely, APUF-I and APUF-II. In APUF-I [25], the output of each multiplexer is given to the same input positions (0, 0; 1, 1) of the next multiplexers in the upper and lower paths as shown in Fig. 4. A closer look at APUF-I design, only one signal is propagate through various routes depending on the challenge bits instead of two signals propagate. Whereas in APUF-II design [8], the output of each multiplexer is given to different input positions (0, 1; 1, 0) of next multiplexers in the upper and lower paths as shown in Fig. 5. A closer look at APUF-II design, two signals are propagate through various routes depending on the challenge bits. In this section, we analyze the resistance of APUF-I and APUF-II against modeling attacks by using LR and DL technique.

LR on APUF. We collected 100,000 CRPs from each of the FPGA implementations of 64-bit APUF-I and also 64-bit APUF-2 for LR-based modeling analysis. We used 50% of CRPs to train the model and 50% CRPs to test the model from the collected CRPs. The estimation of the path delays of the APUF is modeled by using LR algorithm (see Sect. 3). It has been demonstrated that the predication rate is obtained 100% for APUF-I and 78.8% for APUF-II, respectively (see Table 1). Thus, APUF-II construction itself can prevent an LR based attack significantly. This is due to that the wire length of the two lines in APUF-II is almost physically the same when compared to APUF-I.

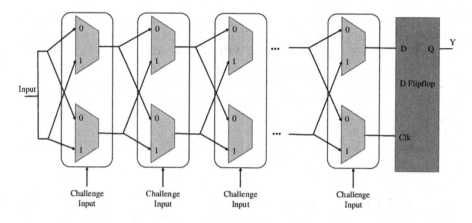

Fig. 4. Schematic diagram of APUF-I

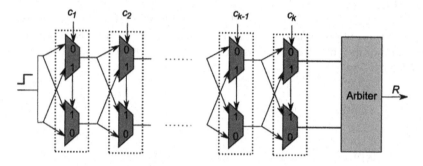

Fig. 5. Schematic diagram of APUF-II

DL on APUF. Once again we collected 100,000 CRPs from each of the implementation of 64-bit APUF-I and also 64-bit APUF-2 for DL based modeling analysis. The generated challenges for APUF-I and APUF-II is converted into a feature vector or parity vector form to train the deep learning network. We have obtained the modeling accuracy of 99.96% for APUF-I and 99.8% for APUF-II, respectively.

It is also clear from the results in Table 1 that the prediction rate of the APUF-I design is higher than the APUF-II design by using the LR technique. However, DL based attack is obtained almost 100% modeling accuracy for both the designs

4.2 Modeling Attacks on XOR Arbiter PUF

An investigation of the modeling effect of XOR Arbiter PUF with a different number of arbiter chains by using the LR and DL is described.

LR on XAPUF. To model the behavior of XAPUF by using LR, we collected 100,000 CRPs from each 64-bit XAPUF FPGA implementation (i.e., XAPUF-I and XAPUF-II) which is incorporated APUF-I and APUF-II styles. The number of test samples is set as the same as the training samples. The results are displayed in Table 1. From the table, we can see that the prediction rate of the XAPUF-I design (96.47%) is higher than the XAPUF-II design (67.12%) by using LR technique. However, the prediction rate of XAPUF designs has been decreased (almost near 50%) when the number of arbiter chains increased from one to seven (i.e. seven XORs are used) in both APUF-I and APUF-II design styles.

DL on XAPUF. To model the behavior of XAPUF by using DL, we used 50% of CRPs for train the model and 50% CRPs to test the model from the collected 100,000 CRPs from each 64-bit XAPUF implementation which is incorporated APUF-I and APUF-II styles. As seen in Table 1, the prediction rate of the XAPUF-I design by using DL is higher than the XAPUF-II design. Moreover, the prediction rate of XAPUF designs has been decreased (almost reached 50%) when the number of arbiter chains increased from one to seven (i.e XAPUF to 7XAPUF).

Table 1. Modeling accuracy of IPUFs and its components

PUF styles	Area (slices)	LR	DL	Collected CRPs
APUF-I	75	100%	99.96%	100,000
APUF- II	74	78.8%	99.8%	100,000
XAPUF-I	143	96.47%	95.57%	100,000
XAPUF-II	154	67.12%	53.15%	100,000
7XAPUF-I	536	50.48%	51.04%	100,000
7XAPUF-II	596	49.76%	50.84%	100,000
IPUF-I	308	78.92%	90.30%	100,000
IPUF-II	282	68.59%	63.04%	100,000
I5PUF-I	1348	49.81%	49.54%	100,000
I5PUF-II	1364	50.30%	49.46%	100,000

4.3   Modeling Attacks on Interpose PUF

ML on IPUF. We have implemented the 64-bit Interpose PUF (see Fig. 2) in two styles, one is incorporated a XAPUF-I (IPUF-I) and another one is incorporated a XAPUF-II (IPUF-II). The LR modeling result of IPUF-I and IPUF-II for 100,000 CRPs is shown in Table 1. The Interpose PUF using XAPUF-I has obtained the highest prediction rate (around 80%) whereas Interpose PUF using XAPUF-II shows a relatively low prediction rate (around 68%). Moreover, the prediction rate of PUF-I and PUF-II designs have been decreased (almost reached 50%) when the number of arbiter chains are increased from one to seven (i.e seven XORs are used in the upper and lower layers)

DL on IPUF. To train the CRPs of interposing PUF by using DL, we used similar technique as used in the XAPUF models. The deep learning result of the interpose PUF by employing XAPUF-I (IPUF-I) and XAPUF-II (IPUF-II) is 90.30% and 64%, respectively. Moreover, very recently, the interpose PUF using the XAPUF-I style is successfully broken by using DL method [20]. Moreover, we identified that the IPUF-I design has obtained low prediction rate when compared to IPUF-II by using ML and DL based modeling attacks. Furthermore, we demonstrated that the prediction rate for I7PUF-I and I7PUF-II (i.e seven XORs are used) decreased if the number of arbiter chains is increased. However, these designs occupies more area (see Table 1) and the percentage of unstable responses also increases exponentially if the number of arbiter chains are increased in XAPUF designs [2,16]. Nguyen et al. [16] also mentioned that IPUF design is vulnerable against ML based attacks if having only two arbiter chains (i.e., only one XORed is used). Therefore, we need efficient and suitable countermeasure solutions to increase the resilience of the IPUF against the modeling attacks.

5   Countermeasures for Thwarting Modeling Attacks on the Interpose PUF

In recent years, various countermeasures have also been developed to improve the resistance of different PUF designs against modeling attacks (see Sect. 2). In this paper, we proposed two efficient countermeasures (based on obfuscating the challenges), namely, OBCIPUF and LROBIPUF, to increase the resilience of the IPUF against ML and DL based modeling attacks.

5.1   OBCIPUF

In OBCIPUF, the outputs of the obfuscation cells are XORed with 64-challenge bits only in the lower layer of IPUF design to generate new challenge bits as shown in Fig. 6. The obfuscation cell (W) is randomly generated from the RS-Latch cell [1]. This countermeasure technique will hide the lower layer of IPUF challenge bits, thereby the mathematical models will become a difficulty. We investigated the resistance of this proposed countermeasure (OBCIPUF) against the modeling attacks. The LR and DL attacks performed on 100,000 CRPs for OBCIPUF when including the PUF-I (OBCIPUF-I) and PUF-II (OBCIPUF-II), respectively. Moreover, the results from the ML and DL based attacks are shown in Fig. 8 and Fig. 9, respectively. In this figure, the horizontal line indicates the number of training data sets, and the vertical indicates the prepared rate of responses for 100,000 data sets. As shown, Fig. 8 and Fig. 9, the predicated rate of the countermeasure (OBCIPUF) is below 64%.

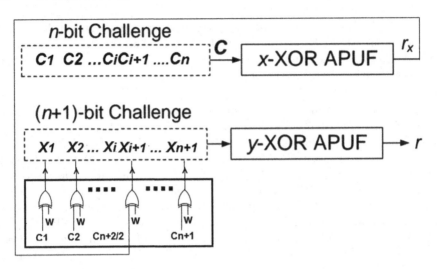

Fig. 6. Challenge bits obfuscation by using obfuscation cell

5.2 LROBIPUF

In LROBIPUF first, we generate the internal challenge from external challenge by using LFSR (Linear-Feedback Shift Register). Then, some of the random bits of internal challenges are XORed with obfuscation cells and fed them into the upper and lower layers of IPUF (as shown in Fig. 7). Here, we are not altering the interpose bit of the lower layer. This countermeasure technique will hide the upper and lower layer of IPUF challenge bits, thereby the model of the IPUF will become more difficult. Moreover, the LR and DL attacks performed on 100,000 CRPs for LROBIPUF when including the PUF-I (LROBIPUF-I) and PUF-II (LROBIPUF-II), respectively. As shown, Fig. 8 and Fig. 9, the predicated rate of the countermeasure (LROBIPUF) was also below 60%.

The Table 2 shows the maximum modeling accuracy of proposed countermeasures with the cost of area overhead (Xilinx Artix-7 FPGA). As seen from the table, our countermeasures increased the resilience of the IPUF against ML and DL based modeling attacks (i.e., the predicated rate of the countermeasure are less than 60%). This is provide an almost equivalent modeling resistance of I5PUF designs (Table 1). Hence our recommendation to use at least 5 number of arbiter chains (i.e., 5 XAPUFs) for securing the IPUF design otherwise to incorporate our countermeasures solution into the secure IPUF design if the less number of arbiter chains. These recommendations also apply whenever APUFs are used as building blocks for larger PUFs, always we must use APUF-II design instead of APUF-I design.

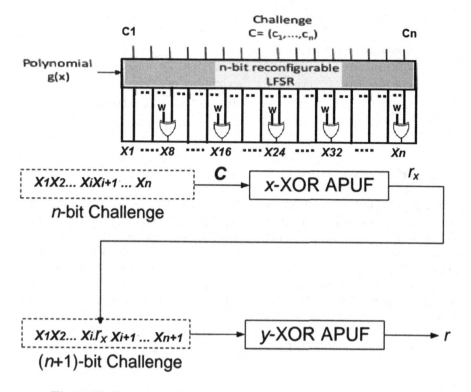

Fig. 7. Challenge bits obfuscation by using obfuscation cell and LFSR

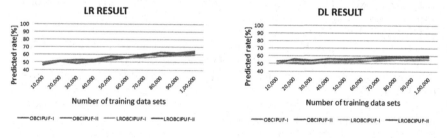

Fig. 8. Modeling accuracy of ML

Fig. 9. Modeling accuracy of DL

Table 2. Modeling accuracy of proposed countermeasures

Countermeasures	Area (slices)	LR	DL	Collected CRPs
OBCIPUF-I	315	65.01%	60.01%	1,00,000
OBCIPUF-II	333	63.57%	55.4%	1,00,000
LROBIPUF-I	432	59.51%	55.54%	1,00,000
LROBIPUF-II	437	62.12%	58.21%	1,00,000

6 Conclusion

In this paper, we demonstrated successful ML and DL based modeling attacks on IPUFs of 64-bit challenge length by changing the input position configuration of switch elements in the APUF and also reducing the number of arbiter chains in the XAPUF. It is necessary to understand that the position configuration of switch elements and the number of arbiter chain selection in the IPUF design. Moreover, experimental results show that our proposed countermeasures to increase the resilience of IPUF to an ML and DL based modeling attack. Furthermore, our countermeasure solutions consumes very little area. Hence, these techniques are suitable for lightweight security devices. In future work, we will investigate if the bias of an IPUF can assist a modeling attack.

References

1. Anandakumar, N.N., Hashmi, M.S., Sanadhya, S.K.: Compact implementations of FPGA-based PUFs with enhanced performance. In: 30th International Conference on VLSI Design and 16th International Conference on Embedded Systems (VLSID), pp. 161–166, January 2017
2. Becker, G.T.: The gap between promise and reality: on the insecurity of XOR arbiter PUFs. In: Güneysu, T., Handschuh, H. (eds.) CHES 2015. LNCS, vol. 9293, pp. 535–555. Springer, Heidelberg (2015). https://doi.org/10.1007/978-3-662-48324-4_27
3. Lim, D., Lee, J.W., Gassend, B., Suh, G.E., van Dijk, M., Devadas, S.: Extracting secret keys from integrated circuits. IEEE Trans. Very Large Scale Integr. (VLSI) Syst. **13**(10), 1200–1205 (2005)
4. Delvaux, J., Verbauwhede, I.: Fault injection modeling attacks on 65 nm arbiter and RO sum PUFs via environmental changes. IEEE Trans. Circ. Syst. I Regul. Pap. **61**(6), 1701–1713 (2014)
5. Delvaux, J., Peeters, R., Gu, D., Verbauwhede, I.: A survey on lightweight entity authentication with strong PUFs. ACM Comput. Surv. **48**(2), 26:1–26:42 (2015)
6. Ganji, F., Tajik, S., Fäßler, F., Seifert, J.-P.: Having no mathematical model may not secure PUFs. J. Cryptogr. Eng. **7**(2), 113–128 (2017). https://doi.org/10.1007/s13389-017-0159-4
7. Ganji, F., Tajik, S., Seifert, J.-P.: Why attackers win: on the learnability of XOR arbiter PUFs. In: Conti, M., Schunter, M., Askoxylakis, I. (eds.) Trust 2015. LNCS, vol. 9229, pp. 22–39. Springer, Cham (2015). https://doi.org/10.1007/978-3-319-22846-4_2

8. Gao, Y., Al-Sarawi, S., Abbott, D., Sadeghi, A.R., Ranasinghe, D.: Modeling attack resilient reconfigurable latent obfuscation technique for PUF based lightweight authentication. ArXiv abs/1706.06232 (2017)
9. Gassend, B., Clarke, D., van Dijk, M., Devadas, S.: Controlled physical random functions. In: 2002 Proceedings of the 18th Annual Computer Security Applications Conference, pp. 149–160 (2002)
10. Gassend, B., Clarke, D.E., van Dijk, M., Devadas, S.: Silicon physical random functions. In: ACM Conference on Computer and Communications Security, pp. 148–160. ACM (2002)
11. Herder, C., Yu, M., Koushanfar, F., Devadas, S.: Physical unclonable functions and applications: a tutorial. Proc. IEEE 102(8), 1126–1141 (2014)
12. Lee, J.W., Lim, D., Gassend, B., Suh, G.E., van Dijk, M., Devadas, S.: A technique to build a secret key in integrated circuits for identification and authentication applications. In: 2004 Symposium on VLSI Circuits. Digest of Technical Papers (IEEE Cat. No.04CH37525), pp. 176–179 (2004)
13. Machida, T., Yamamoto, D., Iwamoto, M., Sakiyama, K.: A new arbiter PUF for enhancing unpredictability on FPGA. Sci. World J. 2015(13) (2015)
14. Majzoobi, M., Koushanfar, F., Potkonjak, M.: Techniques for design and implementation of secure reconfigurable PUFs. ACM Trans. Reconfigurable Technol. Syst. (TRETS) 2(1), 5 (2009)
15. Nandy, T., et al.: Review on security of Internet of Things authentication mechanism. IEEE Access 7, 151054–151089 (2019)
16. Nguyen, P.H., Sahoo, D.P., Jin, C., Mahmood, K., Rührmair, U., van Dijk, M.: The interpose PUF: secure PUF design against state-of-the-art machine learning attacks. IACR Trans. Cryptogr. Hardw. Embed. Syst. 2019(4), 243–290 (2019)
17. Noor, N.Q.M., Daud, S.M., Ahmad, N.A., Maarop, N.: Defense mechanisms against machine learning modeling attacks on strong physical unclonable functions for IOT authentication: a review. Int. J. Adv. Comput. Sci. Appl. 8(10), 99–111 (2017)
18. Rührmair, U., Sehnke, F., Sölter, J., Dror, G., Devadas, S., Schmidhuber, J.: Modeling attacks on physical unclonable functions. In: Proceedings of the 17th ACM Conference on Computer and Communications Security, CCS 2010, pp. 237–249 (2010)
19. Rührmair, U., et al.: Efficient power and timing side channels for physical unclonable functions. In: Batina, L., Robshaw, M. (eds.) CHES 2014. LNCS, vol. 8731, pp. 476–492. Springer, Heidelberg (2014). https://doi.org/10.1007/978-3-662-44709-3_26
20. Santikellur, P., Bhattacharyay, A., Chakraborty, R.S.: Deep learning based model building attacks on arbiter PUF compositions. IACR Cryptology ePrint Archive 2019/566 (2019)
21. Suh, G.E., Devadas, S.: Physical unclonable functions for device authentication and secret key generation. In: 2007 44th ACM/IEEE Design Automation Conference, pp. 9–14 (2007)
22. Surita, R.C., Côrtes, M.L., Aranha, D.F., Araujo, G.: CRPUF: a modeling-resistant delay PUF based on cylindrical reconvergence. Microprocess. Microsyst. 60, 185–195 (2018)
23. Tobisch, J., Becker, G.T.: On the scaling of machine learning attacks on PUFs with application to noise bifurcation. In: Mangard, S., Schaumont, P. (eds.) RFIDSec 2015. LNCS, vol. 9440, pp. 17–31. Springer, Cham (2015). https://doi.org/10.1007/978-3-319-24837-0_2
24. Wisiol, N., et al.: Splitting the interpose PUF: a novel modeling attack strategy. IACR Trans. Cryptogr. Hardw. Embed. Syst. 2020(3), 97–120 (2020)

25. Yanambaka, V.P., Mohanty, S., Kougianos, E.: Making use of manufacturing process variations: a dopingless transistor based-PUF for hardware-assisted security. IEEE Trans. Semicond. Manuf. **31**(2), 285–294 (2018)
26. Ye, J., Guo, Q., Hu, Y., Li, H., Li, X.: Modeling attacks on strong physical unclonable functions strengthened by random number and weak PUF. In: 2018 IEEE 36th VLSI Test Symposium (VTS), pp. 1–6 (2018)
27. Ye, J., Hu, Y., Li, X.: RPUF: physical unclonable function with randomized challenge to resist modeling attack. In: 2016 IEEE Asian Hardware-Oriented Security and Trust (AsianHOST), pp. 1–6, December 2016
28. Zhang, J.-L., Qu, G., Lv, Y.-Q., Zhou, Q.: A survey on silicon PUFs and recent advances in ring oscillator PUFs. J. Comput. Sci. Technol. **29**(4), 664–678 (2014). https://doi.org/10.1007/s11390-014-1458-1
29. Zhang, J., Wan, L.: CMOS: dynamic multi-key obfuscation structure for strong PUFs. CoRR abs/1806.02011 (2018)

Error-Free Lattice-Based Key Encapsulation Mechanism Based on Ring-LWE

Chik How Tan and Theo Fanuela Prabowo[(✉)] [iD]

Temasek Laboratories, National University of Singapore,
5A Engineering Drive 1, #09-02, Singapore 117411, Singapore
{tsltch,tsltfp}@nus.edu.sg

Abstract. As most of the published lattice based encryptions and key encapsulation mechanisms have decryption failure, they are subjected to side-channel attacks. In this paper, we construct an error-free lattice-based key encapsulation mechanism (KEM) which is based on LPR encryption. We also examine some new classes of cyclotomic polynomials for the new error-free lattice-based KEM. The proposed error-free KEM has a reasonable public key size of about 1.472 Kbytes for 128-bit quantum security level. This is comparable to those submitted to the NIST PQC standardization.

Keywords: Lattice-based key encapsulation mechanism ·
Lattice-based encryption · Cyclotomic polynomial

1 Introduction

In 1997, Ajtai and Dwork [1] introduced the first lattice-based encryption. But, the encryption is insecure and the public key size is very large. It was later attacked by [30]. In 2005, Regev [32,33] introduced the learning with error problem (LWE) and proved that LWE is hard to be solved, even using quantum computers, if the shortest vector problem is hard. He also showed that LWE is pseudorandom and constructed a lattice-based encryption that is provably secure against chosen-plaintext attack (CPA). Since then, many variant lattice-based encryption and signature schemes were constructed. In 2010, Lyubashevsky et al. [27,29] extended the LWE problem to Ring-LWE (RLWE) and constructed lattice-based encryption based on RLWE. They also showed that RLWE encryption is secure against chosen-plaintext attack. The advantage of RLWE encryption over LWE encryption is that it has shorter public key size and better efficiency. Since then, many RLWE encryptions, signatures, homomorphic encryptions, attribute-based encryptions, etc. were proposed.

Recently, NIST made a call for post-quantum standardization. There are 27 lattice-based submissions. Twenty-two of them are for public key encryption, key encapsulation mechanism and key exchange; while the other five are lattice-based

© Springer Nature Switzerland AG 2021
G. Nicolescu et al. (Eds.): FPS 2020, LNCS 12637, pp. 163–179, 2021.
https://doi.org/10.1007/978-3-030-70881-8_11

signature schemes. Majority of them are based on the Lyubashevsky-Peikert-Regev (LPR) encryption [27,29] and its variants, except for three of them, which are based on NTRU [7,8,24]. Among these lattice-based submissions, the public key size of the schemes using RLWE is shorter than that of the schemes using LWE.

Most lattice-based NIST PQC submissions (e.g. Frodo [5], LAC [26], NewHope [4], Round 5 [6], Saber [18], Three bears [21], etc.) are variants of LPR encryption [27,29] and their security proofs mostly rely on the security proof in [32,33]. In 2016, Chatterjee et al. [14] found that the security reduction proofs of [32,33] are not tight. In 2019, Sarkar et al. [35] further pointed out that the tightness loss in the security reduction proof is almost exponentiation. Furthermore, most of the lattice-based encryptions, key encapsulation mechanisms and key exchange schemes have decryption failure. Hence, they are subjected to side-channel attacks by exploiting the decryption failure, for example the side channel attacks to recover the private keys on FrodoKEM, Saber, Kyber, LAC, Round 5 [10,15–17,20,37]. In this paper, we will construct lattice-based encryption and key encapsulation mechanism without decryption failure, which we call error-free LPR encryption and error-free LPR KEM respectively. In addition, we also give the parameters for different security levels, which are, 128-bit, 192-bit, and 256-bit quantum security level.

The organization of this paper is as follows. In Sect. 2, we provide a brief review on lattices and ring learning with error problem (RLWE). In Sect. 3, we examine some new cyclotomic polynomials (other than $x^n + 1$). In Sect. 4, we construct error-free encryption by using different classes of cyclotomic polynomials and giving the lower bound for the modulus q in order to have error-free decryption. In Sect. 5, we extend the error-free LPR encryption to key encapsulation mechanism. Sect. 6 gives public/secret key size and ciphertext size for various security levels. Finally, we conclude the paper in Sect. 7.

2   Preliminaries

In this section, we give a brief review on lattices and RLWE. A lattice $\mathcal{L}$ is defined as the set of all integer linear combinations of n vectors $\mathbf{b_1}, \cdots, \mathbf{b_n} \in \mathbb{R}^n$ which are linearly independent over $\mathbb{R}$. We give a formal definition of lattices as follows.

Definition 1. *Let* $\mathbf{b_1}, \cdots, \mathbf{b_n} \in \mathbb{R}^n$ *be* n *linearly independent vectors. Define the lattice generated by* $\mathbf{b_1}, \cdots, \mathbf{b_n}$ *as the set*

$$\mathcal{L}(\mathbf{b_1}, \cdots, \mathbf{b_n}) := \left\{ \sum_{i=1}^{n} x_i \mathbf{b_i} \mid x_i \in \mathbb{Z}, \, i = 1, \cdots, n \right\}.$$

The set of vectors $\{\mathbf{b_1}, \cdots, \mathbf{b_n}\}$ *is called a basis of the lattice* $\mathcal{L}$.
The norm of a vector $\mathbf{v} = (v_1, \cdots, v_n) \in \mathbb{R}^n$ *is defined as* $\|\mathbf{v}\| := \sqrt{\sum_{i=1}^{n} v_i^2}$.

A basis can be represented as a matrix $\mathbf{B} = [\mathbf{b_1}, \cdots, \mathbf{b_n}]^T \in \mathbb{R}^{n \times n}$ having the basis as its row vectors. Then $\mathcal{L}(\mathbf{B}) = \{\mathbf{x}\mathbf{B} \mid \mathbf{x} \in \mathbb{Z}^n\}$. The determinant of a lattice $\mathcal{L}$ is defined as

$$\det(\mathcal{L}) = |\det(\mathbf{B})| = \sqrt{|\det(\mathbf{B}^T\mathbf{B})|},$$

where $\mathbf{B}$ is a basis of $\mathcal{L}$. Note that the determinant of a lattice does not depend on the choice of the basis $\mathbf{B}$. The determinant of $\mathcal{L}$ is also called the volume of a lattice $\mathcal{L}$ as $\mathrm{Vol}(\mathcal{L}) = |\det(\mathbf{B})|$.

Given a lattice, there are three well-known computational problems, namely the shortest vector problem (SVP), the closest vector problem (CVP), and the shortest independent vector problem (SIVP). So far, the closest vector problem (CVP) is proved to be NP-hard [12,25] in the worst case, while SIVP is not yet proved to be NP-hard and SVP is only proved NP-hard in randomized reduction [2]. Now, we describe these three problems as follows.

- **The Shortest Vector Problem (SVP):** Given a basis $\mathbf{B}$ of a lattice $\mathcal{L} \subseteq \mathbb{R}^n$, find the shortest nonzero vector in $\mathcal{L}(\mathbf{B})$.
- **The Closest Vector Problem (CVP):** Given a basis $\mathbf{B}$ of a lattice $\mathcal{L} \subseteq \mathbb{R}^n$ and a vector $\mathbf{y} \in \mathbb{R}^n$, find a lattice point in $\mathcal{L}(\mathbf{B})$, which is closest to $\mathbf{y}$.
- **The Shortest Independent Vector Problem (SIVP):** Given a basis $\mathbf{B}$ of a lattice $\mathcal{L} \subseteq \mathbb{R}^n$, find n linearly independent vectors $\mathbf{v_1}, \cdots, \mathbf{v_n} \in \mathcal{L}(\mathbf{B})$ that minimize $\max_{1 \leq i \leq n}\{\|\mathbf{v_i}\|\}$.

Ring Learning with Error (RLWE). The learning with error problem was first introduced by Regev [32,33]. Given a secret vector $\mathbf{s} \in \mathbb{Z}_q^n$, a uniformly random vector $\mathbf{a} \in \mathbb{Z}_q^n$ and an error $e \leftarrow \chi$, where χ is an error distribution over $\mathbb{Z}_q$. An LWE-sample produces the pair $(\mathbf{a}, b = \langle \mathbf{a}, \mathbf{s} \rangle + e \bmod q) \in \mathbb{Z}_q^n \times \mathbb{Z}_q$. For m LWE-samples $(\mathbf{a_i}, b_i = \langle \mathbf{a_i}, \mathbf{s} \rangle + e_i \bmod q)$, we use matrix notation as follows: $(\mathbf{A}, \mathbf{b} = \mathbf{s}\mathbf{A} + \mathbf{e} \bmod q) \in \mathbb{Z}_q^{n \times m} \times \mathbb{Z}_q^m$, where $\mathbf{A} \in \mathbb{Z}_q^{n \times m}$, the vectors $\mathbf{a_i}$'s form the columns of $\mathbf{A}$, and $\mathbf{b} = (b_1, \cdots, b_m)$, $\mathbf{e} = (e_1, \cdots, e_m)$.

In 2010, Lyubashevsky et al. [27,29] extended the LWE to Ring-LWE (RLWE) which explores the algebraic structure. Let $\mathcal{R}_q = \mathbb{Z}_q[x]/(f(x))$, where $f(x)$ is a cyclotomic polynomial over $\mathbb{Z}$ of degree n. The RLWE-distribution $\mathcal{D}_{\mathbf{s},\chi}$ is $(\mathbf{A}, \mathbf{b} = \mathbf{s}\mathbf{A} + \mathbf{e}) \in \mathcal{R}_q \times \mathcal{R}_q$, where $\mathbf{s} \in \mathcal{R}_q$ is a fixed secret polynomial, $\mathbf{A}$ is sampled uniformly randomly from $\mathcal{R}_q$, and $\mathbf{e} \in \mathcal{R}_q$ is sampled according to the error distribution χ.

One may draw some analogies between RLWE and LWE. Given a polynomial $e \in \mathcal{R}_q$. This polynomial is of degree at most $n - 1$. By taking the coefficients of $x^0, x^1, \cdots, x^{n-1}$ in $e(x)$, we get a vector $\mathbf{e}$ in $\mathbb{Z}_q^n$. Conversely, given a vector $\mathbf{e} = (e_0, e_1, \cdots, e_{n-1}) \in \mathbb{Z}_q^n$, we may obtain an element $e := \sum_{i=0}^{n-1} e_i x^i \in \mathcal{R}_q$. Given $g \in \mathcal{R}_q$, one may construct a matrix $\mathbf{A}_g \in \mathbb{Z}_q^{n \times n}$ as follows. The i-th row of the matrix $\mathbf{A}_g \in \mathbb{Z}_q^{n \times n}$ consists of the coefficients of $x^i g(x) \bmod f(x)$, for $i = 0, \cdots, n - 1$.

Definition 2 (Search RLWE Problem). *Given an RLWE instance* $(\mathbf{A}, \mathbf{b} = \mathbf{s}\mathbf{A} + \mathbf{e}) \in \mathcal{D}_{\mathbf{s},\chi}$, *find* $\mathbf{s} \in \mathcal{R}_q$.

Definition 3 (Decision RLWE Problem). *Given a pair* $(\mathbf{A}, \mathbf{b}) \in \mathcal{R}_q \times \mathcal{R}_q$, *determine whether it is from* $\mathcal{D}_{\mathbf{s},\chi}$ *or uniform distribution over* $\mathcal{R}_q \times \mathcal{R}_q$.

It is well-known that the search RLWE problem is at least as hard as the decision RLWE problem. Lyubashevsky et al. [27–29] showed that the search RLWE problem quantumly reduces to the decision problem. They also showed that $\mathcal{D}_{\mathbf{s},\chi}$ is pseudorandom. This means that the average case decision RLWE problem is hard.

In 2017, Peikert et al. [31] further extended the RLWE based on cyclotomic polynomial to RLWE based on any irreducible polynomial $f(x)$. They also showed some results similar to those of Lyubashevsky et al. [27–29].

IND-CPA Security. The IND-CPA security of an encryption scheme is defined as a security game between a challenger $\mathcal{C}$ and an adversary $\mathcal{A}$ described as follows:

- given security parameter λ, $\mathcal{C}$ sends a public key to $\mathcal{A}$,
- $\mathcal{A}$ chooses two messages m_0, m_1 and sends them to $\mathcal{C}$,
- $\mathcal{C}$ picks $b \in \{0,1\}$ randomly and sends the encryption of m_b to $\mathcal{A}$
- $\mathcal{A}$ outputs $b' \in \{0,1\}$.

The adversary $\mathcal{A}$ wins if $b' = b$. Define $\mathrm{Adv}^{\mathsf{IND\text{-}CPA}}(\lambda) = |\Pr[b' = b] - \frac{1}{2}|$. The scheme is IND-CPA secure if $\mathrm{Adv}^{\mathsf{IND\text{-}CPA}}(\lambda)$ is negligible.

3   Cyclotomic Polynomials

In [27,29], it is shown that the LPR encryption is CPA-secure based on RLWE assumption and their cyclotomic polynomial is $x^{2^k} + 1$, which splits into linear factors over $\mathbb{F}_q$. A polynomial $\Phi_m(x) \in \mathbb{Z}[x]$ is called cyclotomic polynomial if $\Phi_m(x)$ is an irreducible polynomial of degree $\phi(m)$ over $\mathbb{Z}$ and $\Phi_m(x) \mid (x^m - 1)$ for some minimum m, where ϕ is the Euler function. In this section, we will examine more cyclotomic polynomials $\Phi_m(x)$. These polynomials have the property that they split completely into linear factors over $\mathbb{F}_q$ for any prime $q \equiv 1 \bmod m$.

Theorem 1. *Suppose* $e \geq 1$, p *is a prime,* $m = p^e$, *and* q *is a prime with* $q \equiv 1 \bmod m$. *Then* $\Phi_m(x) = \sum_{i=0}^{p-1} x^{p^{e-1}i}$ *and it splits into linear factors over* $\mathbb{F}_q$.

Proof. Consider $x^m - 1 = (x^{p^{e-1}})^p - 1 = (x^{p^{e-1}} - 1) \sum_{i=0}^{p-1} x^{p^{e-1}i}$. Since $\sum_{i=0}^{p-1} x^{p^{e-1}i}$ divides $x^m - 1$ and is of degree $p^{e-1}(p-1) = \phi(m)$, we conclude that $\Phi_m(x) = \sum_{i=0}^{p-1} x^{p^{e-1}i}$.

Since $q \equiv 1 \bmod p^e$, then $q = p^e j + 1$ for some j. Let g be a generator of $\mathbb{F}_q^\times$ and $\hat{g} = g^j$. Then, the order of $\hat{g}$ is p^e. Consider $\hat{g}^l$, where l is coprime to p^e and $l < p^e$. Substituting $x = \hat{g}^l$ into $x^m - 1 = (x^{p^{e-1}} - 1) \sum_{i=0}^{p-1} x^{p^{e-1}i}$ gives

$$0 = (\hat{g}^l)^{p^e} - 1 = ((\hat{g}^l)^{p^{e-1}} - 1) \sum_{i=0}^{p-1} (\hat{g}^l)^{p^{e-1}i} \quad \text{in } \mathbb{F}_q.$$

As $(\hat{g}^l)^{p^{e-1}} - 1 \neq 0$, we have $\sum_{i=0}^{p-1}(\hat{g}^l)^{p^{e-1}i} = 0$ in $\mathbb{F}_q$. Therefore, $\hat{g}^l$ is a root of $\sum_{i=0}^{p-1} x^{p^{e-1}i}$. We note that there are $\phi(p^e) = p^{e-1}(p-1)$ such l (satisfying l coprime to p and $0 < l < p^e$). Hence, we have found $\phi(p^e)$ roots $\hat{g}^l$ of $\sum_{i=0}^{p-1} x^{p^{e-1}i}$ over $\mathbb{F}_q$. We conclude that $\sum_{i=0}^{p-1} x^{p^{e-1}i}$ splits into linear factors over $\mathbb{F}_q$.

Corollary 1. *Let $e \geq 1$, $m = 2^e$, $k = 2^{e-1}$, and q be a prime with $q \equiv 1 \bmod m$. Then $x^k + 1$ is a cyclotomic polynomial and splits into linear factors over $\mathbb{F}_q$.*

Proof. Letting $p = 2$ in Theorem 1 gives the result.

Corollary 2. *Let $e \geq 1$, $m = 3^e$, $k = 3^{e-1}$, and q be a prime with $q \equiv 1 \bmod m$. Then $x^{2k} + x^k + 1$ is a cyclotomic polynomial and splits into linear factors over $\mathbb{F}_q$.*

Proof. Letting $p = 3$ in Theorem 1 gives the result.

Corollary 3. *Let p and q be primes with $q \equiv 1 \bmod p$. Then $\sum_{i=0}^{p-1} x^i$ is a cyclotomic polynomial and splits into linear factors over $\mathbb{F}_q$.*

Proof. Letting $e = 1$ and $m = p$ in Theorem 1 gives the result.

Theorem 2. *Suppose $a, b \geq 1$, $p \geq 3$ is a prime, $m = 2^a p^b$, and q is a prime with $q \equiv 1 \bmod m$. Then $\Phi_m(x) = \sum_{i=0}^{p-1}(-1)^i x^{2^{a-1}p^{b-1}i}$ and it splits into linear factors over $\mathbb{F}_q$.*

Proof. We divide into two cases: (i) $a = 1$ and (ii) $a \geq 2$.
Case (i) $a = 1$: Consider the following factorization of $x^m - 1$.

$$x^{2p^b} - 1 = (x^{p^b} - 1)(x^{p^b} + 1)$$
$$= ((x^{p^{b-1}})^p - 1)((x^{p^{b-1}})^p + 1)$$
$$= (x-1)(x+1)(\sum_{i=0}^{p-1} x^{p^{b-1}i})(\sum_{i=0}^{p-1}(-1)^i x^{p^{b-1}i}).$$

By Theorem 1, $\sum_{i=0}^{p-1} x^{p^{b-1}i} = \Phi_{p^b}(x)$. Note that $\sum_{i=0}^{p-1}(-1)^i x^{p^{b-1}i}$ is a polynomial of degree $p^{b-1}(p-1) = \phi(2p^b)$ dividing $x^{2p^b} - 1$. Hence, $\sum_{i=0}^{p-1}(-1)^i x^{p^{b-1}i}$ must be the cyclotomic polynomial $\Phi_{2p^b}(x)$.

Since $q \equiv 1 \bmod 2p^b$, then $q = 2p^b j + 1$ for some j. Let g be a generator of $\mathbb{F}_q^\times$ and $\hat{g} = g^j$. Then the order of $\hat{g}$ is $2p^b$. Consider $\hat{g}^l$, where l is coprime to $2p^b$ and $0 < l < 2p^b$. Substituting $x = \hat{g}^l$ to $x^{2p^b} - 1 = (x-1)(x+1)(\sum_{i=0}^{p-1} x^{p^{b-1}i})(\sum_{i=0}^{p-1}(-1)^i x^{p^{b-1}i})$, we have

$$0 = (\hat{g}^l)^{2p^b} - 1 = (\hat{g}^l - 1)(\hat{g}^l + 1)\sum_{i=0}^{p-1}(\hat{g}^l)^{p^{b-1}i}\sum_{i=0}^{p-1}(-1)^i(\hat{g}^l)^{p^{b-1}i} \quad \text{in } \mathbb{F}_q.$$

We know that $\hat{g}^l - 1 \neq 0$ and $\hat{g}^l + 1 \neq 0$ in $\mathbb{F}_q$. As $(\hat{g}^l)^{p^b} \neq 1$, then $\sum_{i=0}^{p-1}(\hat{g}^l)^{p^{b-1}i} \neq 0$. Hence, $\sum_{i=0}^{p-1}(-1)^i(\hat{g}^l)^{p^{b-1}i} = 0$ in $\mathbb{F}_q$. Therefore, $\hat{g}^l$ is a root of $\sum_{i=0}^{p-1}(-1)^i x^{p^{b-1}i}$. Note that there are $\phi(2p^b) = p^{b-1}(p-1)$ such l (satisfying l is coprime to $2p^b$ and $0 < l < 2p^b$). Hence, we have found $\phi(2p^b)$ roots $\hat{g}^l$ of $\sum_{i=0}^{p-1}(-1)^i x^{p^{b-1}i}$ over $\mathbb{F}_q$. We conclude that $\sum_{i=0}^{p-1}(-1)^i x^{p^{b-1}i}$ splits into linear factors over $\mathbb{F}_q$.

Case (ii) $a \geq 2$: Consider the following factorization of $x^m - 1$.

$$x^{2^a p^b} - 1 = (x^{2^{a-1}p^b} - 1)(x^{2^{a-1}p^b} + 1)$$
$$= ((x^{2^{a-2}p^b})^2 - 1)((x^{2^{a-1}p^{b-1}})^p + 1)$$
$$= (x^{2^{a-2}p^b} - 1)(x^{2^{a-2}p^b} + 1)(x^{2^{a-1}p^{b-1}} + 1)\sum_{i=0}^{p-1}(-1)^i x^{2^{a-1}p^{b-1}i}.$$

Note that the degree of $\sum_{i=0}^{p-1}(-1)^i x^{2^{a-1}p^{b-1}i}$ is $2^{a-1}p^{b-1}(p-1) = \phi(m)$ and is bigger than that of $x^{2^{a-2}p^b} - 1$, $x^{2^{a-2}p^b} + 1$, and $x^{2^{a-1}p^{b-1}} + 1$. Hence, $\Phi_m(x) = \sum_{i=0}^{p-1}(-1)^i x^{2^{a-1}p^{b-1}i}$.

Since $q \equiv 1 \bmod 2^a p^b$, then $q = 2^a p^b j + 1$ for some j. Let g be a generator of $\mathbb{F}_q^\times$ and $\hat{g} = g^j$. Then the order of $\hat{g}$ is $2^a p^b$. Consider $\hat{g}^l$, where l is coprime to $2^a p^b$ and $0 < l < 2^a p^b$. Substituting $x = \hat{g}^l$ into $x^{2^a p^b} - 1 = (x^{2^{a-2}p^b} - 1)(x^{2^{a-2}p^b} + 1)(x^{2^{a-1}p^{b-1}} + 1)\sum_{i=0}^{p-1}(-1)^i x^{2^{a-1}p^{b-1}i}$ gives

$$(\hat{g}^l)^{2^a p^b} - 1 = ((\hat{g}^l)^{2^{a-2}p^b} - 1)((\hat{g}^l)^{2^{a-2}p^b} + 1)((\hat{g}^l)^{2^{a-1}p^{b-1}} + 1)\sum_{i=0}^{p-1}(-1)^i(\hat{g}^l)^{2^{a-1}p^{b-1}i},$$

where the equality above holds in $\mathbb{F}_q$. Note that the left hand side of the above equation is zero, while $(\hat{g}^l)^{2^{a-2}p^b} - 1$, $(\hat{g}^l)^{2^{a-2}p^b} + 1$, and $(\hat{g}^l)^{2^{a-1}p^{b-1}} + 1$ are nonzero. Hence, $\sum_{i=0}^{p-1}(-1)^i(\hat{g}^l)^{2^{a-1}p^{b-1}i} = 0$ in $\mathbb{F}_q$. Therefore, $\hat{g}^l$ is a root of $\sum_{i=0}^{p-1}(-1)^i x^{p^{e-1}i}$. Note that there are $\phi(2^a p^b) = 2^{a-1}p^{e-1}(p-1)$ such l (satisfying l coprime to $2^a p^b$ and $0 < l < 2^a p^b$). Hence, we have found $\phi(2^a p^b)$ roots $\hat{g}^l$ of $\sum_{i=0}^{p-1}(-1)^i x^{2^{a-1}p^{b-1}i}$ over $\mathbb{F}_q$. We conclude that $\sum_{i=0}^{p-1}(-1)^i x^{2^{a-1}p^{b-1}i}$ splits into linear factors over $\mathbb{F}_q$.

Corollary 4. *Let $a, b \geq 1$, $m = 2^a 3^b$, $k = 2^{a-1}3^{b-1}$ and q be a prime with $q \equiv 1 \bmod m$. Then $x^{2k} - x^k + 1$ is a cyclotomic polynomial and splits into linear factors over $\mathbb{F}_q$.*

Proof. Letting $p = 3$ in Theorem 2 gives the result.

Summarizing the above theorems and corollaries, we listed the above cyclotomic polynomials in the following Table 1.

Table 1. Some cyclotomic polynomials

$f(x) = \Phi_m(x)$	m	k	$n = \phi(m)$	Corollary
$x^k + 1$	2^{e+1}	2^e	k	1
$x^{2k} + x^k + 1$	3^{e+1}	3^e	$2k$	2
$\sum_{i=0}^{k} x^i$	p prime	$p-1$	k	3
$x^{2k} - x^k + 1$	$2^{a+1}3^{b+1}$	$2^a 3^b$	$2k$	4

4 Error-Free LPR Encryption (ER-LPR$_{\mathsf{PKE}}$)

In the following, we give a description of our error-free LPR encryption, which is a modification of the LPR encryption proposed in [27, 29] (the original LPR encryption is only defined on $f(x) = x^n + 1$). We will also show that our proposed error-free LPR encryption is IND-CPA secure.

Let $\mathcal{R}_d = \mathbb{Z}_d[x]/(f(x))$, where d is an integer and $f(x)$ is an irreducible polynomial of degree n over $\mathbb{Z}$. Let q be a prime and p be a positive integer with $p < q$. As usual, we always take $\mathbb{Z}_d = \{-\frac{d-1}{2}, \cdots, \frac{d-1}{2}\}$ for odd integer d. In this way, we may treat $\mathbb{Z}_p \subseteq \mathbb{Z}_q$.

Key Generation: To generate a secret and public key pairs, the receiver performs the following:

(1) Choose a random polynomial $\mathbf{A} \in \mathcal{R}_q^*$.
(2) Choose two secret random polynomials $\mathbf{s}, \mathbf{e} \in \mathcal{R}_p$.
(3) Compute $\mathbf{b} = \mathbf{sA} + \mathbf{e} \in \mathcal{R}_q$.
(4) Then, the public key is $(\mathbf{A}, \mathbf{b})$ and the secret key is $\mathbf{s}$.

Encryption (ER-LPR$_{\mathsf{PKE}}$.Enc): To encrypt a message $\mathbf{m} \in \{0, 1\}^n$, the sender performs the following:

(1) Choose random $\mathbf{z}, \mathbf{d}, \mathbf{a} \in \mathcal{R}_p$.
(2) Compute $\mathbf{c_1} = -\mathbf{zA} + \mathbf{d} \in \mathcal{R}_q$ and $\mathbf{c_2} = \mathbf{zb} + \mathbf{a} + \frac{q-1}{2}\mathbf{m} \in \mathcal{R}_q$.
(3) Output the ciphertext $(\mathbf{c_1}, \mathbf{c_2})$.

Decryption (ER-LPR$_{\mathsf{PKE}}$.Dec): The receiver received the ciphertext $(\mathbf{c_1}, \mathbf{c_2})$. He computes the message $\mathbf{m}$ as follows:

(1) Compute $\mathbf{c} = \mathbf{sc_1} + \mathbf{c_2} \in \mathcal{R}_q$. Note that

$$\mathbf{sc_1} + \mathbf{c_2} = \mathbf{s}(-\mathbf{zA} + \mathbf{d}) + (\mathbf{z}(\mathbf{sA} + \mathbf{e}) + \mathbf{a} + \frac{q-1}{2}\mathbf{m})$$

$$= (\mathbf{ze} + \mathbf{ds} + \mathbf{a}) + \frac{q-1}{2}\mathbf{m} \quad \text{in } \mathcal{R}_q.$$

(2) To recover the message $m_i \in \mathbf{m}$, let c_i and E_i be the coefficient of $\mathbf{c}$ and $\mathbf{E} = \mathbf{ze} + \mathbf{ds} + \mathbf{a}$ respectively. Suppose $E_i \in [-B, B]$ (for some value B to be determined later). Compute $c_i + B$. Then,

$$m_i = \begin{cases} 0 & \text{if } c_i + B < \frac{q-1}{2}, \\ 1 & \text{otherwise.} \end{cases}$$

Thus, the receiver obtains the message $\mathbf{m}$.

Remark 1. *(a) Part (2) in the decryption process above is different from that of LPR [27, 29]. Their decryption is probabilistic. On the other hand, the above encryption scheme has no decryption failure.*
(b) In order to have error-free decryption, we need to determine an upper bound B for the absolute value of each coefficient E_i of $\mathbf{E} = \mathbf{ze} + \mathbf{ds} + \mathbf{a}$. We shall do this in the next proposition and corollary.

Proposition 1. *Let* $u(x) = \sum_{i=0}^{n-1} u_i x^i$, $v(x) = \sum_{i=0}^{n-1} v_i x^i$ *and* $w(x) = u(x)v(x) \in \mathcal{R}_q$. *Then,*

(1) For $f(x) = x^n + 1$, each coefficient of $w(x)$ contains exactly n terms of $u_i v_j$.
(2) For $n = 2k$ and $\sigma \in \{0, 1\}$, $f(x) = x^{2k} + (-1)^\sigma x^k + 1$, each coefficient of $w(x)$ contains at most $3k = \frac{3}{2}n$ terms of $u_i v_j$.

Proof. (1) Let $u(x) = \sum_{i=0}^{n-1} u_i x^i$ and $v(x) = \sum_{i=0}^{n-1} v_i x^i$. Then the coefficient w_i of $w(x) = u(x)v(x) \in \mathcal{R}_q$ is $w_i = \sum_{j=0}^{n-1} s_j u_j v_{n-j+i \bmod n}$, where

$$s_j = \begin{cases} 1 & \text{if } i - j \geq 0, \\ -1 & \text{otherwise.} \end{cases}$$

We conclude that w_i has exactly n terms of $u_i v_j$.
(2) Let $u(x) = \sum_{i=0}^{2k-1} u_i x^i$ and $v(x) = \sum_{i=0}^{2k-1} v_i x^i$. Then the coefficient w_i of $w(x) = u(x)v(x) \in \mathcal{R}_q$ is
(a) For $0 \leq i \leq k - 1$,

$$w_i = \sum_{j=0}^{2k-1} s_j u_j v_{(2k-j+i) \bmod 2k} + \sum_{j=0}^{k-1} s'_j u_{k+j} v_{(2k-j+i) \bmod 2k},$$

where

$$s_j = \begin{cases} 1 & \text{if } i - j \geq 0, \\ -1 & \text{otherwise,} \end{cases} \qquad s'_j = \begin{cases} (-1)^{\sigma+1} & \text{if } i < j \leq k - 1, \\ 0 & \text{otherwise.} \end{cases}$$

(b) For $k \leq i \leq 2k - 1$,

$$w_i = \sum_{j=0}^{2k-1} s_j u_j v_{(2k-j+i) \bmod 2k} + \sum_{j=0}^{2k-1} s'_j u_j v_{(k-j+i) \bmod 2k},$$

where

$$s_j = \begin{cases} 1 & \text{if } i - j \geq 0, \\ 0 & \text{otherwise,} \end{cases} \qquad s'_j = \begin{cases} (-1)^{\sigma+1} & \text{if } i - k < j \leq 2k - 1, \\ 0 & \text{otherwise.} \end{cases}$$

For part (a), w_i has $2k$ terms and at most $k-1$ terms of s_j and s'_j respectively. So, w_i has at most $3k - 1$ terms of $u_i v_j$ for part (a). For part (b), w_i has $i + 1$ terms and $2k - 1 - (i - k + 1) + 1 = 3k - i - 1$ terms of s_j and s'_j respectively. Therefore, w_i has $3k$ terms of $u_i v_j$ for part (b). Hence, w_i has at most $3k$ terms of $u_i v_j$.

Corollary 5. *Suppose each coefficient of* $\mathbf{s}, \mathbf{z}, \mathbf{e}, \mathbf{d}, \mathbf{a}$ *is in* $[-n_1, n_1] \cap \mathbb{Z}$. *Let* E_i *be a coefficient of* $\mathbf{E} = \mathbf{ze} + \mathbf{ds} + \mathbf{a} \in \mathcal{R}_q$. *Then*

(1) For $f(x) = x^n + 1$, *we have* $|E_i| \leq 2nn_1^2 + n_1$.
(2) For $n = 2k$, $\sigma \in \{0, 1\}$, *and* $f(x) = x^{2k} + (-1)^\sigma x^k + 1$, *we have* $|E_i| \leq 3nn_1^2 + n_1$.

Proof. (1) By part (1) of Proposition 1, each coefficient of $\mathbf{ze}$ has n terms of $z_i e_j$, where z_i and e_j are the coefficients of $\mathbf{z}$ and $\mathbf{e}$ respectively. Therefore, the absolute value of each coefficient of $\mathbf{ze}$ is at most nn_1^2. Similarly, the absolute value of each coefficient of $\mathbf{ds}$ is at most nn_1^2. Hence, $|E_i| \leq 2nn_1^2 + n_1$.
(2) By part (2) of Proposition 1 and similar argument as above, we conclude that $|E_i| \leq 3nn_1^2 + n_1$.

Using Corollary 5, we obtain the bound B to be either $2nn_1^2 + n_1$ or $3nn_1^2 + n_1$ depending on whether $f(x) = x^n + 1$ or $f(x) = x^n \pm x^{\frac{n}{2}} + 1$. Recall that $|E_i| \leq B$. In order to achieve error-free decryption, we shall take $\frac{q-1}{2} > 2B$, i.e. $q > 4B + 1$.

Theorem 1. *Let* E_i's *be the coefficients of* $\mathbf{E} = \mathbf{ze} + \mathbf{ds} + \mathbf{a}$. *Suppose* $|E_i| \leq B$ *for all* i. *If* $q > 4B + 1$, *then the decryption in* **ER-LPR**$_{\mathsf{PKE}}$ *is error-free.*

Proof. If $m_i = 0$, then $c_i + B = E_i + B \leq 2B < \frac{q-1}{2}$. If $m_i = 1$, then $c_i + B = E_i + B + \frac{q-1}{2} \geq \frac{q-1}{2}$. This shows that $m_i = 0$ if and only if $c_i + B < \frac{q-1}{2}$. Thus, the decryption is error-free.

We list the results in Table 2 below.

Table 2. Bound B

$f(x)$	m	k	n	B	$q >$
$x^k + 1$	2^{e+1}	2^e	k	$2nn_1^2 + n_1$	$8nn_1^2 + 4n_1 + 1$
$x^{2k} - x^k + 1$	$2^{a+1}3^{b+1}$	$2^a 3^b$	$2k$	$3nn_1^2 + n_1$	$12nn_1^2 + 4n_1 + 1$
$x^{2k} + x^k + 1$	e^{e+1}	3^e	$2k$	$3nn_1^2 + n_1$	$12nn_1^2 + 4n_1 + 1$

In order to further reduce the public key size, we can restrict the number of non-zero coefficients in $\mathbf{s}, \mathbf{z}, \mathbf{e}, \mathbf{d}, \mathbf{a}$. In the following proposition, we give a new bound B for the coefficients of $\mathbf{E} = \mathbf{ze} + \mathbf{ds} + \mathbf{a} \in \mathcal{R}_q$ when we restrict the number of non-zero coefficients in $\mathbf{s}, \mathbf{z}, \mathbf{e}, \mathbf{d}, \mathbf{a}$. We first give an important theorem which will be used to prove the proposition.

Theorem 3 ([22], Sect. 10.2, Theorem 368). *Let $\{u_i\}_{i=0}^{d-1}$ and $\{v_i\}_{i=0}^{d-1}$ be two increasing sequences, where $u_i, v_i \in \mathbb{R}$, that is, $u_0 \leq u_1 \leq \cdots \leq u_{d-2} \leq u_{d-1}$ and $v_0 \leq v_1 \leq \cdots \leq v_{d-2} \leq v_{d-1}$. Let $\rho = \sum_{i=0}^{d-1} u_i v_i$ and $\mu = \sum_{i=0}^{d-1} u_i v_{d-i}$ and σ be a permutation of $\{0, 1, \cdots, d-1\}$. Then, $\mu \leq \sum_{i=0}^{d-1} u_i v_{\sigma(i)} \leq \rho$.*

Proposition 2. *Suppose each coefficient of $\mathbf{s}, \mathbf{z}, \mathbf{e}, \mathbf{d},$ and $\mathbf{a}$ is in $[-n_1, n_1] \cap \mathbb{Z}$. Let $t = \lfloor \frac{3n}{8n_1} \rfloor$ and*

$$\rho = 2 \sum_{i=1}^{n_1} i^2 = \frac{n_1(n_1 + 1)(2n_1 + 1)}{3}.$$

Assume that the coefficients of each of $\mathbf{s}, \mathbf{z}, \mathbf{e}, \mathbf{d}, \mathbf{a}$ consist of t times of any nonzero integer $u \in [-n_1, n_1]$ (and $n - 2tn_1$ zeros). Let E_i be a coefficient of $\mathbf{E} = \mathbf{ze} + \mathbf{ds} + \mathbf{a} \in \mathcal{R}_q$. Then,

(1) For $f(x) = x^n + 1$, we have $|E_i| \leq 2t\rho + n_1$.
(2) For n even, $f(x) = x^n \pm x^{\frac{n}{2}} + 1$, we have $|E_i| \leq 4t\rho + n_1$.

Proof. (1) By part (1) of Proposition 1, each coefficient of $\mathbf{ze}$ has n terms of $z_i e_j$, where z_i and e_j are the coefficients of $\mathbf{z}$ and $\mathbf{e}$ respectively; and $\mathbf{z}$ and $\mathbf{e}$ contain t times of any nonzero integer $u \in [-n_1, n_1]$. Therefore, by Theorem 3, the absolute value of each coefficient of $\mathbf{ze}$ is at most $t\rho$. Similarly, the absolute value of each coefficient of $\mathbf{ds}$ is at most $t\rho$. Hence, $|E_i| \leq 2t\rho + n_1$.

(2) By part (2) of Proposition 1, each coefficient of $\mathbf{ze}$ has $\frac{3n}{2}$ terms of $z_i e_j$, where z_i and e_j are coefficient of $\mathbf{z}, \mathbf{e}$ respectively; and $\mathbf{z}$ and $\mathbf{e}$ contain t times of each nonzero integer $u \in [-n_1, n_1]$. Therefore, by Theorem 3, the absolute value of each coefficient of $\mathbf{ze}$ is at most $2t\rho$. Similarly, the absolute value of each coefficient of $\mathbf{ds}$ is at most $2t\rho$. Hence, $|E_i| \leq 4t\rho + n_1$.

In view of the above proposition and as $q > 4B + 1$, we have the following table for when the coefficients of each of $\mathbf{s}, \mathbf{z}, \mathbf{e}, \mathbf{d}, \mathbf{a}$ consist of t times of any nonzero integer in $[-n_1, n_1]$.

Table 3. Bound B with t number of each non-zero elements

$f(x)$	m	k	n	B	$q >$
$x^k + 1$	2^{e+1}	2^e	k	$2t\rho + n_1$	$8t\rho + 4n_1 + 1$
$x^{2k} - x^k + 1$	$2^{a+1}3^{b+1}$	$2^a 3^b$	$2k$	$4t\rho + n_1$	$16t\rho + 4n_1 + 1$
$x^{2k} + x^k + 1$	3^{e+1}	3^e	$2k$	$4t\rho + n_1$	$16t\rho + 4n_1 + 1$

We end this section by showing that our error-free LPR encryption is IND-CPA secure.

Theorem 4. ER-LPR$_{PKE}$ *is IND-CPA secure.*

Proof. Let $\mathbb{G}_0$ be the usual IND-CPA game, i.e. given two messages $\mathbf{m}_0, \mathbf{m}_1$ and an encryption of one of them, say **ER-LPR$_{PKE}$.Enc($\mathbf{m}_b$)**, where $b \in \{0,1\}$. The adversary is to guess the value of b. He wins if he guesses correctly, and lose otherwise. We shall define other games called $\mathbb{G}_1$ and $\mathbb{G}_2$. For $0 \le i \le 2$, let p_i be the probability that $\mathcal{A}$ wins in $\mathbb{G}_i$.

$\mathbb{G}_1$: the only difference from $\mathbb{G}_0$ is that we choose $\mathbf{b}$ uniformly randomly from $\mathcal{R}_q$ instead of using $\mathbf{b} = \mathbf{sA} + \mathbf{e}$. Distinguishing $\mathbb{G}_0$ and $\mathbb{G}_1$ is the same as solving an instance of Decisional RLWE (D-RLWE) problem. So, $|p_0 - p_1| \le \text{Adv}(\text{D-RLWE})$.

$\mathbb{G}_2$: the only difference from $\mathbb{G}_1$ is that we choose $\mathbf{c}_1$ uniformly randomly from $\mathcal{R}_q$ instead of using $\mathbf{c}_1 = -\mathbf{zA} + \mathbf{d}$. Distinguishing $\mathbb{G}_1$ and $\mathbb{G}_2$ is the same as solving an instance of D-RLWE problem. So, $|p_1 - p_2| \le \text{Adv}(\text{D-RLWE})$.

In $\mathbb{G}_2$, $(\mathbf{c}_1, \mathbf{c}_2)$ is random as $\mathbf{b} \in \mathcal{R}_q, \mathbf{z}, \mathbf{a} \in \mathcal{R}_p$ are chosen randomly. Thus, $p_2 = \frac{1}{2}$. Hence, $\text{Adv}^{\text{IND-CPA}}(\lambda) = |p_0 - \frac{1}{2}| \le |p_0 - p_1| + |p_1 - p_2| + |p_2 - \frac{1}{2}| \le 2\text{Adv}(\text{D-RLWE})$. Therefore, **ER-LPR$_{PKE}$** is IND-CPA secure.

5   CCA2-Secure Key Encapsulation Mechanism (ER-LPR$_{KEM}$)

In this section, we apply the Fujisaki-Okamoto transformation [19] to convert our CPA-secure public key encryption (PKE) to a CCA2-secure key encapsulation mechanism (KEM).

Recently, there are some techniques [23,34] that modify the Fujisaki-Okamoto transformation to produce a provably CCA2-secure KEM in quantum random oracle model. But, Bernstein and Persichetti [9] pointed out that some of the Hofheinz-Hövelmanns-Kiltz [23] transformations are not CCA2-secure KEM and gave a generic construction of the attacks.

The only disadvantage of CCA2-secure KEM constructed using the Fujisaki-Okamoto transformation is that the security reduction proof is quadratic and not tight. But, it is still secure and many NIST submissions of lattice-based KEM are using Fujisaki-Okamoto transformation, such as [4,7,8,21,24,26]. Therefore, we will use Fujisaki-Okamoto transformation to convert our CPA-secure PKE to a CCA2-secure KEM as follows.

Key generation: This is the same as that of **ER-LPR$_{PKE}$**. The public key is $(\mathbf{A}, \mathbf{b})$ and the secret key is $\mathbf{s}$. Let $\mathcal{G}, \mathcal{H}$ be two hash functions.

Encapsulation (ER-LPR$_{KEM}$.Enc)
(1) Let $\mathbf{m} \in \mathcal{R}_2$ be a message. Compute $(\hat{K}, \mathbf{z}, \mathbf{d}, \mathbf{a}) = \mathcal{G}(\mathbf{A}, \mathbf{b}, \mathbf{m})$.
(2) Compute $(\mathbf{c}_1, \mathbf{c}_2) = \mathbf{ER\text{-}LPR}_{PKE}.\mathbf{Enc}(\mathbf{A}, \mathbf{b}, \mathbf{m})$.
(3) Compute $K = \mathcal{H}(\hat{K}, \mathbf{c}_1, \mathbf{c}_2)$.
(4) Output the ciphertext $(\mathbf{c}_1, \mathbf{c}_2)$ and key K.

Decapsulation (ER-LPR$_{\text{KEM}}$.Dec)
(1) Compute $\mathbf{m}' = $ **ER-LPR$_{\text{PKE}}$.Dec**$(\mathbf{c_1}, \mathbf{c_2})$.
(2) Compute $(\hat{K}', \mathbf{z}', \mathbf{d}', \mathbf{a}') = \mathcal{G}(\mathbf{A}, \mathbf{b}, \mathbf{m}')$.
(3) Compute $(\mathbf{c}'_1, \mathbf{c}'_2) = $ **ER-LPR$_{\text{PKE}}$.Enc**$(\mathbf{A}, \mathbf{b}, \mathbf{m}')$.
(4) If $(\mathbf{c}'_1, \mathbf{c}'_2) = (\mathbf{c_1}, \mathbf{c_2})$, then $K = \mathcal{H}(\hat{K}', \mathbf{c}'_1, \mathbf{c}'_2)$, otherwise $K = \mathcal{H}(K'', \mathbf{c}'_1, \mathbf{c}'_2)$,
   where K'' is random.

Remark 2. *Note that the decryption requires a re-encryption after recovering the message. In this process, we ensure that there is no modification of ciphertext by checking the validity of the ciphertext.*

6   ER-LPR$_{\text{KEM}}$ Parameters

In this section, we provide the parameters for our proposed encryption scheme for various security levels and various choices of cyclotomic polynomials. **ER-LPR$_{\text{KEM}}$** is based on ring learning with error problem. So far, there are some techniques to solve the ring learning with error problem, e.g. the BKW algorithm [11] and the BKZ algorithm [36]. The time complexity of BKW algorithm takes exponentiation time, while the complexity of BKZ takes sub-exponentiation time. Hence, the best technique to solve the ring learning with error problem is by solving the unique shortest vector problem (SVP) and is via BKZ algorithm. The solving method for RLWE problem is to first transform a given lattice to a new lattice and solve SVP under this new lattice. Currently, there are two well known attacks on lattices, namely the primal attack and the dual attack. Both attacks use the BKZ algorithm. As the two attacks have approximately equal complexity, we only describe the primal attack in the following.

Primal Attack: The primal attack works by first constructing an Ajtai lattice with a unique-SVP instance from the LWE problem and solving it using BKZ algorithm. Given an LWE instance $\{\mathbf{A}, \mathbf{b} = \mathbf{sA} + \mathbf{e} \bmod q\}$ of a lattice $\mathcal{L} \subseteq \mathbb{Z}^n$, secret short vectors $\mathbf{s}, \mathbf{e} \in \mathbb{Z}^n$, a matrix $\mathbf{A} \in \mathbb{Z}^{m \times n}$. Then, we consider a new lattice of dimension $d = n + m + 1$ with volume q^m defined by:

$$\Lambda(\bar{\mathbf{A}}) = \{\mathbf{x} \mid \mathbf{x}(\mathbf{A}^T \mid \mathbf{I} \mid -\mathbf{b})^T = 0 \bmod q\}.$$

The lattice $\Lambda(\bar{\mathbf{A}})$ has a unique-SVP solution $\mathbf{v} = (\mathbf{s}, \mathbf{e}, 1)$ of norm $\|\mathbf{v}\| \approx \zeta\sqrt{n+m}$, where ζ is the standard deviation of the distribution used to sample $\mathbf{s}, \mathbf{e}$.

Following the technique used in [3], the behavior of BKZ (with block size β) is modelled using the geometric series assumption to find a basis, whose Gram-Schmidt norm is given by

$$\|\mathbf{b}_i^*\| = \delta^{d-2i+1} \cdot \text{Vol}(\Lambda(\bar{\mathbf{A}}))^{\frac{1}{d}}, \quad \text{where } \delta = ((\pi\beta)^{\frac{1}{\beta}} \cdot \frac{\beta}{2\pi e})^{\frac{1}{2(\beta-1)}}.$$

In the above, δ is the estimated root Hermite factor which is an important parameter for successful running of BKZ algorithm [13].

The unique vector $\mathbf{v}$ is detected if the projection of $\mathbf{v}$ onto the vector space spanned by the last β Gram-Schmidt vectors is shorter than $\mathbf{b}^*_{d-\beta}$. Its projected norm is expected to be $\zeta\sqrt{\beta}$. Then, the attack is successful if

$$\zeta\sqrt{\beta} \le \delta^{2\beta-d+1} \cdot q^{\frac{m}{d}}.$$

In order to select secure parameters, we shall take into account the primal attack. We now compute the standard deviation of the distribution we are interested in as follows.

Lemma 1. *Let $t \ge 1$. Consider the distribution on $[-d, d] \cap \mathbb{Z}$ where each non-zero integer in $[-d, d]$ appears t times and 0 appears $n - 2dt > 0$ times. Then, the mean and standard deviation of this distribution are 0 and $\sqrt{\frac{2t}{n}\sum_{i=1}^{d} i^2}$ respectively.*

Combining the conditions for primal attack, Lemma 1, Proposition 2, Table 3 and assuming that $\mathbf{A}$ is generated by hash function with 2λ-bit seed, we obtain the parameters n, q for various quantum security levels λ (SLQ). We list them in Table 4 below.

Table 4. Parameters for **ER-LPR**$_{\mathsf{KEM}}$ according to Table 3

SLQ	$f(x)$	n	n_1	t	q	PK (byte)	SK (byte)	CT (byte)
80	$x^n + 1$	$512 = 2^9$	1	192	12289	916	128	1344
			2	96	12289	916	192	1344
			3	64	15361	916	192	1344
			4	48	25601	980	256	1440
	$x^n - x^{\frac{n}{2}} + 1$	$648 = 2^3 3^4$	1	243	9721	1154	162	1701
			2	121	19441	1235	243	1823
			3	81	52489	1316	243	1944
			4	60	58321	1316	324	1944
128	$x^n + 1$	$1024 = 2^{10}$	1	384	12289	1824	256	2688
			2	192	18433	1952	348	2880
			3	128	40961	2080	348	3072
			4	96	59393	2080	512	3072
	$x^n - x^{\frac{n}{2}} + 1$	$768 = 2^8 3$	1	288	18433	1472	192	2160
			2	144	32257	1472	288	2160
			3	96	43777	1568	288	2304
			4	72	87553	1664	384	2448
192	$x^n - x^{\frac{n}{2}} + 1$	$1296 = 2^4 3^4$	1	486	19441	2478	324	3645
			2	243	58321	2640	486	3888
			3	162	77761	2802	486	4131
			4	121	139969	2964	648	4374
256	$x^n + 1$	$2048 = 2^{11}$	1	768	40961	4160	512	6144
			2	384	40961	4160	768	6144
			3	256	61441	4160	768	6144
			4	192	114681	4416	1024	6528
	$x^n - x^{\frac{n}{2}} + 1$	$1458 = 2 \cdot 3^6$	1	546	17497	2798	365	4101
			2	273	52489	2980	547	4374
			3	182	87481	3163	547	4648
			4	136	131221	3345	729	4921

Remark 3. *Only $\frac{n}{2}$ coordinates of $\mathbf{c_2}$ is needed to be sent as part of the cipher-text as it is enough to perform the decapsulation.*

Table 5. Comparisons with lattice-based KEM in NIST PQC standardization

Scheme	PK (byte)	SK (byte)	CT (byte)	Security level
NewHope1024	1,824	3,680	2,208	5
LAC256	1,056	2,080	1,424	5
Round 5	978	1,042	1,285	5
FireSaber	1,312	3,040	1,472	5
PapaBear	1,584	40	1,697	5
Frodo-1344	21,520	43,088	21,632	5
NTRU prime	1,218	1,600	1,047	5
This paper	1,472	192	2,160	5

In Table 5, we compare our proposed key encapsulation mechanism with other lattice-based key encapsulation mechanisms submitted to the NIST PQC standardization with the same security level (defined in NIST standardization, for example, level 5 is equivalent to key search of AES-256, which has 128-bit quantum security). In the comparison, we use $f(x) = x^n - x^{\frac{n}{2}} + 1$, $n = 768$, and $n_1 = 1$. We remark that out of all the KEMs listed in Table 5, only NTRU prime [7,8] and our proposed KEM do not have decryption failure. Our error-free KEM is based on the LPR encryption, while NTRU prime is not.

As can be seen in Table 5, the public/secret key size of our error-free LPR KEM is slightly better than that of NewHope1024 [4] and comparable to others, for example, PapaBear [21] and Round 5 [6].

7   Conclusion

In this paper, we examined some cyclotomic polynomials which are useful for lattice-based encryptions. We also constructed error-free encryption and error-free key encapsulation mechanism which are based on LPR encryption. In our constructions, we gave more options on the choice of cyclotomic polynomials. Furthermore, we also gave the parameters of the error-free KEM and showed that the public key size is about 1.472 Kbytes for 128-bit quantum security level. This parameter size is comparable to those KEMs which are based on variants of LPR encryptions with decryption failure.

References

1. Ajtai, M., Dwork, C.: A public-key cryptosystem with worst-case/average-case equivalence. In: 29th ACM STOC, pp. 284–293. ACM Press, May 1997

2. Ajtai, M.: The shortest vector problem in L_2 is NP-hard for randomized reductions (extended abstract). In: Vitter, J.S. (ed.) Proceedings of the Thirtieth Annual ACM Symposium on the Theory of Computing, Dallas, Texas, USA, 23–26 May 1998, pp. 10–19. ACM (1998). https://doi.org/10.1145/276698.276705

3. Albrecht, M.R., Player, R., Scott, S.: On the concrete hardness of learning with errors. J. Math. Cryptol. **9**(3), 169–203 (2015)

4. Alkim, E., et al.: NewHope. https://newhopecrypto.org/data/NewHope_2019_04_10.pdf

5. Alkim, E., et al.: FrodoKEM learning with errors key encapsulation. https://frodokem.org/files/FrodoKEM-specification-20190702.pdf

6. Baan, H., et al.: Round5: KEM and PKE based on (ring) learning with rounding. https://round5.org/Supporting_Documentation/Round5_Submission.pdf

7. Bernstein, D.J., Chuengsatiansup, C., Lange, T., van Vredendaal, C.: NTRU Prime: reducing attack surface at low cost. In: Adams, C., Camenisch, J. (eds.) SAC 2017. LNCS, vol. 10719, pp. 235–260. Springer, Cham (2018). https://doi.org/10.1007/978-3-319-72565-9_12

8. Bernstein, D.J., Chuengsatiansup, C., Lange, T., van Vredendaal, C.: NTRU Prime. NIST submission "Supporting Documentation". https://ntruprime.cr.yp.to/nist.html

9. Bernstein, D.J., Persichetti, E.: Towards KEM unification. Cryptology ePrint Archive, report 2018/526 (2018). https://eprint.iacr.org/2018/526

10. Bindel, N., Schanck, J.M.: Decryption failure is more likely after success. In: Ding, J., Tillich, J.-P. (eds.) PQCrypto 2020. LNCS, vol. 12100, pp. 206–225. Springer, Cham (2020). https://doi.org/10.1007/978-3-030-44223-1_12

11. Blum, A., Kalai, A., Wasserman, H.: Noise-tolerant learning, the parity problem, and the statistical query model. J. ACM (JACM) **50**(4), 506–519 (2003)

12. van Emde Boas, P.: Another NP-complete partition problem and the complexity of computing short vectors in lattices. Technical report 81-04, Mathematics Department, University of Amsterdam (1981)

13. Chen, Y., Nguyen, P.Q.: BKZ 2.0: better lattice security estimates. In: Lee, D.H., Wang, X. (eds.) ASIACRYPT 2011. LNCS, vol. 7073, pp. 1–20. Springer, Heidelberg (2011). https://doi.org/10.1007/978-3-642-25385-0_1

14. Chatterjee, S., Koblitz, N., Menezes, A., Sarkar, P.: Another look at tightness II: practical issues in cryptography. In: Phan, R.C.-W., Yung, M. (eds.) Mycrypt 2016. LNCS, vol. 10311, pp. 21–55. Springer, Cham (2017). https://doi.org/10.1007/978-3-319-61273-7_3

15. Dachman-Soled, D., Ducas, L., Gong, H., Rossi, M.: LWE with side information: attacks and concrete security estimation. In: Micciancio, D., Ristenpart, T. (eds.) CRYPTO 2020. LNCS, vol. 12171, pp. 329–358. Springer, Cham (2020). https://doi.org/10.1007/978-3-030-56880-1_12

16. D'Anvers, J.-P., Guo, Q., Johansson, T., Nilsson, A., Vercauteren, F., Verbauwhede, I.: Decryption failure attacks on IND-CCA secure lattice-based schemes. In: Lin, D., Sako, K. (eds.) PKC 2019. LNCS, vol. 11443, pp. 565–598. Springer, Cham (2019). https://doi.org/10.1007/978-3-030-17259-6_19

17. D'Anvers, J.-P., Rossi, M., Virdia, F.: *(One) failure is not an option*: bootstrapping the search for failures in lattice-based encryption schemes. In: Canteaut, A., Ishai, Y. (eds.) EUROCRYPT 2020. LNCS, vol. 12107, pp. 3–33. Springer, Cham (2020). https://doi.org/10.1007/978-3-030-45727-3_1

18. D'Anvers, J.-P., Karmakar, A., Sinha Roy, S., Vercauteren, F.: Saber: module-LWR based key exchange, CPA-secure encryption and CCA-secure KEM. In: Joux, A., Nitaj, A., Rachidi, T. (eds.) AFRICACRYPT 2018. LNCS, vol. 10831, pp. 282–305. Springer, Cham (2018). https://doi.org/10.1007/978-3-319-89339-6_16

19. Fujisaki, E., Okamoto, T.: Secure integration of asymmetric and symmetric encryption schemes. J. Cryptol. **26**(1), 80–101 (2013). https://doi.org/10.1007/s00145-011-9114-1

20. Guo, Q., Johansson, T., Yang, J.: A novel CCA attack using decryption errors against LAC. In: Galbraith, S.D., Moriai, S. (eds.) ASIACRYPT 2019. LNCS, vol. 11921, pp. 82–111. Springer, Cham (2019). https://doi.org/10.1007/978-3-030-34578-5_4

21. Hamburg, M.: Post-quantum cryptography proposal: THREEBEARS. https://www.shiftleft.org/papers/threebears/nist-submission.pdf

22. Hardy, G.H., Littlewood, J.E., Pólya, G.: Inequalities, Cambridge Mathematical Library, 2nd edn. Cambridge University Press, Cambridge (1952)

23. Hofheinz, D., Hövelmanns, K., Kiltz, E.: A modular analysis of the Fujisaki-Okamoto transformation. In: Kalai, Y., Reyzin, L. (eds.) TCC 2017. LNCS, vol. 10677, pp. 341–371. Springer, Cham (2017). https://doi.org/10.1007/978-3-319-70500-2_12

24. Hoffstein, J., Pipher, J., Silverman, J.H.: NTRU: a ring-based public key cryptosystem. In: Buhler, J.P. (ed.) ANTS 1998. LNCS, vol. 1423, pp. 267–288. Springer, Heidelberg (1998). https://doi.org/10.1007/BFb0054868

25. Karp, R.M.: Reducibility among combinatorial problems. In: Miller, R.E., Thatcher, J.W., Bohlinger, J.D. (eds.) Complexity of Computer Computations. IRSS, pp. 85–103. Springer, Boston (1972). https://doi.org/10.1007/978-1-4684-2001-2_9

26. Lu, X., et al.: LAC: lattice-based cryptosystems. https://cs.rit.edu/~ats9095/csci762/pdfs/LAC.pdf

27. Lyubashevsky, V., Peikert, C., Regev, O.: On ideal lattices and learning with errors over rings. In: Gilbert, H. (ed.) EUROCRYPT 2010. LNCS, vol. 6110, pp. 1–23. Springer, Heidelberg (2010). https://doi.org/10.1007/978-3-642-13190-5_1

28. Lyubashevsky, V., Peikert, C., Regev, O.: A toolkit for ring-LWE cryptography. In: Johansson, T., Nguyen, P.Q. (eds.) EUROCRYPT 2013. LNCS, vol. 7881, pp. 35–54. Springer, Heidelberg (2013). https://doi.org/10.1007/978-3-642-38348-9_3

29. Lyubashevsky, V., Peikert, C., Regev, O.: On ideal lattices and learning with errors over rings. J. ACM **60**(6), 1–35 (2013). Article no. 43. Early version in EUROCRYPT 2010. https://doi.org/10.1145/2535925

30. Nguyen, P., Stern, J.: Cryptanalysis of the Ajtai-Dwork cryptosystem. In: Krawczyk, H. (ed.) CRYPTO 1998. LNCS, vol. 1462, pp. 223–242. Springer, Heidelberg (1998). https://doi.org/10.1007/BFb0055731

31. Peikert, C., Regev, O., Stephens-Davidowitz, N.: Pseudorandomness of ring-LWE for any ring and modulus. In: STOC, pp. 461–473. ACM (2017)

32. Regev O.: On lattices, learning with errors, random linear codes, and cryptography. In: STOC, pp. 84–93. ACM (2005)

33. Regev, O.: On lattices, learning with errors, random linear codes, and cryptography. J. ACM **56**(6), 1–40 (2009). Preliminary version in STOC 2005

34. Saito, T., Xagawa, K., Yamakawa, T.: Tightly-secure key-encapsulation mechanism in the quantum random oracle model. In: Nielsen, J.B., Rijmen, V. (eds.) EUROCRYPT 2018. LNCS, vol. 10822, pp. 520–551. Springer, Cham (2018). https://doi.org/10.1007/978-3-319-78372-7_17

35. Sarkar, P., Singha, S.: Verifying solutions to LWE with implications for concrete security. Adv. Math. Commun. (2020). https://www.aimsciences.org/article/doi/10.3934/amc.2020057

36. Schnorr, C.-P., Euchner, M.: Lattice basis reduction: improved practical algorithms and solving subset sum problems. Math. Program. **66**, 181–199 (1994). https://doi.org/10.1007/BF01581144

37. Xu, Z., et al.: Magnifying side-channel leakage of lattice-based cryptosystems with chosen ciphertexts: the case study of Kyber. Cryptology ePrint Archive, report 2020/912 (2020). https://eprint.iacr.org/2020/912

Pisces: A New Zero-Knowledge Protocol for Blockchain Privacy

Shihui Fu$^{(\boxtimes)}$ and Guang Gong

Department of Electrical and Computer Engineering, University of Waterloo,
200 University Avenue West, Waterloo, ON N2L 3G1, Canada
{shihui.fu,ggong}@uwaterloo.ca

Abstract. Applications of blockchain in banking, health care, transportation, asset and supply chain require to maintain the privacy of transactions, which can be achieved through anonymity using generic non-interactive zero-knowledge proof systems. In this work, we design and evaluate a simple zero-knowledge argument protocol for arithmetic circuit satisfiability to present verifiable encryption proof, which can offer good concrete efficiency and sublinear communication in the circuit size when combined with the regular signing process of the blockchain transactions. The proposed zero-knowledge protocol is an improved and optimized version of the lightweight sublinear protocol called Ligero (CCS 2017). The proof system requires no trusted setup, is plausibly post-quantum secure and uses only lightweight cryptography. We report on experiments for evaluating the performance of our proposed protocol. For instance, for verifying a SHA-256 preimage in zero-knowledge with 128 bits security, the communication cost can be roughly reduced to 1/4 and the proof size can be shortened to 3/4, compared with the original protocol. While the prover running time has a slight improvement, the verifier running time is 4× shorter than Ligero. This brings great advantages in practice, as the transactions conducted on a block (created by a miner in general) must be verified by the network (many nodes in general) before the block can be added to the chain.

Keywords: Blockchain privacy · Circuit-SAT · interactive PCP · Zero-knowledge proofs · zkSNARKs

1 Introduction

Arising from the Bitcoin cryptocurrency in 2008, distributed ledger technology (DLT) has great potential to revolutionize the way governments, institutions and corporations work. The fundamental promise of DLT is the ability to construct self-reconciling workflows between untrusted participants that maintain integrity across all participants. Maintaining privacy constitutes a challenge problem within any distributed ledger. Initially, Bitcoin considers only sender privacy, which is achieved by pseudonyms. This is a very weak protection, since pseudonyms can be linked [30]. Since Bitcoin, there have been a

© Springer Nature Switzerland AG 2021
G. Nicolescu et al. (Eds.): FPS 2020, LNCS 12637, pp. 180–204, 2021.
https://doi.org/10.1007/978-3-030-70881-8_12

number of research articles for blockchain privacy. Blockchain privacy includes sender, transaction and receiver privacy. Notable approaches include the use of ring signatures [29] to achieve sender privacy and stealth addresses for receiver privacy. Moreover, almost all existing solutions employ advanced "cryptographic engines", i.e., zero-knowledge verifiable computation schemes. Verifiable computation [26] provides integrity of computation and solves the problem how users can be assured the validity of the results of a cloud service provider computed on his behalf without actually recomputing it. Other approaches include deploying multiparty computation (MPC) [25] or fully homomorphic encryption (FHE) [18]. The fundamental challenge associated with maintaining transactions privacy is that participants must be able to agree on the state of the network and reject any invalid transactions or unfair play while still respecting the external privacy constraints endowed by the workflows. Simply, participants must be able to agree that something is the same without seeing it. Many applications further require that a transaction consists of a single non-interactive message that can be verified by anyone; such messages are cheap to communicate and can be stored for later use (e.g., on a public ledger). Constructions that satisfy these properties are known as zero-knowledge succinct non-interactive arguments (zkSNARGs) [16], and refer to the proof constructions where one can prove possession of certain information, e.g., a secret key, without revealing that information, and without any interaction between the prover and verifier. Additionally, if the prover can convince the verifier not only that the secret exists, but that they in fact know such a secret – again, without revealing any information about the secret, such a proof construction is referred as zero-knowledge succinct non-interactive argument of knowledge (zkSNARK).

1.1 General Model of zkSNARK Based Protocols

In recent years, significant progress has been made to bring zkSNARKs from purely theoretical interest to practical implementations, leading to its numerous applications in delegation of computations, anonymous credentials, privacy-preserving cryptocurrencies and smart contracts. A general approach for zkSNARK design consists of the following four steps:

1 convert computational problems to arithmetic circuits;
2 convert arithmetic circuit satisfiability (Circuit-SAT) to (univariate or multivariate) polynomial satisfiability;
3 build an argument to prove some claims about the polynomial satisfiability using algebraic methods for (non-) interactive proofs;
4 add zero-knowledge and then convert interactive to non-interactive variant if not done in steps 2 and 3, such as applying the Fiat-Shamir heuristic [14] or commitments with efficient opening proofs.

According to whether the proof systems depend on a trusted setup or not, there are two different approaches which will be surveyed in Sects. 1.2 and 1.3.

1.2   Approaches for the Design of zkSNARKs with Trusted Setup

One of the celebrated zkSNARKs is the quadratic arithmetic program/quadratic span program (QAP/QSP) based zkSNARK [15] in 2013. It first converts a Circuit-SAT into a QAP/QSP, then constructs a zero-knowledge verifiable computation schemes from the QAP/QSP using pairing-based homomorphic encryption to verify the satisfiability of a QAP-SAT (QSP-SAT) (e.g., Pinocchio [28] for verifiable computation, Zcash [3] for cryptocurrency, and Hawk [22] for smart contract). This line of research on zkSNARKs has been the subject of extensive research [4,8,19,32] since then. For example, Groth [19] further reduced the verification to a single pairing product equations and the proof only consists of three group elements in total. The main feature of this approach is that proofs are very short (a few hundred bytes) and very cheap to verify (a few milliseconds). However, the zkSNARK approach along this line requires a trusted setup to generate parameters for the argument system, and incurs a high overhead in the prover running time and memory consumption, which makes it hard to scale to large statements. Furthermore, common reference strings (CRSs) may suffer threats from physical channels since CRSs are hard coded. There has been a great number of research for generating the structured reference strings (SRSs) through secure MPCs [5] and making the SRS universal and updatable [21].

1.3   Approaches for the Design of zkSNARKs Without Trusted Setup

More recent improvements for QAP/QSP based zkSNARKs have been proposed in the directions for removing the need for a trusted setup and construct transparent zkSNARK schemes. First, Spartan [31] achieves sublinear verification costs for statements expressed in R1CS through the sum-check protocol to build low degree multilinear polynomials (LDPs) where it employs a polynomial commitment scheme as a black box to commit some polynomial computations. Bulletproof [12] is also along this line, but it is to iteratively check inner products committed by discrete logarithm computation, which suffers the heavy cost for both communication between provers and verifiers, since it leverages some benefits from MPC.

Based on "(MPC)-in-the-head", Ames et al. [1] proposed a zero-knowledge interactive probabilistically checkable proofs (IPCPs) called Ligero. It only uses symmetric key operations and the prover time is fast in practice and the verification time is linear to the size of the circuit. Later, it is categorized as interactive oracle proofs (IOPs, a multi-round variant of IPCPs), and in the same model Ben-Sasson et al. built Stark [2], a transparent zero-knowledge proof in the RAM model of computation. Its verification time is also linear to the description of the RAM program, and succinct (polylogarithmic) in the time required for program execution. Recently, Ben-Sasson et al. proposed Aurora [6], in the IOP model with a logarithmic factor reduction of the proof size and prover time than Stark. All these proof systems have the verifier oracle access to an encoding of the input using a Reed-Solomon (RS) code, and achieve non-interactivity through the Fiat-Shamir transform. We summarize the properties of these three coding based zkSNARKs in Table 1.

Table 1. A comparison of prior RS coding based zkSNARKs

	Round complexity	Proof length	Prover time	Verifier time	Computational model
Ligero [1]	1	$O(\sqrt{N})$	$O(N \log N)$	$O(N)$	Arithmetic circuits
Stark [2]	$O(\log N)$	$O(\log^2 N)$	$O(N \log^2 N)$	$O(N)$	Uniform circuits
Aurora [6]	$O(\log N)$	$O(\log^2 N)$	$O(N \log N)$	$O(N)$	R1CS

Therefore, the major challenge is how to make it practical for large circuit sizes, since the circuit sizes of NP languages or their equivalent algorithms are always large in blockchain systems. For example, the circuit of SHA-256 tested in Ligero [1] has the circuit size about 34 000 multiplication gates (by customized optimized methods), and the implementation only achieves the overall 80 bits or less security.

1.4 Our Results

In this work, we continue to focus on the coding based approach. Those proof systems listed in Table 1 are provided by (multi-round) IPCPs [11] using error correcting codes to encode circuit computations (e.g., the schemes in Ligero [1] and Aurora [6] use interleaved RS codes, and Stark [2] uses an RS code). The advantage of this approach is that it is lightweight, since it does not need to employ an enormously large cryptographical engine as those used in [15], Pinocchio [28], Hawk [22] and Bulletproof [12], and also it is post-quantum secure. The only cryptographic primitive needed is a collision resistance hash function.

Following this approach, we propose a new zero-knowledge argument protocol for NP problems. We now describe the main contributions.

(1) IPCP for arithmetic Circuit-SAT. We construct a zero-knowledge IPCP protocol for arithmetic Circuit-SAT problem with sublinear proof length and sublinear query complexity. The core of our protocol can be seen as an improved and optimized variant of the argument of Ligero [1].

In the original protocol of Ligero, the prover needs to generate an extended witness which consists of two parts: The first part is the public input bits of the circuit, for example, the 256 bits image for the SHA-256 circuit. And the second part is the private output values of all interior addition and multiplication gates (we assume that the arithmetic circuit contains only addition and multiplication gates). Inspired by the idea of QAP, we make a first optimization via considering only the multiplication gates by expressing the input wires of a multiplication gate as an affine function of the output wires of lower multiplication gates. This is to say, the addition gates will be compressed into their contributions to the multiplication gates. The length of the extended witness could be significantly reduced. For example, to the best of our knowledge, the optimum SHA-256 circuit contains 22 272 AND gates, 91 780 XOR gates and 2 194 INV gates [13] respectively. If we consider only the AND gates, the length of the extended witness will roughly be reduced to one fifth, compared with the original protocol in which they take account of all the AND, XOR and INV gates.

In Ligero, the prover and verifier need to construct three matrices that are used to transform the extended witness vector to the left input, right input and output vectors of the multiplication gates. Therefore, in Ligero, it needs to enforce three linear checks to test whether these three vectors are computed correctly. With the additional linear check for the addition gates, the protocol in Ligero needs to run four linear tests in each repetition. Since we do not consider the addition gates, we do not need the linear test for the addition gates. In addition, instead of enforcing the three linear checks for the three vectors separately, we can do the linear check for these three vectors simultaneously in each repetition. This leads to a second improvement. The communication cost can be roughly 3–4× fewer, compared with the original protocol which needs to run four linear checks in each repetition. Since the final soundness error comes from applying a union bound to all the sub-protocols engaged in the final IPCP protocol, we can also obtain an improved soundness error.

For example, in Ligero the communication complexity of proving the satisfiability of the SHA-256 circuit over a finite field of size greater than 2^{128} with soundness error 2^{-40} consists of roughly $95\sqrt{s}$ field elements, where s is the number of gates. Our improved protocol can achieve a security level of 128 bits with almost the same communication cost over a finite field of size greater than 2^{140}.

(2) zkSNARK for arithmetic Circuit-SAT. We design and evaluate **Pisces**, a zkSNARK for arithmetic Circuit-SAT with the following notable features: (1) it only employs the black-box use of fast symmetric cryptography primitives (any cryptographic hash function modeled as a random oracle); (2) it has a transparent setup, namely the users merely need to agree on which cryptographic hash function to use; (3) it is plausibly post-quantum secure as there are no known efficient quantum attacks against this construction. These features follow from the fact that Pisces is obtained by applying the Fiat-Shamir transformation or the transformation described in [7] to our IPCP for the arithmetic Circuit-SAT. The transformation preserves both zero-knowledge and proof of knowledge of the underlying IPCP. For verifying a SHA-256 preimage in zero-knowledge, the prover and verifier running times are about 70% and 40% of those in Ligero, respectively.

2   Preliminaries

Let $\mathcal{L} \subset \{0,1\}^*$ be a language and $\mathcal{R}$ be an NP relation. For each instance $x \in \mathcal{L}$, let $\mathcal{R}_x \subset \{0,1\}^*$ denote the corresponding set of witnesses for the fact that $x \in \mathcal{L}$. Namely, $\mathcal{R}_x = \{w : (x,w) \in \mathcal{R}\}$. Let $\mathcal{R}_\mathcal{L}$ denote the corresponding language of valid (instance, witness) pairs, i.e., $\mathcal{R}_\mathcal{L} = \{(x,w) : x \in \mathcal{L} \text{ and } w \in \mathcal{R}_x\}$.

We denote by $\mathsf{negl}(n)$ a negligible function defined over the integers, meaning that for every polynomial $p(\cdot)$ and all sufficiently large n's, $\mathsf{negl}(n) < \frac{1}{p(n)}$. We use "PPT algorithms" to refer to probabilistic polynomial time algorithms.

Definition 1 (Interactive proofs). *A pair of probabilistic interactive algorithms $(\mathcal{P}, \mathcal{V})$ is called an interactive proof system for a language $\mathcal{L}$ with soundness ϵ if the algorithm $\mathcal{V}$ is polynomial time and the following two conditions hold:*

1. *Completeness: For every instance-witness pair $(x, w) \in \mathcal{R}_{\mathcal{L}}$,*

$$\Pr[\langle \mathcal{P}(w), \mathcal{V} \rangle(x) = 1] = 1.$$

2. *Soundness: For every instance $x \notin \mathcal{L}$, every malicious prover $\mathcal{P}^*$, and every $w \in \{0, 1\}^*$,*

$$\Pr[\langle \mathcal{P}^*(w), \mathcal{V} \rangle(x) = 1] \leq \epsilon.$$

An argument system for an NP relationship $\mathcal{R}$ is a protocol between a computationally-bounded prover $\mathcal{P}$ and a verifier $\mathcal{V}$ [17]. We formalize interactive zero-knowledge arguments in the following:

Definition 2 (Public-coin succinct interactive zero-knowledge arguments). *Let $(\mathcal{P}, \mathcal{V})$ denote a pair of PPT interactive algorithms and pp public parameters given as input the security parameter λ. Then a protocol between $\mathcal{P}$ and $\mathcal{V}$ is called a public-coin succinct interactive argument for a language $\mathcal{L}$ if:*

- *Completeness: For every instance-witness pair $(x, w) \in \mathcal{R}_{\mathcal{L}}$,*

$$\Pr[\langle \mathcal{P}(\mathsf{pp}, w), \mathcal{V}(\mathsf{pp}) \rangle(x) = 1] \geq 1 - \mathsf{negl}(\lambda).$$

- *Soundness: For every instance $x \notin \mathcal{L}$, every malicious PPT prover $\mathcal{P}^*$, and every $w \in \{0, 1\}^*$,*

$$\Pr[\langle \mathcal{P}^*(\mathsf{pp}, w), \mathcal{V}(\mathsf{pp}) \rangle(x) = 1] \leq \mathsf{negl}(\lambda).$$

- *(Perfect) zero-knowledge: There exists a PPT algorithm $\mathcal{S}$, called the simulator, running in time polynomial in the length of its first input, such that for every instance-witness pair $(x, w) \in \mathcal{R}_{\mathcal{L}}$, every $z \in \{0, 1\}^*$, and every PPT interactive machine $\mathcal{V}^*$, $\mathsf{View}(\langle \mathcal{P}(\mathsf{pp}, w), \mathcal{V}^*(\mathsf{pp}, z) \rangle(x))$ and $\mathcal{S}^{\mathcal{V}^*}(x, z)$ are identically distributed.*
- *Succinctness: The total communication between $\mathcal{P}$ and $\mathcal{V}$ is sublinear in the size of the NP statement $x \in \mathcal{L}$.*
- *Public coin: $\mathcal{V}$'s challenge in each round is independent of $\mathcal{P}$'s messages in previous rounds.*

Our zero-knowledge argument also satisfies a proof of knowledge property. Intuitively, this means that in order to produce a convincing proof of a statement, the prover must convince the verifier that it "knows" a witness w for the statement x such that $(x, w) \in \mathcal{R}$. In this paper, knowledge means that the argument has witness-extended emulation. To define this notion formally, we follow Groth and Ishai [20] who borrowed the notion of statistical witness-extended emulation from Lindell [24].

Definition 3 (Witness-extended emulation). *An interactive argument system* $(\mathcal{P}, \mathcal{V})$ *for* $\mathcal{L}$ *has witness-extended emulation if for all deterministic polynomial time* $\mathcal{P}^*$ *there exists an expected polynomial time emulator* $\mathcal{E}$ *such that for all non-uniform polynomial time adversaries* $\mathcal{A}$ *and all* $z_{\mathcal{V}} \in \{0, 1\}^*$, *the following probabilities differ by at most* $\mathsf{negl}(\lambda)$:

$$\Pr\left[\mathcal{A}(t) = 1 : \begin{array}{c}(x, z_{\mathcal{P}}) \leftarrow \mathcal{A}(\mathsf{pp}) \\ t \leftarrow \mathsf{tr}\langle \mathcal{P}^*(z_{\mathcal{P}}), \mathcal{V}(z_{\mathcal{V}})\rangle(x)\end{array}\right]$$

and

$$\Pr\left[\begin{array}{c}\mathcal{A}(t) = 1 \text{ and} \\ t \text{ accepting} \Rightarrow (x, w) \in \mathcal{R}_{\mathcal{L}}\end{array} : \begin{array}{c}(x, z_{\mathcal{P}}) \leftarrow \mathcal{A}(\mathsf{pp}) \\ (t, w) \leftarrow \mathcal{E}^{\mathcal{P}^*(z_{\mathcal{P}})}(x)\end{array}\right],$$

where tr *denotes the random variable that corresponds to the transcript of the interaction between* $\mathcal{P}^*$ *and* $\mathcal{V}$.

Here, the oracle called by $\mathcal{E}$ permits rewinding the prover to a specific point and resuming with fresh randomness for the verifier from this point onwards.

3   Pisces: A New Zero-Knowledge Argument for Arithmetic Circuit-SAT

For $n \in \mathbb{N}$, let $[n] = \{1, 2, \ldots, n\}$. Let $\langle \cdot, \cdot \rangle$ denote the inner product. We use $(-1)^n$ (respectively, $\mathbf{0}^n$) to denote the vector in $\mathbb{F}^n$ whose entries are all equal to -1 (respectively, 0). Let I_n be the $n \times n$ identity matrix. For a matrix $A \in \mathbb{F}^{m \times n}$ and $i \in [m], j \in [n]$, we denote by A_i the ith row of A, by $A[j]$ the jth column of A, and by $A[i, j]$ the entry lying in the ith row and the jth column of A.

Any arithmetic circuit may be viewed as being composed of addition, multiplication-by-scalar (i.e., one of the operands is constant) and non-scalar multiplication gates. Let $C : \mathbb{F}^\tau \to \mathbb{F}$ be an arithmetic circuit over a finite field $\mathbb{F}$, we use s to denote the number of non-scalar multiplication gates in the circuit. After labeling the non-scalar multiplication gates of the circuit C in topological order from inputs to outputs, we can express each input value to a non-scalar multiplication gate as an affine function of the values lower in the circuit, where each of these values is either an output of a lower non-scalar multiplication gate (for which there is a non-scalar multiplication gate path from this lower non-scalar multiplication gate to the original non-scalar multiplication gate), or is an input value to the circuit. This is to say, the addition and multiplication-by-scalar gates will be compressed into their contributions to the non-scalar multiplication gates.

However, in general the output wires of an arithmetic circuit are not outputs exclusively of multiplication-by-scalar or non-scalar multiplication gates. Therefore, these output values cannot be compressed into any multiplication gates. In order to handle this case, we may need to modify the arithmetic circuit slightly. In particular, we create one more input variable which is always required to be assigned the number '1', and create multiplication-by-scalar gates at the top of the circuit which multiply this new variable '1' with the "old" outputs that are outputs of addition gates.

We denote by $\alpha_1, \ldots, \alpha_\tau$ the τ input values of the circuit C, and β_i the output value of the ith non-scalar multiplication gate when evaluating the circuit $C(\alpha_1, \ldots, \alpha_\tau)$. Define the extended witness

$$w = (1, \alpha_1, \ldots, \alpha_\tau, \beta_1, \ldots, \beta_s).$$

For the final output wires we also include the output values in the extended witness if they are outputs of multiplication-by-scalar gates. Then for every non-scalar multiplication gate $g \in [s]$ in the circuit C, we have the following quadratic constraint

$$\gamma_l \cdot \gamma_r - \beta_g = 0,$$

where γ_l and γ_r are the left input and right input values to the gate g respectively, and β_g is the output value of the gate g in the extended witness. Combining all the quadratic constrains together, we obtain three vectors x, y and z such that

$$x \odot y - z = \mathbf{0}, \tag{1}$$

where $\odot$ denotes entry-wise product. The dimension of the vectors x, y and z is equal to the number of quadratic constraints.

Furthermore, as mentioned above, there exist two vectors $a_g, b_g \in \mathbb{F}^{1+\tau+s}$ such that

$$\gamma_l = \langle a_g, w \rangle, \quad \gamma_r = \langle b_g, w \rangle.$$

Actually, the entries in each of the vectors a_g, b_g corresponding to the gate $g \in [s]$ are always equal to 0 except the first $\tau + g$ entries (which might or might not be equal to 0). Therefore, we can construct three matrices A_x, A_y, A_z such that

$$x = A_x w, \quad y = A_y w, \quad z = A_z w,$$

or equivalently, in a combined form

$$\begin{bmatrix} A_x & -I & 0 & 0 \\ A_y & 0 & -I & 0 \\ A_z & 0 & 0 & -I \end{bmatrix} \begin{bmatrix} w \\ x \\ y \\ z \end{bmatrix} = \begin{bmatrix} 0 \\ 0 \\ 0 \end{bmatrix}. \tag{2}$$

Informally, we need to test the arithmetic Circuit-SAT by relying on two building blocks, one for testing the entry-wise vector product (1) and the other for testing the linear constraint systems induced by (2). We thus consider protocols for the following two problems.

- Lcheck: given a vector $x \in \mathbb{F}^\ell$ and a matrix $A \in \mathbb{F}^{m \times \ell}$, test whether $Ax = \mathbf{0}$.
- Qcheck: given three vectors $x, y, z \in \mathbb{F}^m$, test whether $x \odot y - z = \mathbf{0}$.

Now the goal is how to efficiently test the linear constraints system and the quadratic constraints system respectively. Clearly, once we get interactive protocols for the Lcheck and Qcheck problems, we can immediately obtain an interactive protocol for the arithmetic Circuit-SAT. The prover first generates and sends proof oracles to the verifier, namely the extended witness w and its linear transformations $x = A_z w$, $y = A_y w$, $z = A_z w$. Then the prover and verifier engage in two tests in parallel, namely checking the linear constraints system induced by (2) and the quadratic constraints system (1). Of course, the verifier must still verify that w is consistent with the public input α against a cheating prover. Loosely speaking, if α is not a satisfiable circuit assignment, a malicious prover cannot generate a valid witness with noticeable success probability.

However, naively applying the Lcheck and Qcheck problems only admits a trivial protocol, therefore, we cannot benefit from them. The verifier needs to query all entries of the vectors in order to check the required properties. The query complexity is $O(s)$. In order to allow for sublinear query complexity, we need the vectors w, x, y, z to be encoded via some error-correcting code. We follow the approaches in [1,2,6] and use an RS code to encode these vectors.

3.1   Interleaved RS Codes

We follow the notations used in Ligero [1]. For a code $C \subseteq \mathbb{F}^n$ and a vector $v \in \mathbb{F}^n$, we denote by $d_H(v, C)$ the minimal Hamming distance of v from C, namely the number of positions in which v differs from the closest codeword in C, and by $\Delta(v, C)$ the set of positions in which v differs from such a closet codeword (if not unique, take the lexicographically first closest codeword).

For two positive integers n, k, and an evaluation vector $\eta = (\eta_1, \ldots, \eta_n) \in \mathbb{F}^n$ of distinct field elements, the RS code, denoted by $\mathrm{RS}_{\eta,k}$, is the $[n, k, n - k + 1]$ linear code L over $\mathbb{F}$ that consists of all n-tuples $(p(\eta_1), \ldots, p(\eta_n))$, where p is a polynomial of degree $< k$ over $\mathbb{F}$.

For a positive integer m, we denote by $L^m \subseteq \mathbb{F}^{m \times n}$ the linear "interleaved" code with alphabet $\mathbb{F}^m$ that equals to the set of all $m \times n$ matrices whose rows are codewords in L. Since the alphabet is $\mathbb{F}^m$, the Hamming distance is taken column-wise. For a codeword $U \in L^m$ and $j \in [n]$, we denote also by $U[j]$ the jth column of U.

Given an encoding set $S = \{\zeta_1, \ldots, \zeta_\ell\} \subseteq \mathbb{F}$, the encoding of a vector $v = (v_1, \ldots, v_\ell) \in \mathbb{F}^\ell$ is defined as the vector $(p_v(\eta_1), \ldots, p_v(\eta_n)) \in \mathbb{F}^n$, where p_v is the Lagrange interpolation polynomial of degree $< \ell$ such that $p_v|_S = (p_v(\zeta_1), \ldots, p_v(\zeta_\ell)) = (v_1, \ldots, v_\ell)$. When $\ell \leq k$, the polynomial p_v has degree less than k, thus we can obtain a codeword $((p_v(\eta_1), \ldots, p_v(\eta_n))) \in L$.

Given this encoding, we can consider the "encoded" variants of the Lcheck and Qcheck problems.

- Encoded Lcheck: given a codeword $c \in \mathrm{RS}_{\eta,k}$, and a matrix $A \in \mathbb{F}^{m \times \ell}$, check that $\sum_{j \in [\ell]} A_{i,j} \cdot p_c(\zeta_j) = 0$ for all $i \in [m]$, where p_c is the polynomial corresponding to c.
- Encoded Qcheck: given three codewords $x, y, z \in \mathrm{RS}_{\eta,k}$, check that $p_x(\zeta_j) \cdot p_y(\zeta_j) - p_z(\zeta_j) = 0$ for all $j \in [\ell]$, where p_x, p_y, p_z are the polynomials corresponding to x, y, z respectively.

Given interactive protocols for the above problems, we can now get an interactive protocol for the arithmetic Circuit-SAT as before. Instead of sending w, x, y and z to the verifier, the prover sends their encodings $p_w(\eta)$, $p_x(\eta)$, $p_y(\eta)$ and $p_z(\eta)$ to the verifier. The prover and verifier then engage in Lcheck and Qcheck protocols as before, but with respect to their encoded variants.

3.2   The Fast Fourier Transform

In this paper, we use an (interleaved) RS code to encode the messages in order to allow for sublinear query complexity. Therefore, we need frequently move from univariate polynomials over a finite field to their evaluations on chosen subsets and back. Many fast polynomial-related algorithms are based on fast Fourier transforms (FFTs).

In [23], the authors presented a basis of polynomial over finite fields of characteristic two and then applied it to the encoding/decoding of RS codes. The proposed polynomial basis allows that n-point polynomial evaluation and interpolation over a finite field can be computed in $O(n \log n)$ finite field operations with small leading constant. Strictly, for an $[n, k, n - k + 1]$ RS code, an additive FFT evaluates a polynomial of degree $k - 1$ on a subspace of size k. In order to allow an evaluation on a larger subspace, for example the fixed evaluation subspace of size n, one can run an FFT over each coset of the smaller subspace inside the larger one at a cost of $\frac{n}{k} \cdot O(k \log k) = O(n \log k)$ finite field operations.

In practical implementations of the FFT algorithms, Victor Shoup's NTL library is a very popular high-performance C++ library in computational number theory and cryptography. NTL provides high quality implementations of state-of-the-art algorithms for polynomial arithmetic over finite fields. Some further optimization leveraging register cache and the GPU's computational power can be found in [9].

In the following subsections, we give a self-contained description of our zero-knowledge IPCP protocol. This protocol is an improved version of the protocol proposed in [1]. At a high level, the proposed protocol is a sequential efficient procedure for testing whether a message $[w, x, y, z]^T$ encoded by an interleaved RS code satisfies the given linear constraints system (2), and whether three vectors x, y, z encoded by an interleaved RS code satisfy the quadratic constraints system (1). Simultaneously, the verifier challenges the prover to reveal $O(\sqrt{s})$ linear combinations of the entries of the interleaved codeword, and checks their consistency with t randomly selected columns of this codeword to reduce the success probability for a malicious prover. Finally, by adding to the rows of the matrix an additional random RS codeword that is used for blinding, the actual protocol can achieve zero-knowledge.

3.3   Interleaved Linear Check

We first describe the Encoded Lcheck protocol, an RS-encoded IPCP for verifying linear constraints on RS codewords: Given a codeword $c \in \mathsf{RS}_{\eta, k}$ and a coefficient matrix $A \in \mathbb{F}^{m \times \ell}$, check that $\sum_{j \in [\ell]} A_{i,j} \cdot p_c(\zeta_j) = 0$ for all $i \in [m]$, where p_c is the polynomial corresponding to c.

To build intuition, consider that, given a vector $x \in \mathbb{F}^\ell$ and a matrix $A \in \mathbb{F}^{m \times \ell}$, a simple probabilistic test for the claim $Ax = \mathbf{0}$ is to check that $\langle r, Ax \rangle = 0$ for a random $r \in \mathbb{F}^m$. Indeed, if $Ax \neq \mathbf{0}$ then $\Pr_r[\langle r, Ax \rangle = 0] = 1/|\mathbb{F}|$.

We now return to the RS-encoded version of the problem, and explain how the prover can handle the claim $\sum_{j \in [\ell]} A_{i,j} \cdot p_c(\zeta_j) = 0$ for all $i \in [m]$. The RS-encoded version works as follows.

- The verifier samples and sends a uniformly random vector $r \in \mathbb{F}^m$ to the prover.
- The prover and verifier each computes the polynomial p_r of degree less than ℓ that evaluates to $r^T A \in \mathbb{F}^\ell$ on the encoding set S.
- The prover sends the $k + \ell - 1$ coefficients of the polynomial $q(\cdot) = p_r(\cdot) \cdot p_c(\cdot)$ to the verifier.
- The verifier accepts if and only if $\sum_{j \in [\ell]} q(\zeta_j) = 0$.

The foregoing protocol has the communication complexity of $k + \ell - 1 = O(s)$ field elements. To make the test sublinear, we let the encoding of s field elements consist of $O(\sqrt{s})$ RS codewords of block length $O(\sqrt{s})$ rather than a single RS codeword of length $O(s)$. We restate the Encoded Lcheck problem to the following interleaved variant.

- Interleaved Lcheck: given an $m_1 \ell \times m_2 \ell$ matrix A over $\mathbb{F}$ for two positive integers m_1 and m_2, check whether the oracle $U \in L^{m_2}$ encodes a message $x \in \mathbb{F}^{m_2 \ell}$ such that $Ax = \mathbf{0}$.

The protocol below is an interleaved variant of the Encoded Lcheck protocol, which also takes care of the input consistency check. The parameter t controls the number of queries.

Protocol 1

1. The verifier $\mathcal{V}$ samples vectors $s_1, \ldots, s_{m_1} \in \mathbb{F}^\ell$ uniformly at random and sends them to the prover $\mathcal{P}$.
2. The verifier $\mathcal{V}$ and prover $\mathcal{P}$ compute:
   - $(r_1, \ldots, r_{m_2})^T := (s_1, \ldots, s_{m_1})^T A$;
   - for $i \in [m_2]$, the polynomial $p_i^r(\cdot)$ of degree less than ℓ that evaluates to $r_i \in \mathbb{F}^\ell$ on the encoding set S.
3. The prover $\mathcal{P}$ sends the $k + \ell - 1$ coefficients of the polynomial $q(\cdot) = \sum_{i \in [m_2]} p_i^r(\cdot) \cdot p_i^x(\cdot)$ to $\mathcal{V}$, where $p_i^x(\cdot)$ is the polynomial of degree less than k corresponding to the ith row of U.
4. The verifier $\mathcal{V}$ samples a uniformly random index set $Q \subset [n]$ of size t, queries U at the jth column for all $j \in Q$ and checks that:
   (a) $\sum_{i \in [\ell]} q(\zeta_i) = 0$;
   (b) $q(\eta_j) = \sum_{i \in [m_2]} p_i^r(\eta_j) \cdot U[i, j]$ for all $j \in Q$.

We next give the security analysis of the above interleaved linear check protocol.

Proposition 1. *Protocol 1 is an RS-encoded IPCP for* Interleaved Lcheck *with soundness* $1/|\mathbb{F}| + ((k + \ell - 2)/n)^t$. *The communication cost is* $k + \ell - 1$ *field elements.*

Proof. **Completeness.** If $Ax = 0$ and $\mathcal{P}$ sends the correct $q(\cdot)$, then letting $r = (r_1, \ldots, r_{m_2})$,

$$\sum_{i \in [\ell]} q(\zeta_i) = \sum_{i \in [\ell]} \left(\sum_{j \in [m_2]} p_j^r(\zeta_i) \cdot p_j^x(\zeta_i) \right) = \sum_{i \in [\ell]} \left(\sum_{j \in [m_2]} r_j[i] \cdot x_j[i] \right) = r^T x = (s_1, \ldots, s_{m_1})^T Ax = 0,$$

so the verifier's first test passes. Correctness of the second test follows easily form the definition of $q(\cdot)$.

Soundness. If $Ax \neq 0$, there is a probability of $1/|\mathbb{F}|$ over the choice of $s_1, \ldots, s_{m_1}$ such that $(s_1, \ldots, s_{m_1})^T Ax = 0$. If $(s_1, \ldots, s_{m_1})^T Ax \neq 0$ then q does not sum to 0 over the encoding set S. If the polynomial q' sent by the prover is equal to q, then the verifier always rejects. Otherwise, as both are polynomials of degree less than $k + \ell - 1$, q and q' agree on at most $k + \ell - 2$ points. The verifier accepts only if all of its queries lie in this set. By a union bound, the protocol has a soundness error $1/|\mathbb{F}| + \binom{k+\ell-2}{t} / \binom{n}{t} \leq 1/|\mathbb{F}| + ((k + \ell - 2)/n)^t$.

Efficiency. The prover and the verifier perform matrix multiplication $(s_1, \ldots, s_{m_1})^T A$, whose cost depends on the number of nonzero entries in A. Each also performs interpolations to obtain the polynomial $p_i^r(\cdot)$. The prover obtains the polynomial $q(\cdot)$ by suitably combining evaluations of p_i^r, p_i^x and then interpolating. The verifier also evaluates q on the encoding set S for the first test, and performs simple arithmetic to check the answer of each of its queries. The communication cost is $k + \ell - 1$ field elements. ☐

Look in more detail at the above protocol, it cannot ensure zero-knowledge since the individual evaluations of q on the encoding set S themselves may reveal information about the witness. To hide this, we make a small modification to our construction via standard techniques from [1]. In particular, instead, we apply the Interleaved Lcheck with an extended oracle U' whose first m_2 rows contain U and last row is u' that encodes a message $(\mu_1, \ldots, \mu_\ell)$ such that $\sum_{i \in [\ell]} \mu_i = 0$. Let $q(\cdot) = \sum_{i \in [m_2]} p_i^r(\cdot) \cdot p_i^x(\cdot) + r_{\mathsf{blind}}(\cdot)$ be the polynomial sent from the prover to the verifier, where $r_{\mathsf{blind}}(\cdot)$ is a polynomial (of degree less than $k + \ell - 1$) corresponding to u'. It was shown that the soundness error of the resulting scheme will be the same as above.

Remark 1. With the additional Interleaved Lcheck for the addition gates in Ligero, the prover and verifier also need to conduct three tests that are used to test whether these three vectors are computed correctly. Since we do not consider the addition gates, we do not need the linear test for the addition gates. Moreover, as stated early in this section, instead of enforcing the three linear checks separately, we do the linear check only once in a combined form. The communication cost is still $k + \ell - 1$ field elements, compared with $4 \cdot (k + \ell - 1)$ in Ligero. As we will see later, this can also lead to an improved soundness error.

3.4   Interleaved Quadratic Check

In this subsection, we will deal with how to check the quadratic constraints system. We first describe the Encoded Qcheck protocol, an RS-encoded IPCP for verifying quadratic constraints system on RS codewords. Given three codewords $x, y, z \in \mathrm{RS}_{\eta,k}$, check that $p_x(\zeta_j) \cdot p_y(\zeta_j) - p_z(\zeta_j) = 0$ for all $j \in [\ell]$, where p_x, p_y, p_z are the polynomials corresponding to x, y, z respectively.

Intuitively speaking, consider that, given three vectors $x, y, z \in \mathbb{F}^\ell$, a simple probabilistic test for the claim $x \odot y - z = \mathbf{0}$ is to check that $\langle r, x \odot y - z \rangle = 0$ for a random $r \in \mathbb{F}^\ell$. Indeed, if $x \odot y - z \neq \mathbf{0}$ then $\Pr_r[\langle r, x \odot y - z \rangle = 0] = 1/|\mathbb{F}|$.

Now we return to the RS-encoded version of the problem, and explain how the prover can handle the claim $p_x(\zeta_j) \cdot p_y(\zeta_j) - p_z(\zeta_j) = 0$ for all $j \in [\ell]$. The RS-encoded version works as follows.

- The verifier samples and sends a uniformly random vector $r \in \mathbb{F}^\ell$ to the prover.
- The prover and verifier each computes the polynomial p_r of degree less than ℓ that evaluates to $r \in \mathbb{F}^\ell$ on the encoding set S.
- The prover sends the $2k + \ell - 2$ coefficients of the polynomial $q(\cdot) = p_r(\cdot) \cdot (p_x(\cdot) \cdot p_y(\cdot) - p_z(\cdot))$ to the verifier.
- The verifier accepts if and only if $\sum_{j \in [\ell]} q(\zeta_j) = 0$.

The foregoing protocol has a communication complexity of $2k + \ell - 2 = O(s)$ field elements. To make the test sublinear, we also let the encoding of s field elements consist of $O(\sqrt{s})$ RS codewords of block length $O(\sqrt{s})$ rather than a single RS codeword of length $O(s)$. We restate the Encoded Qcheck problem to the following interleaved variant.

- Interleaved Qcheck: check whether the three oracles $U^x, U^y, U^z \in L^m$ encode messages $x, y, z \in \mathbb{F}^{m\ell}$ such that $x \odot y - z = \mathbf{0}$.

The protocol below is an interleaved variant of the Encoded Qcheck protocol, which also takes care of the input consistency check. In order to further reduce the communication complexity, we borrow an idea from [1] and make a modification to the construction. In particular, the prover computes a random linear combination $q(\cdot)$ by using the random vector $r \in \mathbb{F}^m$ directly rather than its interpolation polynomial. The parameter t controls the number of queries.

Protocol 2

1. The verifier $\mathcal{V}$ samples a vector $r = (r_1, \ldots, r_m) \in \mathbb{F}^m$ uniformly at random and sends it to the prover $\mathcal{P}$.
2. The prover $\mathcal{P}$ sends the $2k - 1$ coefficients of the polynomial $q(\cdot) = \sum_{i \in [m]} r_i \cdot (p_i^x(\cdot) \cdot p_i^y(\cdot) - p_i^z(\cdot))$ to $\mathcal{V}$, where $p_i^x(\cdot), p_i^y(\cdot)$ and $p_i^z(\cdot)$ are the polynomials of degree less than k corresponding to the ith row of U^x, U^y, U^z respectively.
3. The verifier $\mathcal{V}$ samples a uniformly random index set $Q \subset [n]$ of size t, queries U^x, U^y, U^z at the jth column for all $j \in Q$, and checks that:
   (a) $q(\zeta_i) = 0$ for every $i \in [\ell]$;
   (b) $q(\eta_j) = \sum_{i \in [m]} r_i \cdot (U^x[i,j] \cdot U^y[i,j] - U^z[i,j])$ for all $j \in Q$.

We next give the security analysis of the above interleaved quadratic check protocol.

Proposition 2. *Protocol 2 is an RS-encoded IPCP for* Interleaved Qcheck *with soundness* $1/|\mathbb{F}|+((2k-2)/n)^t$. *The communication cost is* $2k-1$ *field elements.*

Proof. **Completeness.** If $x \odot y - z = 0$ and $\mathcal{P}$ sends the correct $q(\cdot)$, then for every $j \in [\ell]$,

$$q(\zeta_j) = \sum_{i\in[m]} r_i \cdot (p_i^x(\zeta_j) \cdot p_i^y(\zeta_j) - p_i^z(\zeta_j)) = \sum_{i\in[m]} r_i \cdot (x[i,j] \cdot y[i,j] - z[i,j]) = \sum_{i\in[m]} r_i \cdot 0 = 0,$$

where x, y, z are viewed as $m \times \ell$ matrices. So the verifier's first test passes. Correctness of the second test follows easily form the definition of $q(\cdot)$.

Soundness. If $x \odot y - z \neq 0$, then there is a probability of $1/|\mathbb{F}|$ over the choice of r such that $r^T(x \odot y - z) = 0$. If $r^T(x \odot y - z) \neq 0$ then q does not vanish over the encoding set S. If the polynomial q' actually sent by the prover is equal to q, then the verifier always rejects. Otherwise, as both are polynomials of degree less than $2k - 1$, q and q' agree on at most $2k - 2$ points. The verifier accepts only if all of its queries lie in this set. By a union bound, the protocol has a soundness error $1/|\mathbb{F}| + \binom{2k-2}{t}/\binom{n}{t} \leq 1/|\mathbb{F}| + ((2k-2)/n)^t$.

Efficiency. The prover obtains the polynomial q by suitably combining evaluations of the rows of oracles U^x, U^y, U^z, and then interpolating. The verifier evaluates q on the encoding set S for the first test, and performs simple arithmetic to check the answer of each of its queries. The communication cost is $2k-1$ field elements. $\qquad\square$

Clearly, the above protocol cannot ensure zero-knowledge since the individual evaluations of q on the encoding set S themselves may reveal information about the witness. To hide this, we make a small modification to the construction in the same way as we did in the case of Interleaved Lcheck via a standard technique from [1]. In particular, we apply the Interleaved Qcheck with an extended oracle U' whose first $3m$ rows contain U^x, U^y, U^z and last row is u' that encodes a message $\mathbf{0}^\ell$. Let $q(\cdot) = \sum_{i\in[m]} r_i\cdot(p_i^x(\cdot)\cdot p_i^y(\cdot) - p_i^z(\cdot))+r_{\mathsf{blind}}(\cdot)$ be the polynomial sent from the prover to the verifier, where $r_{\mathsf{blind}}(\cdot)$ is a polynomial of degree less than $2k - 1$ corresponding to u'. It was shown that the soundness error of the resulting scheme will be the same as above.

3.5 Proximity Test of RS Codewords

The protocols of the Interleaved Lcheck and Interleaved Qcheck in the prior subsections are RS-encoded because soundness assumes that the oracle sent by the prover is an interleaved RS codeword (a list of RS codewords over the same domain). Therefore, in order to obtain a regular IPCP for the arithmetic Circuit-SAT, we need to combine these protocols with any proximity test. Informally, the verifier tests whether a suitable linear combination of words in the oracle is close to the RS code. A straightforward way for the proximity test is that the prover sends, as a message, the coefficients of the polynomial that interpolates the linear combination, and the verifier probabilistically checks that this polynomial is consistent with the oracle. This subroutine actually corresponds to the "Test-Interleaved" protocol in [1].

We now describe this simple testing sub-protocol for checking whether a given matrix $U \in \mathbb{F}^{m \times n}$ is close to an interleaved RS code L^m.

1. The verifier $\mathcal{V}$ samples a vector $r \in \mathbb{F}^m$ uniformly at random and sends r to the prover $\mathcal{P}$.
2. The prover $\mathcal{P}$ responds the linear combination $w = r^T U \in \mathbb{F}^n$ to the verifier $\mathcal{V}$.
3. The verifier $\mathcal{V}$ samples a random index set $Q \subset [n]$ of size t, queries $U[j]$ for all $j \in Q$, and checks that:
   - $w \in L$.
   - $\sum_{i=1}^{m} r_i \cdot U[i,j] = w_j$, for every $j \in Q$.

Completeness. Correctness of the test follows easily from the description.
Efficiency. The communication cost is n field elements.
Soundness. The soundness analysis relies on the following lemmas.

Lemma 1 (See [10]). *Let $L \subseteq \mathbb{F}^n$ be a linear space over a finite field $\mathbb{F}$ with minimal distance λ. Let U be an affine space and suppose $d_H(U, L) > \delta$. For any $\epsilon > 0$ such that $\delta - \epsilon < \lambda/3$,*

$$\Pr_{u \in U}[d_H(u, L) < \delta - \epsilon] \leq \frac{1}{\epsilon |\mathbb{F}|}.$$

The following lemma follows directly by setting $\epsilon = 1/(n + \mathbb{F}^{-m})$.

Lemma 2. *Let L be an $[n, k, d]$ RS code, U^* a matrix in $\mathbb{F}^{m \times n}$ and e a positive integer such that $e < d/3$. Suppose $d_H(U^*, L^m) > e$. Then for a random w^* in the row-span of U^*, we have*

$$\Pr[d_H(w^*, L) \leq e] \leq \frac{n}{|\mathbb{F}|}.$$

For any matrix $U^* \in \mathbb{F}^{m \times n}$ with $d_H(U^*, L^m) > e$, letting $w^* = r^T U^*$ for a random vector $r \in \mathbb{F}^m$. Observe that

$$\begin{aligned}
&\Pr[\mathcal{V} \text{ accepts } U^*] \\
&= \Pr[\mathcal{V} \text{ accepts } U^* | d_H(w^*, L) > e] \cdot \Pr[d_H(w^*, L) > e] \\
&\quad + \Pr[\mathcal{V} \text{ accepts } U^* | d_H(w^*, L) \leq e] \cdot \Pr[d_H(w^*, L) \leq e] \\
&\leq \Pr[\mathcal{V} \text{ accepts } U^* | d_H(w^*, L) > e] + \Pr[d_H(w^*, L) \leq e] \\
&\leq \frac{\binom{n-e-1}{t}}{\binom{n}{t}} + \frac{n}{|\mathbb{F}|} \leq \left(1 - \frac{e}{n}\right)^t + \frac{n}{|\mathbb{F}|},
\end{aligned}$$

which gives the following soundness error.

Proposition 3. *Let e be a positive integer such that $e < d/3$. Suppose $d_H(U^*, L^m) > e$. Then for any malicious prover $\mathcal{P}^*$, the oracle U^* is rejected by $\mathcal{V}$ except with at most $(1 - e/n)^t + n/|\mathbb{F}|$ probability.*

To achieve zero-knowledge, we make a slight modification to the above protocol. We apply the proximity test to L^{m+1}, with an extended oracle U' whose first m rows contain the matrix U and whose last row is a random codeword $u' \in L$. The verifier still sends a uniformly random vector $r \in \mathbb{F}^m$ to $\mathcal{P}$ as before, but the prover responds with $w' = r^T U + u'$, instead. It is easy to see that we can get the same soundness error as in Proposition 3.

3.6   Zero-Knowledge IPCP Protocol for Arithmetic Circuit-SAT

In this subsection, we provide a self-contained description of the final zkIPCP protocol, combining all the previous sub-protocols.

Protocol zkIPCP $(C, \mathbb{F})$.

Input: The prover $\mathcal{P}$ and the verifier $\mathcal{V}$ share a common input arithmetic circuit $C : \mathbb{F}^\tau \to \mathbb{F}$ and input statement x. $\mathcal{P}$ additionally has input $\overline{\alpha} = (\alpha_1, \ldots, \alpha_\tau)$ such that $C(\overline{\alpha}) = 1$.

Oracle: Let m_1, m_2, ℓ be integers such that $m_1 \cdot \ell > 1 + \tau + s$ and $m_2 \cdot \ell$ great than the number of quadratic constraints in (1). Then the prover $\mathcal{P}$ generates an extended witness $w \in \mathbb{F}^{m_1 \ell}$ whose first $1 + \tau + s$ entries are

$$(1, \alpha_1, \ldots, \alpha_\tau, \beta_1, \ldots, \beta_s),$$

where β_i is the output of the ith non-scalar multiplication gate when evaluating $C(\overline{\alpha})$. For the final output wires we also include the output values in the extended witness if they are the outputs of multiplication-by-scalar gates. $\mathcal{P}$ constructs three vectors $x, y, z \in \mathbb{F}^{m_2 \ell}$ such that the jth entries of x, y, z contain the left input value, right input value and output value corresponding to the jth quadratic constraint respectively. $\mathcal{P}$ and $\mathcal{V}$ construct three matrices A_x, A_y and A_z in $\mathbb{F}^{m_2 \ell \times m_1 \ell}$ such that

$$x = A_x w, \quad y = A_y w, \quad z = A_z w,$$

and set A^{Lin} as the following matrix

$$\begin{bmatrix} A_x & -I & 0 & 0 \\ A_y & 0 & -I & 0 \\ A_z & 0 & 0 & -I \end{bmatrix} \in \mathbb{F}^{(3m_2\ell) \times (m_1\ell + 3m_2\ell)}.$$

The prover samples random codewords $U^w \in L^{m_1}$ and $U^x, U^y, U^z \in L^{m_2}$ that encode messages w, x, y, z respectively, where $L = \mathsf{RS}_{\eta, k}$ and $\eta = (\eta_1, \ldots, \eta_n)$. The encoding set S is selected as $\{\zeta_1, \ldots, \zeta_\ell\}$, a sequence of distinct elements disjoint from $\eta = (\eta_1, \ldots, \eta_n)$. We select a suitable parameter σ to control the number of repetitions of the protocol. Let u_ι^{Mem}, u_ι^{Lin}, u_ι^{Qua} be auxiliary rows sampled uniformly at random from L for every $\iota \in [\sigma]$, where u_ι^{Lin} encodes an independently sampled random message $(\mu_1, \ldots, \mu_\ell)$ of length ℓ subject to $\sum_{i=1}^\ell \mu_i = 0$ and u_ι^{Qua} encodes $\mathbf{0}^\ell$. Finally, $\mathcal{P}$ sets the oracle as $U \in L^{m_1+3m_2}$ which is set as the vertical juxtaposition of the matrices $U^w \in L^{m_1}$, U^x, U^y, $U^z \in L^{m_2}$.

The Interactive Protocol

1. For every $\iota \in [\sigma]$, $\mathcal{V}$ picks the following random vectors and sends them to $\mathcal{P}$:
   - $r_\iota^{\mathsf{Mem}} \in \mathbb{F}^{m_1+3m_2}$,
   - $r_\iota^{\mathsf{Lin}} \in \mathbb{F}^{3m_2\ell}$,
   - $r_\iota^{\mathsf{Qua}} \in \mathbb{F}^{m_2}$.

2. For every $\iota \in [\sigma]$, $\mathcal{P}$ responds with:
   - $v_\iota = (r_\iota^{\mathsf{Mem}})^T U + u_\iota^{\mathsf{Mem}} \in \mathbb{F}^n$,
   - The $k + \ell - 1$ coefficients of the polynomial

$$q_\iota^{\mathsf{Lin}}(\cdot) = r_{\mathsf{blind},\iota}^{\mathsf{Lin}}(\cdot) + \sum_{i=1}^{m_1} r_{\iota,i}^{\mathsf{Lin}}(\cdot) \cdot p_i^w(\cdot) + \sum_{i=1}^{m_2} r_{\iota,m_1+i}^{\mathsf{Lin}}(\cdot) \cdot p_i^x(\cdot)$$
$$+ \sum_{i=1}^{m_2} r_{\iota,m_1+m_2+i}^{\mathsf{Lin}}(\cdot) \cdot p_i^y(\cdot) + \sum_{i=1}^{m_2} r_{\iota,m_1+2m_2+i}^{\mathsf{Lin}}(\cdot) \cdot p_i^z(\cdot),$$

   where $p_i^w(\cdot)$, $p_i^x(\cdot)$, $p_i^y(\cdot)$ and $p_i^z(\cdot)$ are the polynomials of degree $< k$ corresponding to the ith rows of U^w, U^x, U^y, U^z respectively, $r_{\iota,i}^{\mathsf{Lin}}(\cdot)$ is the unique polynomial of degree $< \ell$ such that $r_{\iota,i}^{\mathsf{Lin}}(\zeta_c) = ((r_\iota^{\mathsf{Lin}})^T A^{\mathsf{Lin}})_{i,c}$ for every $c \in [\ell]$, and $r_{\mathsf{blind},\iota}^{\mathsf{Lin}}(\cdot)$ is the polynomial of degree $< k + \ell - 1$ corresponding to u_ι^{Lin}.
   - The $2k - 1$ coefficients of the polynomial
   $q_\iota^{\mathsf{Qua}}(\cdot) = r_{\mathsf{blind},\iota}^{\mathsf{Qua}}(\cdot) + \sum_{i=1}^{m_2} r_\iota^{\mathsf{Qua}}[i] \cdot (p_i^x(\cdot) \cdot p_i^y(\cdot) - p_i^z(\cdot))$,
   where $r_{\mathsf{blind},\iota}^{\mathsf{Qua}}(\cdot)$ is the polynomial of degree $< 2k - 1$ corresponding to u_ι^{Qua}.

3. $\mathcal{V}$ picks a random index set $Q \subset [n]$ of size t, queries $U[j]$ (which is the vertical juxtaposition of $U^w[j]$, $U^x[j]$, $U^y[j]$ and $U^z[j]$), $u_\iota^{\mathsf{Mem}}[j]$, $u_\iota^{\mathsf{Lin}}[j]$ and $u_\iota^{\mathsf{Qua}}[j]$ for every $j \in Q$, and accepts if the following conditions hold for every $\iota \in [\sigma]$:
   - $\sum_{c \in [\ell]} q_\iota^{\mathsf{Lin}}(\zeta_c) = 0$ and $q_\iota^{\mathsf{Qua}}(\zeta_c) = 0$ for every $c \in [\ell]$,
   - For every $j \in Q$,
     - $v_\iota[j] = \sum_{i=1}^{m_1+3m_2} r_\iota^{\mathsf{Mem}}[j] \cdot U[i,j] + u_\iota^{\mathsf{Mem}}[j]$,
     - $q_\iota^{\mathsf{Lin}}(\eta_j) = u_\iota^{\mathsf{Lin}}[j] + \sum_{i=1}^{m_1+3m_2} r_{\iota,i}^{\mathsf{Lin}}(\eta_j) \cdot U[i,j]$,
     - $q_\iota^{\mathsf{Qua}}(\eta_j) = u_\iota^{\mathsf{Qua}}[j] + \sum_{i=1}^{m_2} r_\iota^{\mathsf{Qua}}[i] \cdot (U^x[i,j] \cdot U^y[i,j] - U^z[i,j])$.

The following theorem follows from the constructions of the sub-protocols described in the prior subsections.

Theorem 1. *Fix parameters n, k, m_1, m_2, ℓ, e such that $e < (n - k)/3$. Let $C : \mathbb{F}^\tau \to \mathbb{F}$ be an arithmetic circuit with size s of non-scalar multiplication gates, where $|\mathbb{F}| \geq \ell + n$, $m_1 \cdot \ell > 1 + \tau + s$ and $m_2 \cdot \ell > s$. Then the protocol $zkIPCP(C, \mathbb{F})$ satisfies the following:*

- *Completeness: If $\overline{\alpha}$ is such that $C(\overline{\alpha}) = 1$ and oracle π is generated honestly as described in the protocol, then*

$$\Pr[(\mathcal{P}(C, w), \mathcal{V}^\pi(C)) = 1] = 1.$$

- *Soundness: If there exists no $\overline{\alpha}$ such that $C(\overline{\alpha}) = 1$, then for every (unbounded) prover strategy $\mathcal{P}^*$ and every $\tilde{\pi} \in \mathbb{F}^{(m_1+3m_2)n}$,*

$$\Pr[(\mathcal{P}^*, \mathcal{V}^{\tilde{\pi}}(x)) = 1] \leq \frac{n+2}{|\mathbb{F}|^\sigma} + \left(1 - \frac{e}{n}\right)^t + 2\left(\frac{e+2k}{n}\right)^t.$$

- *Zero-knowledge: For every adversary verifier $\mathcal{V}^*$, there exists a simulator S such that the output of $S^{\mathcal{V}^*}(C)$ is distributed identically to the view of $\mathcal{V}$ in the $\langle \mathcal{P}(C, w), \mathcal{V}^\pi(C) \rangle(x)$.*
- *Complexity: The number of field $\mathbb{F}$ operations performed is $\mathsf{poly}(|C|, n)$. The number of field elements communicated by $\mathcal{P}$ to $\mathcal{V}$ is $\sigma \cdot n + \sigma \cdot (k + \ell - 1) + \sigma \cdot (2k - 1)$ whereas $\mathcal{V}$ reads $\sigma \cdot t$ symbols from $\mathbb{F}^{m_1+3m_2+3}$.*

Proof. The completeness and complexity follow directly from the sub-protocols described in the prior subsections, i.e., Propositions 1, 2 and 3. We now focus on arguing the soundness and zero-knowledge properties. The proof is almost identical to [1], we include it here for the sake of completeness.

Soundness. Let $U^* \in L^{m_1+3m_2}$ be the vertical juxtaposition of the matrices $U^{w*} \in L^{m_1}$ and $U^{x*}, U^{y*}, U^{z*} \in L^{m_2}$, and let $E = \Delta(U^*, L^{m_1+3m_2})$. Then we argue soundness by considering the following two cases and applying a union bound.

- Case $d_\mathsf{H}(U^*, L^{m_1+3m_2}) > e$. Since $e < (n-k)/3 < d/3$, from Proposition 3, we conclude that the verifier rejects in the proximity test of RS codewords except with probability $(1 - e/n)^t + n/|\mathbb{F}|$.
- Case $d_\mathsf{H}(U^*, L^{m_1+3m_2}) \leq e$. We consider the interleaved linear test and assume that the oracle U^* encodes $w \in \mathbb{F}^{m_1 \ell \times n}$, $x, y, z \in \mathbb{F}^{m_2 \ell \times n}$ such that $A^\mathsf{Lin}(w; x; y; z) \neq (\mathbf{0}; \mathbf{0}; \mathbf{0})$. Then there is a probability of $1/|\mathbb{F}|$ over the choice of r such that $r^T(A^\mathsf{Lin}(w; x; y; z)) = (\mathbf{0}; \mathbf{0}; \mathbf{0})$. Therefore, the polynomial q_ι^Lin fails to satisfy the tests in Step 3 except with probability $1/|\mathbb{F}|$.
  Now let $\hat{q}_\iota^\mathsf{Lin}$ be the polynomial sent by the prover. If $\hat{q}_\iota^\mathsf{Lin} = q_\iota^\mathsf{Lin}$, the verifier $\mathcal{V}$ rejects in Step 3. If $\hat{q}_\iota^\mathsf{Lin} \neq q_\iota^\mathsf{Lin}$, then the number of indices $j \in [n]$ for which $\hat{q}_\iota^\mathsf{Lin}(\eta_j) = q_\iota^\mathsf{Lin}(\eta_j)$ is at most $k+\ell-2$ as both polynomials are of degree at most $k + \ell - 2$. Let Q' be the set of indices on which they agree. Then $\mathcal{V}$ rejects in Step 3 whenever Q selected contains an index $i \notin Q' \cup E$. This fails to happen with probability at most $\binom{e+k+\ell-2}{t}/\binom{n}{t} \leq ((e+k+\ell-2)/n)^t$. Hence, for any malicious $\mathcal{P}^*$, U^* is rejected by $\mathcal{V}$ except with at most $((e+k+\ell-2)/n)^t + 1/|\mathbb{F}|$ probability.
  With a similar argument, we can obtain that if the oracle U^* encodes $w \in \mathbb{F}^{m_1 \ell \times n}$, $x, y, z \in \mathbb{F}^{m_2 \ell \times n}$ such that $x \odot y - z \neq \mathbf{0}$, then for any malicious $\mathcal{P}^*$, U^* is rejected by $\mathcal{V}$ except with at most $((e + 2k - 2)/n)^t + 1/|\mathbb{F}|$ probability.

Zero-Knowledge. To demonstrate zero-knowledge against honest verifier, we need to construct a simulator $\mathcal{S}$ that can be able to generate a transcript given the randomness provided by the honest verifier $\mathcal{V}$. For every $\iota \in [\sigma]$, the simulator $\mathcal{S}$ first generates:

- random polynomial $q_\iota^{\mathsf{Lin}}(\cdot)$ of degree $< k + \ell - 1$ such that $\sum_{c \in [\ell]} q_\iota^{\mathsf{Lin}}(\zeta_c) = 0$.
- random polynomial $q_\iota^{\mathsf{Qua}}(\cdot)$ of degree $< 2k - 1$ such that $q_\iota^{\mathsf{Qua}}(\zeta_c) = 0$ for every $c \in [\ell]$.
- random vector $v_\iota \in \mathbb{F}^n$.

Next, for every $j \in Q$ the simulator $\mathcal{S}$ samples random vectors $U^w[j] \in \mathbb{F}^{m_1}$, $U^x[j], U^y[j], U^z[j] \in \mathbb{F}^{m_2}$ and sets $U[j] \in L^{m_1 + 3m_2}$ as the vertical juxtaposition of the vectors $U^w[j]$, $U^x[j]$, $U^y[j]$ and $U^z[j]$. Finally, given the random challenges from $\mathcal{V}$, the simulator $\mathcal{S}$ sets:

- $u_\iota^{\mathsf{Mem}}[j] = \sum_{i=1}^{m_1 + 3m_2} r_\iota^{\mathsf{Mem}}[j] \cdot U[i, j] - v_\iota[j]$.
- $u_\iota^{\mathsf{Lin}}[j] = \sum_{i=1}^{m_1 + 3m_2} r_{\iota,i}^{\mathsf{Lin}}(\eta_j) \cdot U[i, j] - q_\iota^{\mathsf{Lin}}(\eta_j)$.
- $u_\iota^{\mathsf{Qua}}[j] = \sum_{i=1}^{m_2} r_\iota^{\mathsf{Qua}}[i] \cdot \left(U^x[i, j] \cdot U^y[i, j] - U^z[i, j] \right) - q_\iota^{\mathsf{Qua}}(\eta_j)$.

The zero-knowledge follows from the fact that in an honest execution with the prover $\mathcal{P}$, the distribution of $\{U^x[j], U^y[j], U^z[j], U^w[j]\}_{j \in Q}$ are uniformly distributed and given that u_ι^{Mem}, u_ι^{Lin}, u_ι^{Qua} are chosen uniformly at random, polynomials $q_\iota^{\mathsf{Lin}}(\cdot)$, $q_\iota^{\mathsf{Qua}}(\cdot)$ and vector v_ι are uniformly distributed in their respective spaces. $\qquad\square$

3.7   The Non-interactive Variant

Blockchain requires that the proof of a transcript is a single non-interactive message that can be verified by anyone. Therefore, before applying the previous protocol to the protection of the blockchain privacy, we need to transform the protocol to a non-interactive version. We can use a random oracle to directly compile our previous protocol into a non-interactive protocol. In this mode, the verifier's messages are emulated by applying the random oracle on the partial transcript in each round following the Fiat-Shamir transform [14]. A formal description and analysis of this transformation is presented in [7] for IOP model which generalizes (public-coin) IPCP.

In slightly more detail, the BCS transformation in [7] uses a cryptographic hash function (modeled as a random oracle) to compile any public-coin IOP into a SNARG that is: 1) transparent (the only global parameter needed to produce/validate proof strings is the hash function); 2) post-quantum (it is secure in the quantum random oracle model); 3) lightweight (no cryptography beyond the hash function is used). In the BCS transformation, the prover uses the random oracle to generate the verifier's messages and complete the execution (computing its own messages) based on the emulated verifier's messages, where instead of using an oracle, the prover commits to its proof and messages using Merkle hash trees. The (statistical) zero-knowledge property is preserved [7].

In [7], the soundness of the transformed protocol is shown to essentially match the soundness of the original protocol up to an additive term that roughly depends on the product of t_q^2 and $2^{-\lambda}$ where t_q is an upper bound on the number of queries to the random oracle that a malicious prover can make, and λ is a security parameter setting up the output length of the random oracle. The aforementioned soundness is tight up to small factors. More precisely, the authors related the soundness of the transformed protocol to the state restoration soundness of the underlying IPCP and collision-probability of queries to the random oracle. State restoration soundness refers to the soundness of the IOP protocol against cheating prover strategies that may rewind the verifier back to any previously seen state, where every new continuation from a state invokes the next-message function of the verifier with fresh randomness [1,7]. They showed that for any IOP the state restoration soundness of an IOP protocol is bounded by $\binom{t_q}{k(x)} \cdot \epsilon(x)$ and the soundness of the transformed protocol is $\binom{t_q}{k(x)} \cdot \epsilon(x) + 3(t_q^2 + 1) \cdot 2^{-\lambda}$ where $k(x)$ is the round complexity of the IOP and $\epsilon(x)$ is the (standard) soundness of the IOP for an instance x. In particular, in our zero-knowledge IPCP model, since the round complexity is 1, the soundness of the transformed protocol can be further tighten to $t_q \cdot \epsilon(x) + 3(t_q^2 + 1) \cdot 2^{-\lambda}$. See [1,7] for more details.

In addition, the authors in [6] also provide an open library libiop (see https://github.com/scipr-lab/libiop), a codebase that enables the design and implementation of certain types of IOP-based non-interactive arguments. The library provides a tool chain for transforming IOPs into zkSNARKs with preserving both zero-knowledge and proof of knowledge of the underlying IOPs via the BCS transformation [7]. It also contains an implemented zkSNARK obtained by applying the BCS transformation to the Ligero-IOP protocol presented in the Appendix of [6]. As our protocol is a Ligero-based improved and optimized variant, it is easy to apply to our case by a slight modification to our zero-knowledge IPCP.

4   Evaluation

In this section, we evaluate the performance of Pisces. As our zero-knowledge argument is an improved and optimized version of Ligero, they have the same asymptotic complexity. More specifically, the round complexity is 1, the length of proof is $O(\sqrt{N})$ field elements, the query complexity is $O(\sqrt{N})$, prover time and verifier time are $O(N \log N)$ and $O(N)$ field operations respectively. Therefore, in this section we give a comparison between our protocol and Ligero.

First, we describe how to set the parameters of our zero-knowledge argument protocol. We assume that the finite field $\mathbb{F}$ is friendly to FFT algorithms, namely $\mathbb{F}$ is a binary field or its multiplicative group is smooth. We consider Pisces at the standard security level of 128 bits over a binary field. Following the transformation in Sect. 3.7, the communication complexity of the zero-knowledge protocol that is compiled based on our zero-knowledge IPCP is

$$\sigma \cdot [n + (k + \ell - 1) + (2 \cdot k - 1) + t \cdot (m_1 + 3 \cdot m_2 + 3)] \cdot \lceil \log |\mathbb{F}| \rceil + t \cdot \lceil \log |\mathbb{F}| \rceil \cdot h,$$

where h is the output length of the hash function. For security parameter λ, when $\mathbb{F}$ is large (i.e., $|\mathbb{F}| > O(2^\lambda)$), we can set $\sigma = 1$ for λ bits security.

For the circuit, we use the optimum SHA-256 circuit to the best of our knowledge, which contains 22 272 AND gates, 91 780 XOR gates and 2 194 INV (can be converted to an XOR gate) gates respectively [13]. Since all the final 256 output wires are output values of XOR and INV gates, we need to create 256 additional dummy multiplication-by-1 gates in order to contain them in the extended witness. Therefore, we obtain an extended witness of length 23 041. The total number of quadratic constraints in (1) is equal to 22 528. In order to take advantage of the FFT algorithms over a binary field, we choose an affine subspace as the definition set of the RS code and another disjoint affine subspace as the encoding set $S = \{\zeta_1, \dots, \zeta_\ell\}$ similarly as Aurora [6]. Hence, the length n of the RS codeword and the length ℓ of the blocks in the messages are set to equal to the powers of 2. We list all the parameters that are used in our protocol as follows:

σ	$|\mathbb{F}|$	m_1	m_2	ℓ	t	k	n	e
1	$>2^{140}$	23	22	1024	310	1334	4096	920

Soundness Error: According to the proof of Theorem 1, the soundness error comes from applying a union bound to all the soundness errors of these sub-protocols engaged in the final IPCP protocol. With the additional linear check for the addition gates, the original protocol in Ligero needs to run four linear tests in each repetition. Since we do not consider the addition gates, we do not need the linear test for the addition gates. In addition, instead of enforcing the three linear checks for the three vectors separately, we do the linear check only once in each repetition. Therefore, this leads to a direct reduction in the final soundness error.

Ligero	$\frac{e+6}{|\mathbb{F}|^\sigma} + \left(1 - \frac{e}{n}\right)^t + 5\left(\frac{e+2k}{n}\right)^t$
Our protocol	$\frac{n+2}{|\mathbb{F}|^\sigma} + \left(1 - \frac{e}{n}\right)^t + 2\left(\frac{e+2k}{n}\right)^t$

Proximity Error e: In Ligero, the authors conjectured that the condition $e < d/4$ can be relaxed to $e < d/3$ with essentially the same soundness error bound [1, Theorem 4.3]. Under this conjecture, the corresponding variant, they called Ligero-Strong, would yield roughly up to 25% improvement in the size of the zero-knowledge argument and a 20% reduction in communication on the average. Due to a remarkable result in [10, Theorem 7], we can give this improvement and relax directly the condition $e < d/4$ to $e < d/3$ with almost the same soundness error bound.

Communication Cost: In Ligero, for each linear check, the prover needs to send the $k + \ell - 1$ coefficients of a polynomial to the verifier. So when we reduce the number of linear checks performed in each repetition, the communication cost can be reduced to $4\times$ fewer than Ligero in each repetition. The total communication costs of these two protocols are list in the following table (up to identical additive and multiplicative terms).

Ligero	$[n + 4(k + \ell - 1) + (2k - 1) + t(4m_1 + 5)]$
Pisces	$[n + (k + \ell - 1) + (2k - 1) + t(m_1 + 3m_2 + 3)]$

Argument Size, Prover and Verifier Running Times: We give the argument size, prover and verifier running times for both arguments in the following table respectively. We ran both experiments for the SHA-256 circuit at the security level of 128 bits on an Intel Corel i7-6700 CPU 3.60 GHz and 16 GB RAM platform.

	Argument size (KB)	Prover running time (ms)	Verifier running time (ms)
Ligero	96*	794	502
Pisces	67	567	197

* For the Ligero-Strong variant, this would have a 25% reduction.

5 Conclusions

In this work, we presented Pisces, a new zero-knowledge argument for the arithmetic Circuit-SAT problem that has a sublinear proof size. This argument is an improved and optimized variant of Ligero. For instance, for verifying a SHA-256 preimage in zero-knowledge with 128 bits security, the proof size is 1–2× shorter and the verification is 4× faster than the original protocol Ligero.

There are some research problems that need to be done to develop general solutions to the fundamental problems on privacy blockchain and implementations before they are largely deployed. For example, the vulnerability found in [27] in 2019. In addition, there is still a sizable gap between the argument sizes of IOP-based zkSNARKs and other zkSNARKs that use public-key cryptographic assumptions vulnerable to quantum adversaries [2]. It remains an exciting open problem to close this gap.

Acknowledgments. We thank the anonymous FPS reviewers for their careful reading of our manuscript and their many insightful comments and suggestions.

References

1. Ames, S., Hazay, C., Ishai, Y., Venkitasubramaniam, M.: Ligero: lightweight sublinear arguments without a trusted setup. In: Thuraisingham, B.M., Evans, D., Malkin, T., Xu, D. (eds.) Proceedings of the 2017 ACM SIGSAC Conference on Computer and Communications Security, CCS 2017, pp. 2087–2104. ACM (2017)
2. Ben-Sasson, E., Bentov, I., Horesh, Y., Riabzev, M.: Scalable, transparent, and post-quantum secure computational integrity. IACR Cryptology ePrint Archive 2018/46 (2018)
3. Ben-Sasson, E., et al.: Zerocash: decentralized anonymous payments from bitcoin. In: 2014 IEEE Symposium on Security and Privacy, SP 2014, pp. 459–474. IEEE Computer Society (2014)
4. Ben-Sasson, E., Chiesa, A., Genkin, D., Tromer, E., Virza, M.: SNARKs for C: verifying program executions succinctly and in zero knowledge. In: Canetti, R., Garay, J.A. (eds.) CRYPTO 2013. LNCS, vol. 8043, pp. 90–108. Springer, Heidelberg (2013). https://doi.org/10.1007/978-3-642-40084-1_6
5. Ben-Sasson, E., Chiesa, A., Green, M., Tromer, E., Virza, M.: Secure sampling of public parameters for succinct zero knowledge proofs. In: 2015 IEEE Symposium on Security and Privacy, SP 2015, pp. 287–304. IEEE Computer Society (2015)
6. Ben-Sasson, E., Chiesa, A., Riabzev, M., Spooner, N., Virza, M., Ward, N.P.: Aurora: transparent succinct arguments for R1CS. In: Ishai, Y., Rijmen, V. (eds.) EUROCRYPT 2019. LNCS, vol. 11476, pp. 103–128. Springer, Cham (2019). https://doi.org/10.1007/978-3-030-17653-2_4
7. Ben-Sasson, E., Chiesa, A., Spooner, N.: Interactive oracle proofs. In: Hirt, M., Smith, A. (eds.) TCC 2016. LNCS, vol. 9986, pp. 31–60. Springer, Heidelberg (2016). https://doi.org/10.1007/978-3-662-53644-5_2
8. Ben-Sasson, E., Chiesa, A., Tromer, E., Virza, M.: Succinct non-interactive zero knowledge for a von neumann architecture. In: Fu, K., Jung, J. (eds.) 2014 Proceedings of the 23rd USENIX Security Symposium, pp. 781–796. USENIX Association (2014)
9. Ben-Sasson, E., Hamilis, M., Silberstein, M., Tromer, E.: Fast multiplication in binary fields on GPUs via register cache. In: Ozturk, O., Ebcioglu, K., Kandemir, M.T., Mutlu, O. (eds.) Proceedings of the 2016 International Conference on Supercomputing, ICS 2016, pp. 35:1–35:12. ACM (2016)
10. Ben-Sasson, E., Kopparty, S., Saraf, S.: Worst-case to average case reductions for the distance to a code. In: Servedio, R.A. (ed.) 33rd Computational Complexity Conference, CCC 2018, volume 102 of LIPIcs, pp. 24:1–24:23. Schloss Dagstuhl - Leibniz-Zentrum für Informatik (2018)
11. Ben-Sasson, E., Sudan, M.: Short PCPs with polylog query complexity. SIAM J. Comput. **38**(2), 551–607 (2008)
12. Bünz, B., Bootle, J., Boneh, D., Poelstra, A., Wuille, P., Maxwell, G.: Bulletproofs: short proofs for confidential transactions and more. In: Proceedings of the 2018 IEEE Symposium on Security and Privacy, SP 2018, pp. 315–334. IEEE Computer Society (2018)
13. Campanelli, M., Gennaro, R., Goldfeder, S., Nizzardo, L.: Zero-knowledge contingent payments revisited: attacks and payments for services. In: Thuraisingham, B.M., Evans, D., Malkin, T., Xu, D. (eds.) Proceedings of the 2017 ACM SIGSAC Conference on Computer and Communications Security, CCS 2017, pp. 229–243. ACM (2017)

14. Fiat, A., Shamir, A.: How to prove yourself: practical solutions to identification and signature problems. In: Odlyzko, A.M. (ed.) CRYPTO 1986. LNCS, vol. 263, pp. 186–194. Springer, Heidelberg (1987). https://doi.org/10.1007/3-540-47721-7_12

15. Gennaro, R., Gentry, C., Parno, B., Raykova, M.: Quadratic span programs and succinct NIZKs without PCPs. In: Johansson, T., Nguyen, P.Q. (eds.) EURO-CRYPT 2013. LNCS, vol. 7881, pp. 626–645. Springer, Heidelberg (2013). https://doi.org/10.1007/978-3-642-38348-9_37

16. Gentry, C., Wichs, D.: Separating succinct non-interactive arguments from all falsifiable assumptions. In: Fortnow, L., Vadhan, S.P. (eds.) Proceedings of the 43rd ACM Symposium on Theory of Computing, STOC 2011, pp. 99–108. ACM (2011)

17. Goldwasser, S., Micali, S., Rackoff, C.: The knowledge complexity of interactive proof-systems (extended abstract). In: Sedgewick, R. (ed.) Proceedings of the 17th Annual ACM Symposium on Theory of Computing, pp. 291–304. ACM (1985)

18. Gorbunov, S., Vaikuntanathan, V., Wichs, D.: Leveled fully homomorphic signatures from standard lattices. In: Servedio, R.A., Rubinfeld, R. (eds.) Proceedings of the Forty-Seventh Annual ACM on Symposium on Theory of Computing, STOC 2015, pp. 469–477. ACM (2015)

19. Groth, J.: On the size of pairing-based non-interactive arguments. In: Fischlin, M., Coron, J.-S. (eds.) EUROCRYPT 2016. LNCS, vol. 9666, pp. 305–326. Springer, Heidelberg (2016). https://doi.org/10.1007/978-3-662-49896-5_11

20. Groth, J., Ishai, Y.: Sub-linear zero-knowledge argument for correctness of a shuffle. In: Smart, N. (ed.) EUROCRYPT 2008. LNCS, vol. 4965, pp. 379–396. Springer, Heidelberg (2008). https://doi.org/10.1007/978-3-540-78967-3_22

21. Groth, J., Kohlweiss, M., Maller, M., Meiklejohn, S., Miers, I.: Updatable and universal common reference strings with applications to zk-SNARKs. In: Shacham, H., Boldyreva, A. (eds.) CRYPTO 2018. LNCS, vol. 10993, pp. 698–728. Springer, Cham (2018). https://doi.org/10.1007/978-3-319-96878-0_24

22. Kosba, A.E., Miller, A., Shi, E., Wen, Z., Papamanthou, C.: Hawk: the blockchain model of cryptography and privacy-preserving smart contracts. In: IEEE Symposium on Security and Privacy, SP 2016, pp. 839–858. IEEE Computer Society (2016)

23. Lin, S.-J., Al-Naffouri, T.Y., Han, Y.S., Chung, W.-H.: Novel polynomial basis with fast Fourier transform and its application to Reed-Solomon erasure codes. IEEE Trans. Inf. Theory 62(11), 6284–6299 (2016)

24. Lindell, Y.: Parallel coin-tossing and constant-round secure two-party computation. J. Cryptol. 16(3), 143–184 (2003). https://doi.org/10.1007/s00145-002-0143-7

25. Lindell, Y., Pinkas, B.: An efficient protocol for secure two-party computation in the presence of malicious adversaries. J. Cryptol. 28(2), 312–350 (2015). https://doi.org/10.1007/s00145-014-9177-x

26. Micali, S., Rabin, M.O., Vadhan, S.P.: Verifiable random functions. In: 40th Annual Symposium on Foundations of Computer Science, FOCS 1999, pp. 120–130. IEEE Computer Society (1999)

27. NIST: common vulnerabilities and exposures, March 2019. https://nvd.nist.gov/vuln/detail/cve-2019-7167

28. Parno, B., Howell, J., Gentry, C., Raykova, M.: Pinocchio: nearly practical verifiable computation. In: 2013 IEEE Symposium on Security and Privacy, SP 2013, pp. 238–252. IEEE Computer Society (2013)

29. Rivest, R.L., Shamir, A., Tauman, Y.: How to leak a secret. In: Boyd, C. (ed.) ASIACRYPT 2001. LNCS, vol. 2248, pp. 552–565. Springer, Heidelberg (2001). https://doi.org/10.1007/3-540-45682-1_32

30. Ron, D., Shamir, A.: Quantitative analysis of the full bitcoin transaction graph. In: Sadeghi, A.-R. (ed.) FC 2013. LNCS, vol. 7859, pp. 6–24. Springer, Heidelberg (2013). https://doi.org/10.1007/978-3-642-39884-1_2
31. Setty, S.: Spartan: efficient and general-purpose zkSNARKs without trusted setup. In: Micciancio, D., Ristenpart, T. (eds.) CRYPTO 2020. LNCS, vol. 12172, pp. 704–737. Springer, Cham (2020). https://doi.org/10.1007/978-3-030-56877-1_25
32. Wahby, R.S., Tzialla, I., Shelat, A., Thaler, J., Walfish, M.: Doubly-efficient zkSNARKs without trusted setup. In: Proceedings of the 2018 IEEE Symposium on Security and Privacy, SP 2018, pp. 926–943. IEEE Computer Society (2018)

Author Index

Printed in the United States
By Bookmasters